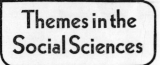

Themes in the Social Sciences

Families in former times

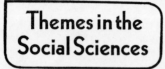

Themes in the Social Sciences

Editors: Jack Goody and Geoffrey Hawthorn

The purpose of this series is to publish discussions of general interest to anthropologists, demographers and sociologists, and to those economists, historians and students of politics who are concerned with issues that extend beyond the conventional limits of their disciplines. The books will be both theoretical and empirical, and often comparative. They will deal with non-industrial and industrial societies, and with those in transition. They will not necessarily be introductions to their subjects, but should appeal to more advanced undergraduates as well as to graduate students and teachers.

Other books in the series

Edmund Leach: *Culture and communication: the logic by which symbols are connected. An introduction to the use of structuralist analysis in social anthropology*

Anthony Heath: *Rational choice and social exchange: a critique of exchange theory*

Philip Abrams and Andrew McCulloch: *Communes, sociology and society*

Jack Goody: *The domestication of the savage mind*

Families in former times

Kinship, household and sexuality

by Jean-Louis Flandrin

Translated by Richard Southern

Cambridge University Press

Cambridge
London   New York   Melbourne

Published by the Syndics of the Cambridge University Press
The Pitt Building, Trumpington Street, Cambridge CB2 1RP
Bentley House, 200 Euston Road, London NW1 2DB
32 East 57th Street, New York, NY 10022, USA
296 Beaconsfield Parade, Middle Park, Melbourne 3206, Australia

English translation first published 1979

This work was originally published in French in 1976 by
Librairie Hachette under the title *Familles: parenté, maison, sexualité
dans l'ancienne société*.

Printed in Great Britain by
Western Printing Services Ltd, Bristol

Library of Congress Cataloguing in Publication Data
Flandrin, Jean-Louis.
Families in former times.

(Themes in the social sciences)
Translation of *Familles*.
Bibliography: p.
Includes index.
1. Family – France – History.   I. Title.   II. Series.
HQ623.F5513   301.42′0944   78–18095
ISBN 0 521 22323 7 hard covers
ISBN 0 521 29449 5 paperback

Contents

Contents

Contents

Tables

ix

Figures

Introduction

The historian, in his capacity as a former or informer of the civic sense in others, has for a long time restricted himself to the study of public life. Even when he has set out to analyse the structure of the economies of past times, and the situations and social conflicts to which they have given rise, he has done so from a political point of view. The history of domestic life and of institutions has been left to the sociologists and the legal historians.

If, nowadays, historians are beginning to discuss the family, this is perhaps because the problems of private life have irrupted into the sphere of current events, and the respective rights and duties of husband and wife, their authority over their children, and the possibilities of divorce, contraception and abortion have become affairs of State. In the face of a transformation of moral conduct that is more evident with every day that passes, some people are, in effect, calling upon the State to preserve traditional morality, others are demanding that it accelerate certain 'necessary' changes, while yet others are trying to make these changes a weapon in an all-out war against the prevailing political system. How, then, can a historian conscious of the political conflicts of his own time fail to be interested in the 'private life' of our forefathers?

This is especially true because to make a clear-cut distinction between private and public life – a distinction so fundamental in our liberal societies – is of limited relevance to the analysis of the old-style monarchical societies. In the latter case, the family as an institution had many of the characteristics of a public institution, and the relations of kinship served as a model for social and political relations.

The authority of a king over his subjects, and that of a father over his children, were of the same nature, as we shall observe: neither authority was based on contract, and both were considered 'natural'. The king and the father were accountable for their governance to God alone. Both normally acted for the best interests of their family, however unfortunate this might turn out to be for their subjects or their children. How can one comprehend the marriages that took place in past times if one considers marriages as a purely private affair, in which the only objective is the happiness of the spouses? How can one understand the War of the Spanish

1

Succession, at the end of the reign of Louis XIV, or the Italian wars, if one reasons only from the point of view of the interests of State?

It is true that there was in foreign as in domestic policy a logic of sovereignty that imposed its criteria on the princes of past times just as it imposes them on the States of the present day, impelling them to fight all other powers that might cast a shadow over their own power. We should not conclude, however, that there was nothing but vanity and hypocrisy in such formulas as 'my brother' or 'my cousin', which princes in former times used when they addressed another prince or some great lord of their realm. These formulas are highly significant: they constitute one indication, among many others, of the fact that relations of kinship helped to mould political relations; and, conversely, they provide information concerning the ties of fraternity and cousinhood for the historian of family relations.

Furthermore, particular families played a major role in political life. It was normal, when one possessed a share of the public authority, to govern with the aid of one's relations and for their profit. The greatest servants of the State – Richelieu, for example, or Colbert – did not decline this privilege. On the other hand, when the magnates were removed from power, they did not hesitate to take up arms against the king, with the collusion of their kinsfolk and clients.

The history of the Ancien Régime cannot, of course, be reduced to that of conflicts between families: some wars can be explained as being essentially confrontations between ideological fanaticisms, and others as class struggles; and sometimes ideological confrontations and class struggles closely combined. But this was not always the case. Rather than distorting the evidence in order to find, in all the conflicts of former times, the class nature of each party to the conflict, one might at times be better advised to investigate the ties of kinship, alliance or clientele which always bound them to a greater or lesser extent. Even when a group was ostensibly defending class interests, it often happened that the latter were in fact merely a mask for family interests.

For these reasons, too, and for others, the analysis of political, economic and social life under the Ancien Régime would seem to require that one take into consideration the structure of the family and the relations of kinship. There is, however, a further consideration: to us, who transfer into the public domain the problems of our private life and who are conscious of the upsetting of our traditional moral values, it is important in itself to know about the family life of our ancestors, more important, fundamentally, than the vicissitudes and the anachronistic annals of public life in olden times. Rather than the family affairs of the great, which constitute the thread of these events, it is the structures of the private lives of the masses that arouse our curiosity. In what ways did the families of past times differ from, and in what ways did they resemble, those of today? What, precisely, do we know about their dimensions? About the age and the ties of kinship of those who composed those families? About the relations between husband and wife? About the attitude of parents towards their children? About the role of the family in the upbringing of children?

With regard to all these points, research is in progress, and the results will probably make more explicit or modify the ideas developed in this book. Nevertheless, it appears to us necessary to carry out, here and now, a preliminary evaluation of our knowledge as regards the family in former times – principally French families of the sixteenth, seventeenth and eighteenth centuries. This is because, for some years past, historians have perceptibly modified the image that had been presented by sociologists and legal historians. They have made fresh enquiries; they have approached the traditional questions on the basis of fresh documentary evidence and using new methods of analysis; and they have reached conclusions that are at times directly contrary to those that had been considered as firmly established.

However, it must be borne in mind that each of these sources, each of these methods, allows us to discover only one aspect, only one dimension of the real structure of the family in former times. The 'families' reconstructed by the French demographers on the basis of the registers of baptisms, marriages and burials are nothing more than a demonstration of the fertility of couples; they tell us nothing at all about the dimensions of the domestic group. The 'families' which British historians discover in censuses of households are merely, as it were, a snapshot of the occupants of accommodation in a given locality at a given moment. Neither of these sets of results could simply replace the images which, on the basis of different documents – less numerous but providing fuller information – legal historians and sociologists had presented of the families of past times.

Today, therefore, it is necessary to achieve a synthesis between the old images and the new ones, for the benefit of an educated public which is showing an increasing interest in these questions. The synthesis will be critical, provisional and at times speculative – let us acknowledge this here and now – but it will, perhaps, be useful to those specialists who, each on his own path, work without always considering what is happening on the neighbouring paths. Displaying a curiously provincial attitude, British historians and those of the Paris Basin attempt to relegate the extended family to the museum of sociological myths, in complete ignorance of the censuses held in southern France which confirm its existence. Many historians, both in France and in Britain, also confuse the extended household with the *lignage*, and the *lignage* with the *race* or the 'household', without taking account of the distinctions which legal historians have,

nevertheless, shown to have existed between these different concepts.*
Moreover, the distinction that the ethnologists have established between
the notion of *lignage* and that of kindred is not always familiar to the
historians. What has probably happened is that the historians of the
family, like the demographers and the sociologists, have been too exclusively interested in the domestic family 'cell', and have not shown enough
interest in the systems of kinship and alliance with which the ethnologists,
by contrast, are obsessed.

It is true that the concept of the family is not entirely free from
ambiguity. Let us attempt, therefore, to define it, before we begin our
study of the actual facts of family life.

THE CONCEPT OF THE FAMILY

Nowadays the word 'family' refers to different things. In the widest sense
of the word, it is 'the entirety of persons mutually connected by marriage
or filiation', or 'the succession of individuals who descend from one
another', that is to say, 'a line', 'a *race*', 'a dynasty' (*Petit Robert*
dictionary). There is also, however, a narrower sense, in much more
common use, which the dictionaries usually put in first place and which is
the only one, generally speaking, taken into account by the sociologists.
In this sense, the word designates 'related persons living under the same
roof', and 'more especially, the father, the mother and the children' (*Petit
Robert* dictionary). These two elements defining the family in the narrower
sense can be reconciled in so far as, and only in so far as, it is rare, in our
society, for persons other than the father, the mother and the children to
live together in the same house.

This apparently was not the case from the sixteenth to the eighteenth
centuries. If one consults the older English and French dictionaries, one
finds that the concept of the family was divided between the notions of
co-residence and kinship, which one finds amalgamated in the definition
that has become most current today. In former times, the word 'family'
more often referred to a set of kinsfolk who did not live together, while
it also designated an assemblage of co-residents who were not necessarily
linked by ties of blood or marriage.

It was the *notion of co-residence* which was mentioned first in the older
English dictionaries. That of Samuel Johnson (1755) gives, as the first sense
of the word 'family', 'those who live in the same house' and, as a synonym,

* *Lignage* is used here in its medieval and early modern sense, very different from its
current meaning. The most approximate modern English translation would be
'branch'. *Race* is also used in its medieval and early modern sense. The most
approximate modern English translation would be 'stock'.

4

'household'. Abel Boyer, in the first edition of his *Dictionnaire royal françoys et anglois*, understood by the word 'famille' 'all those who live in the same house, under the same head'; and he gave as English equivalents 'family' and 'household'. Similarly, Cotgrave, writing in 1673, translated *famille* as 'a family or household', and 'family' as 'famille, maisonnée', even though he went on to add other equivalents corresponding to other senses of the word. Not one of these dictionaries restricted the concept of the family to those who, living in one house, are united by ties of kinship. Moreover, usage confirmed the fact that the servants and other domestics were part of the family. Thus, Samuel Pepys wrote in 1660, at the beginning of his famous *Diary*, 'I lived in Axe Yard, having my wife, and servant Jane, and no more in family than us three.'[1]

This sense of 'household' (especially common in English) is also found in seventeenth- and eighteenth-century French. It is this definition which appears as the principal one in the entry under 'famille' in the first edition of the *Dictionnaire de l'Académie* (1694): 'Toutes les personnes qui vivent dans une même maison, sous un même chef.' Moreover, as early as 1690, Furetière had clearly stated that, in this sense, the word 'famille' is understood to mean a household composed of a head and his domestics, be they women, children or servants. This definition reappeared in all subsequent editions of his dictionary, and in all those of the *Dictionnaire de Trévoux*, published between 1704 and 1771. One observes, incidentally, the classing of the wife and children together with the servants in the concept of 'domestiques'. Furthermore, it sometimes happened that the word 'famille' designated only the domestic staff, as a collective noun, even including at times those who did not live with the master. Thus, the dictionaries of both Furetière and Trévoux noted that among the people of quality, one understands by the term 'famille' all the domestic servants, all the major and minor household officials. The use of the word in this sense was probably no longer very frequent in the eighteenth century, because from 1740 onwards dictionaries find it necessary to situate this usage geographically, e.g. when speaking of the Grandees of Italy (*Dictionnaire de l'Académie*), and to illustrate it by such examples as 'the family of a cardinal' and 'the lower family [*basse famille*] of the Ambassador (of France in Italy)'. Nevertheless, it was still the case in the second half of the eighteenth century, both in France and England, and whatever the social milieu concerned, that the members of the family were held to include both the kinsfolk residing in the house and the domestic servants, in so far as they were all subject to the same head of the family.

The concept of kinship, without any indication of co-residence, was, on the other hand, given a prominent place in all the French dictionaries and most of the English ones. Nicot, writing in 1606, gave only this sense;

Furetière and the *Dictionnaire de Trévoux*, a century later, recognized other senses, but always placed this one at the beginning of their entries under the word 'famille'; Richelet, the *Dictionnaire de l'Académie* and the English dictionaries put it second or third. 'It is used in this sense of those who are of the same blood in the male line' (*Dictionnaire de l'Académie*); 'all those who descend from one and the same stock and who are, consequently, of the same blood' (*Encyclopédie*); and of 'those descended or claiming descent from a common ancestor; a house, kindred, lineage' (Murray). The *Encyclopédie* adds a significant nuance of meaning when it asserts that the word 'famille' is usually understood to mean the entirety of several persons united by ties of blood or of affinity. Moreover, the dictionaries give as synonyms of the word 'family' understood in this sense, 'race', 'house' (*maison*); 'descent', 'extraction' (*extraction, naissance*); 'stock' (*souche, tige*); 'branch', 'parentage', 'issue' (*lignage, parentage, parentelle*).

When one speaks of 'house', in this context, this does not imply co-residence. At that time (the beginning of the eighteenth century), the House of France had a branch established on the throne of Spain, as the House of Austria had had before it. This was too well known for the authors of the time to consider it worth mentioning. On the other hand, it did seem to them important to emphasize the differences in usage of the words 'family' and 'house'. 'In France [the word *famille*] is hardly ever used except for the Houses of the *noblesse de robe* or the bourgeoisie... It would be speaking improperly to say of a great lord "he is of the family of...", to describe his descent. One must say, "he is of the House of..."' (*Furetière*, Trévoux). *Famille*, according to the Abbé Girard, 'is more properly used of the bourgeoisie, and *Maison* of people of quality'. Certain usages, however, cannot be explained in this way: 'One says, in speaking of birth, that someone is of an honourable family and a good house, one speaks of a Royal Family, and of a reigning House' (Trévoux, 1771).

In the *Encyclopédie*, the Chevalier de Jaucourt took up arms against the affectation implied in the use of the word 'house'.

> It is vanity that has imagined the word *house*, in order to mark even more blatantly the distinctions effected by fortune and chance. Pride has therefore decreed in our language, as in past times among the Romans, that the titles, the great dignities and the great appointments continuously held by people of the same name should form what one calls the *houses* of the people of quality, whereas one describes as *families* those of citizens who, clearly distinguished from the dregs of the populace, perpetuate themselves in an Estate, and transmit their line from father to son in honourable occupations, in useful employments, in well-matched alliances, a proper

upbringing, and agreeable and cultivated manners; thus, taking everything into account, the *families* are worth just as much as the *houses*...

'Families', therefore, were not to be found among the 'dregs of the populace', any more than 'houses' were. The 'family', like the 'house', was a social assemblage characteristic of the élites; and a kinsman by blood, if he did not have the social status and the culture required of the members of the family, would doubtless be excluded from it. This is suggested, too, by the *Dictionnaire de Trévoux* in 1771: 'Families are formed by matrimonial alliances, by polite behaviour, by conduct distinguished from that of the lower orders, and by cultivated manners, which are passed on from father to son.'

Were these social criteria in the definitions very long established? One may well doubt it, because they do not appear before 1750. Moreover, one has to wait for the fifth edition of the *Dictionnaire de l'Académie* (1798) to learn that one 'calls an *Enfant de famille* a young man of honourable birth'. Previously, all French dictionaries had applied to the term *fils de famille* the legal definition: 'a young man living under the authority of his father and his mother'. This would carry complete conviction were it not for the fact that Cotgrave, as early as 1673, had translated *Enfant ou fils de famille* as 'Youths of good houses, rich young men (whose parents are living)'. Perhaps this was because the child of the poor man, living as a domestic servant under the authority of a master, was not included in the legal definition of a 'son of the family'.

'The word *family* is understood in an even narrower sense', according to the French dictionaries: 'that of the nearest kinsfolk. In this sense, it is used of people of quality as well as of the bourgeoisie and the people' (Furetière, Trévoux). This sense of the word approximates so much more closely to the sense in which the word is used today that it was given after that of 'household'. But who were these kinsfolk? What were the criteria and the limitations of their proximity? The few dictionaries that concern themselves with this question give different answers, of varying degrees of explicitness. 'In this sense, under the name of the *Royal Family*, one includes the children and grandchildren of Kings', according to Furetière and the *Dictionnaire de Trévoux*. The Academy understood in this restricted sense 'all those of the same blood, such as children, brothers, nephews'. This did not prevent it from reproducing verbatim Furetière's entry under the heading 'Royal Family'. To Richelet, 'family' signified essentially 'the father and the mother with the children'. The same definition was given by the Chevalier de Jaucourt in the *Encyclopédie*.

Is it possible to discern any progression in this third sense of the word, any tendency to separate from the rest of the extended family the father,

the mother and the children? The sense of close kinship was not emphasized by Nicot (1606 and 1621), or Cotgrave (1611 and 1673), or the Abbé
Boyer (1702). It does not appear in France until 1680, with the first edition
of Richelet's dictionary. After that date, it appears in all the great French
dictionaries. In England there was an analogous, though later, development: this sense of the word 'family' is still missing from Johnson's
Dictionary (1755), but it is given by Murray, in the nineteenth century,
with the first indisputable example dating from 1829. Moreover, the
evolution of the concept of the family is illustrated by the definitions
that are given of the 'Holy Family'. In all the editions of Furetière, from
1690 to 1732, in the first five editions of the *Dictionnaire de Trévoux*
(published between 1704 and 1752) and in the first two editions of the
Academy dictionary, the Holy Family is held to include 'Our Lord, the
Virgin, Saint Joseph and Saint John'. Subsequently, the presence of Saint
John was not automatic, and it seems to have raised a problem: the
Dictionnaire de Trévoux in 1771, and those of the Academy in 1740, 1762,
1798 and 1835 describe the Holy Family as 'a picture representing Our
Lord, the Virgin, Saint Joseph and *sometimes* Saint John'. There is a fresh
nuance in Littré (1863), who observes: '*The Holy Family*, Joseph, the
Virgin and the infant Jesus. A *Holy Family*, a picture representing the
Holy Family, sometimes with Saint John.' Today, in the *Petit Robert*
dictionary, Saint John has disappeared altogether.

At the same time as this reduction in the members of the family, there
occurred the conflation of the two concepts of kinship and co-residence,
which were still dissociated as late as the mid eighteenth century. Instead
of listing the different senses of the word 'family', the Chevalier de
Jaucourt, writing in the *Encyclopédie*, made efforts to unite them in one
whole. According to him, the family is a

> domestic society which constitutes the first of the accessory and
> natural states of Man. Indeed, the family is a civil society estab-
> lished by Nature: this society is the most natural and the most
> ancient of all societies; it serves as a foundation for the national
> society; for a people or a nation is nothing more than an entirety
> compounded of several families. Families are established by mar-
> riage, and it is nature herself that invites men to form this union;
> from it are born children who, perpetuating the families, maintain
> human society in being, and make good the losses which death
> causes in it every day.

One sees at work in this preamble the ideology of the Enlightenment: it
was probably needed to mask the separation – which was frequent in the
circles where one could read the *Encyclopédie* – between close kinship
and the assemblage of co-residents. If the family has been established by
Nature, then such a separation is without significance. It is only once these

principles are established that Jaucourt goes on to distinguish two senses of the word 'family', with a plethora of justifications that reveals the innovative character of his interpretation.

> In a narrow sense, it is composed, firstly, only of the father of the family; secondly of the mother of the family who, according to the almost universally accepted interpretation, becomes a member of the family of her husband; thirdly, of the children, who are, as it were, formed of the substance of their father and mother, and ineluctably belong to the *family*. However, when one considers the word *family* in a broader sense, one includes in it all the kinsfolk; for although, after the death of the father of the family, each child establishes his or her own family, nevertheless all those who descend from the same stock, and who are in consequence issue of the same blood, are regarded as members of the same *family*.

One has to wait until the nineteenth century for the concepts of co-residence and of close kinship to be united in concise formulas, in definitions whose very succinctness bears witness to the fact that they no longer constitute any problem. 'Persons of the same blood living under the same roof, and more especially the father, the mother and the children', in the words of Littré, writing in 1869. Even so, he still puts this definition in fourth place; and the Academy dictionary, in its sixth edition, suggests that this interpretation was still not widely accepted in 1835: 'The word is *sometimes* used of kinsfolk who live together, and, more especially, of the father, the mother and the children, or even of the children alone.' The concept of the family, therefore, as it is most commonly defined today, has only existed in our western culture since a comparatively recent date.

This conceptual analysis provides us with several working hypotheses. It suggests that the concept of the *lignage* was more deeply rooted among the élites than among the people; that in France, as in England, what united the members of a domestic group – kinsfolk and servants – in one 'family', was their common dependence on the 'father of the family'; and that, in both countries, the father–mother–children triad acquired an ever-increasing independence with respect to the *lignage* and to the servants, until in the nineteenth century it became the fundamental nucleus of our society. It is true that the chronology of the transformations of the concept of the family, as defined in the dictionaries, probably suffers from a time-lag with respect to the actual evolution of the institution itself. There is no lack, however, of other indications of the lateness of this evolution. In the eighteenth century, it was 'Enlightened' opinion that militated in favour of the intimacy of the family circle, and that interpreted the family as a 'natural society' and made of it the privileged haven of felicity. In contrast to this, since the beginning of the twentieth century, it has been innovative writers who have attacked the family, and conservative opinion which has defended it.

We are not, however, thereby prevented from giving a privileged place in our historical researches to the relations between spouses and between them and their children, because it is these relations that lie at the heart of our preoccupations today. It is, however, important to emphasize that what was referred to in past times as the 'family' was not identical with the father–mother–children triad, and that one cannot study this triad, in the sixteenth, seventeenth and eighteenth centuries, without taking into account its relations with *lignage* or kindred on the one hand, and the domestic staff on the other.

1. *The ties of kinship*

1. THE NATURE OF KINSHIP

The house and the 'race'

'Kinsfolk', *lignage*, *race*, 'house' and, of course, 'family' appear in the dictionaries of the seventeenth and eighteenth centuries as more or less synonymous, and we have ourselves seemed to admit this when we were drawing the distinction between 'family' in the sense of 'kinship' and 'family' in the sense of 'household'. In fact, they were not synonymous, or at least were not always so.

One of the most difficult concepts to grasp has been that of the 'house'. In his *Essays*, in the chapter entitled 'Of names', Montaigne speaks of a maid of honour of Catherine de Medici, of whom Henri II was 'of the opinion that she should be called by the general name of her *race*, because that of her paternal "house" appeared to him too outlandish'.[1] What did this mean? What the king understood by the 'name of her *race*' was the patronymic surname, or name of the family. The use of this was not customary, among the aristocracy of that era, any more than the use of the person's baptismal name. This custom had its drawbacks, as Montaigne emphasizes in the same chapter.

> It is a wretched custom, and with most injurious consequences in our land of France, to call each person by *the name of his estate*, and it is the usage that most leads to confusion between different *races*. The younger son of a good *house*, having had as his appanage a piece of land under the name of which he has been known and honoured, cannot honourably abandon it; ten years after his death, the land passes into the hands of a stranger, who follows the same usage: you may well guess how confused we become when we try to ascertain the origin of these men.[2]

Whereas in the first passage he distinguishes between the 'name of the paternal house' and the 'name of the *race*', in the second he distinguishes between the 'name of the land' and that of the house and the *race*, which are apparently confused. Let us observe, in an example cited from Brantôme,[3] how the different terms were used.

11

Monsieur le Comte du Lude of today is the son of that gallant Messire Guy de Daillon, whose father and my mother were first cousins, both being descended from Louise de Daillon, known as the Seneschalle of Poictou, my grandmother, who was the aunt of M. du Lude, first cousin of my aforesaid mother...From the said M. du Lude, Guy de Daillon, and Madame du Lude, of the house of La Fayette, there issued the present M. du Lude and three daughters...M. du Lude [Jean de Daillon] had several sons and daughters. The sons were Messieurs des Chastelliers..., de Sarterre and de Briançon, who died without issue. The daughters were Mademoiselle du Lude, who died unmarried at Court, Madame la Maréchale de Matignon, whose son was Monsieur le Comte de Torigny, married to a daughter of Longueville, and the third daughter was married to Monsieur de Ruffec, Governor of the Angoûmois, and their sons were the Messieurs de Ruffec of today, who are four male offspring...

The *name of the 'race'* – what we would call the 'patronymic' or 'family name' – was Daillon. By way of exception, Brantôme uses it for his grand-mother, the 'Seneschalle de Poictou', and for the 'gallant Messire Guy de Daillon', who had, perhaps, become well known under this name during his father's lifetime. However, rather than call his own father Jean de Daillon or his son François de Daillon by their surnames and first names, he prefers to use paraphrases such as 'M. du Lude, first cousin of my aforesaid mother' and 'the present M. le Comte du Lude', or incur the risk of misleading the reader.

The *name of the paternal house* was used to designate the unmarried daughters, such as that 'Mademoiselle du Lude, who died unmarried at Court'. It was also used to record publicly matrimonial alliances between houses, e.g. 'Madame du Lude, of the house of La Fayette' and 'Monsieur le Comte de Torigny, married to a daughter of Longueville'. The sons used this name only during their childhood. An example of this was the case of the 'Messieurs de Ruffec of today, who are four male offspring'. When they grew older, the eldest son once again took the name of the paternal house, whereas the younger sons customarily took the *names of their estates*: thus, one speaks of the 'Messieurs des Chastelliers..., de Sarterre and de Briançon'. All three continued to belong to the *race* of the Daillons, but they no longer belonged to the 'du Lude house'. Were they each going to found a new 'house'? Their status as younger sons would have made this hardly possible; it was not entirely fortuitous that all three died without issue. These 'names of estates', therefore, which were always less long established than the names of *houses*, were also, in general, less enduring. It even happened that a younger son lost this name during his lifetime, as did Emmanuel de Gondi, lord of Dampierre:[4] 'Monsieur de

12

Dampierre still calls himself by this name, even though the place has been sold; others call him Monsieur the General of the Galleys, which is certainly a very fine and great estate.' This had been sheer good fortune! It remains no less certain that the custom of calling each person by his title – whether it were the title of an office or appointment or that of the lordship over a piece of land – was, as Montaigne put it, 'the usage that most leads to confusion between different *races*'.

This 'wretched custom' did not exist only in France, as Montaigne suggests. It existed also in Spain, and among the higher nobility of certain other countries. In England, where gentlemen were known by their first names and surnames, lords bore their titles. Thus, the royal favour created George Villiers Duke of Buckingham, Sir Edward Hyde the first Earl of Clarendon, and Sir Edward Montagu, Lord Sandwich. These titles, like the names of 'houses' in France, passed only to the heir, whereas the younger sons, in general, had to be content with their patronymic preceded by their Christian name, for example, Sir James Montagu, sixth son of Lord Sandwich.

It would be safe to assert that the French gentlemen were as pretentious as the great English lords. But was the use of the name of the house characteristic, in France, only of the nobility? In fact, one finds this usage even among the poorest peasants in many parts of the south-west, such as the Béarn or the Basque country. 'In Labourt', wrote the Bordeaux magistrate Pierre de Lancre at the beginning of the seventeenth century,

> the most beggarly men and women in the villages style themselves lord or lady of such-and-such a house, and these are the houses that each one has in his village, even though they be no more than pigsties. . .to such an extent that they usually abandon their 'cognomen' and the name of their families, and the women even abandon the name of *their* husbands, to take the names of their houses. . .[5]

The Basque house not only gave its name to its occupants, causing their official civil status to be completely forgotten, but it even decided their social rank: the house was called free, and noble, and displayed its coat of arms, enjoying a certain degree of juridical personality.[6] And even the priests, in their parish registers, in addition to recording the family names and baptismal names, indicated the name of the house and the relation to it – master, heir, younger son, son-in-law, etc. – of the person concerned.[7]

The concept of the 'house' is, fundamentally, intermediate between those of *race* and of 'household', which we distinguished above. We shall return to this subject in the following chapter. However, it must be emphasized at this point that the concept of the 'house' linked the continuity of the family with the perenniality of settlement in a particular place. Designation by the patronymic surname, which has become the universal custom today, does not permit a family to survive the interruption of its male line of descent, whereas designation by the name of the house did make this possible. Let us take as an example the house of Le Vigean, founded in the sixteenth century by a younger son of the house of Le Fou.[8] François du Fou, lord of Le Vigean, the son of the founder, 'died without male heirs', leaving only three daughters. The eldest, Madeleine du Fou, inherited the fief, which she bequeathed to her only daughter, Ester de Pons, the lady of Le Vigean, known in her time under the name of 'Madame de Fors' because she had married Charles Pesnart, lord of Fors, who was apparently the younger son of a good house. Nevertheless, the eldest of the children, instead of assuming the paternal title, became 'Baron du Vigean', thus reviving the house of Le Vigean, which had 'fallen to the distaff' for two generations.

Some embittered commentators – from the end of the sixteenth century, and perhaps earlier – complained of a custom which, by 'making the lines of descent unrecognizable', made it possible for those of ignoble birth to graft themselves onto illustrious stocks. One must note, however, the advantages of the system. It maintained, in the face of the hazards of demography and economics, a certain continuity of names and families, thus disguising, as far as possible, the upheavals suffered by the social hierarchy. The use of the patronymic, on the other hand, increases the risk of the extinction of lines of descent, emphasizes the impudence of social-climbers, and, if one reflects on the matter, is no better guarantee of purity of blood than is the name of the house.

Why, indeed, link the *line of descent* to the patrilinearity of the sur-name? The physicians of the sixteenth century acknowledged, for the most part, that in the constitution of the genetic patrimony of the descendants – if one may, for the sake of brevity, risk using this anachronistic formula – the mother played as important a part as the father. Or, rather, the genetic privileges of the father were too widely disputed to serve as a solid basis for the patrilinearity of the line of descent. Moreover, it was common knowledge that it was less easy to discover the identity of the father of a child than that of its mother: the obsession with cuckoldry manifested itself in the writings of the jurists and theologians, and in stories, comedies and tragedies. Furthermore, in real life, the suspicion of illegitimacy was not absent from even the greatest families. Thus, the line of descent of the Condés probably owed its salvation from extinction in 1588 to the arbitrary decision of Henri IV to deem legitimate the father of the victor of Rocroy, a child born in gaol to a mother imprisoned for adultery and for poisoning her husband. The line of descent, in so far as it was denoted by the patronymic, was not, therefore, so much a biological as a juridical reality. It seems to have become solidly established in the course of the thirteenth and fourteenth centuries, at the same time as the legal status of women

was deteriorating, in circumstances that have not yet been fully elucidated.

The 'lignage'

Before the line of descent became recognized, there had been the *lignage*,
an assemblage of individuals who descended or claimed to descend from
a common ancestor, either in the male or the female line. By reason of this
cognatic character, therefore, the *lignage* was more comprehensive than
the line of descent, and, clearly, was quite distinct from the *house*. What,
however, remained of it in the period with which we are concerned?

In the England of the seventeenth century it still happened that, rather
than the name of the patrilinear line of descent, one adopted that of the
maternal *lignage*. A famous example is provided for us by the genealogy
of Oliver Cromwell. Through the male line, he was connected with a
Welsh family of the name of Morgan, members of which had come to seek
their fortune in England in the early sixteenth century. One of them
married a sister of Thomas Cromwell, the favourite of Henry VIII. The
children of this man Morgan abandoned his patronymic surname and
adopted that of the now illustrious *lignage* to which they belonged on their
mother's side. It does appear, however, that at that time such a practice
was exceptional.

Can we regard as sufficient evidence of the survival of the *lignage* in
England the survival of the word *lignage* in the dictionaries as late as the
eighteenth century? In France the word itself was considered antiquated
and had fallen into disuse by the dictionaries from the end of the seventeenth century onwards. Still current at the beginning of the sixteenth
century – but in the vague sense of 'kinship' – it then disappeared from
use, and only a hazy recollection of it was retained in its derivative 'lineal'
(from *lignage*) in the expression 'lineal shrinkage', to which we shall have
occasion to return. Finally, from the mid sixteenth century, the notion of
the *lignage* survived in France only among the jurists. Let us observe,
therefore, what they have to tell us about ties of solidarity based on the
lignage.

In the tenth and eleventh centuries, in a society in which the royal power
had become almost non-existent, the *lignage* had had, as an essential
function, the protection of its members. All were, in effect, obliged to
avenge the injury done to one of them, or to punish his murderer. This
duty of *faide* was sacred, and was recognized by law. The sovereign could
pardon a murderer only if the latter came to an arrangement with the
lignage of the victim by paying the blood-price. In such cases, the necessary sum was usually collected by the kinsfolk of the murderer and shared

out among those of the victim. This custom suggests that the individual was, at that time, less a person in his own right than a member of the *lignage,* in the most concrete sense of the term.

The gradual resurgence of the royal power, and the opposition of the Church to private wars, effected a progressive reduction in *the necessity and the exercise* of vengeance by members of the branch. In the era with which we are concerned, it no longer had any legal sanction. It doubtless still figured in the news, especially during the turbulent times of the wars of religion. It appears, however, to have been more a question of clienteles; these included the members of a *lignage,* even though the two groups were not co-terminous. It subsisted in an institutionalized form only in Corsica. 'They kill one another like Barbarians', wrote the missionaries from France in the sixteenth century,

> and are not willing to pardon nor even to discuss any arrangement, until they are avenged. And not only do they make war on him who has done the injury, but also, in general, on all his kinsfolk, as far as the third degree of relationship. So that, if one has offended another, it is necessary for all his kinsfolk to be on their guard, for the first one to be found, even though he be innocent, and perhaps knowing nothing of the injury that has been done, will nevertheless be treated as though he were an accomplice.[9]

The surprise and emotion evinced by these missionaries bears witness to the fact that this Corsican vendetta contrasted strongly with the customs of continental France. In France, the most obvious reminder of the traditional *lignage* solidarities, in this sphere, were the crowds of kinsfolk who came to throw themselves at the feet of the king to plead for justice to be done to a murderer or, instead, to beg for pardon for a guilty man. It was still the kinsfolk who, almost exclusively, enacted this role.

The strength of the ties of lineal solidarity, in medieval western Europe, did not imply that all the members of the *lignage* lived as a community and possessed an undivided patrimony inherited from a common ancestor. This would have been even more difficult in view of the fact that, since kinship was transmitted by women as well as men, each individual had two grandfathers, four great-grandfathers, etc., and therefore belonged to several *lignages.* Nevertheless, the descendants of a common ancestor preserved certain rights over the entirety of a property that had been parcelled out. When one of them wished to alienate all or part of his patrimonial possessions, he had to obtain the agreement of his kinsfolk of the same *lignage*: the deeds of alienation of the eleventh and twelfth centuries provide evidence of this. From the twelfth century onwards, the renaissance of the economy based on the exchange of goods and services, and that of Roman Law, had the effect of diminishing these prerogatives of the *lignage.* From the thirteenth century, the kinsfolk of the person who

sold or gave away his patrimony had no other recourse than that of the possibility of obliging the person acquiring it to resell it to them. This was the law of 'lineal repurchase right' (*retrait lignager*).[10]

In the thirteenth century, this privilege appears to have fulfilled the function of protecting the rights of the most immediate heirs. After the fourteenth century, however, there was established a new principle, whereby in the case of alienation in favour of a kinsman, a closer relation could not exercise this lineal repurchase right. The lineal repurchase right was no longer the exclusive privilege of the most immediate heirs, but of the *lignage* as a whole. It resisted the onslaughts of the jurists inspired by Roman Law, and had from then on, as its essential function, the maintenance of the power and glory of the great families. In the fourteenth century, the *Grand coutumier de France* declared that 'the repurchase right was first introduced for the benefit of the *lignage*, so that inheritance might remain in the lines of descent from which they came, and for the honour of the said *lignage*'.[11] There is one further indication of the aristocratic character of this institution: the right of repurchase could be exercised within a year and a day in the case of the alienation of a fief, while the time limit was very much less in the case of a censive holding. This distinction, which had legal force in Picardy, Artois and Flanders, also became established at the end of the Middle Ages.[12]

Being an institution based on custom, lineal repurchase right never became fully established in the written-law provinces – with the exception of Provence – even though Henri III, for revenue purposes, tried to introduce it by edict in 1581.[13] This was, perhaps, because it was not necessary for the continuity of houses in southern France, where Roman Law gave the heads of families the right to bequeath the entirety of their patrimony to a sole heir, after the deduction of certain meagre 'legitimate shares' for the younger sons.

In what one might, therefore, call 'lineal' France, how was the property of the *lignage* defined? Lineal redemption, in general, only applied to the inherited property – and not subsequent acquisitions. The inherited property was transmitted according to the rule of *paterna paternis, materna maternis*, that is to say, only the kinsfolk on the father's side had any rights over the property which had come from the father, and only those on the mother's side had rights over that which had come from the mother. This principle was unquestioned, but it received, owing to variations between customs, diverse interpretations. The latter can be divided into three systems. According to the *simple côté* system, all the kinsfolk of the vendor, on the side from which the property derived, had the right of redemption. This interpretation was exceptional: in the eighteenth century it was found only in the customs of Chauny, Meaux, Etampes and Chaumont. In contrast to this, the *soucher* (stock) system granted the right of redemption only to the descendants in the direct line of the first person to acquire the property being sold. This interpretation was more common, and examples have been found in Mantes, Dourdan, Melun, the Nivernais, the Bourbonnais and Touraine. Finally, there was the 'system of *côté et ligne*' which occupied an intermediate position between the other two systems, and was the most widespread. According to this system, the right of repurchase was granted to all the descendants of the first person to acquire the property, whether their descent were direct or collateral.[14]

In other words, the two most widely accepted interpretations of the *paterna paternis, materna maternis* rule defined the *lignage* as the entirety of the descendants of a common ancestor. This definition, which tallies with that accepted by anthropologists today, clearly distinguished it from what the latter call a *parentela*,* that is to say, the entirety of the relations of a particular individual. Moreover, the rule itself is evidence of the invariably cognatic nature of the ties of kinship, despite the appearance of patronymic surnames in the fourteenth century. This is not, however, evidence in favour of the reality with which we are concerned. In other words, it is not likely that individuals, in their daily lives, felt closer ties of solidarity with those whom the laws of succession called their 'lineal' kinsfolk than with their other relations.

The rules defining the ability to inherit or redeem in fact concerned themselves with the past history of the property claimed, rather than with the real extent of the ties of solidarity between kinsfolk at the time when the repurchase took place. Conversely, how could these rules have imposed a special solidarity between the individual and his kinsfolk of the same *lignage*, when – by the process, continued for several generations, of acquisitions, contributions from dowries and division among heirs – the majority of individuals possessed property derived from a multiplicity of ancestors, and belonged to as many different *lignages*? The relations who were not 'lineal' kinsfolk in connection with some property or other must have been extremely rare.

Rather than the status of 'lineal' kinship, what made for the strength of family solidarities was the line of descent – in other words, the sharing of the same patronymic surname – and the closeness of relationships. As evidence of this, one may quote a passage from *La Vie de mon père*, in which the lawyer Rétif de Noyer, in order to overcome the possible jealousy of the young Edme Rétif towards a cousin named Daiguesmortes, says to him 'he is my first cousin [whereas Edme was only the offspring of a first cousin], and the son of an aunt who has been like a mother to me...

---

* 'By a person's *parentela* is meant the sum of those persons who trace their blood from him. My issue are my *parentela*, my father's issue are his *parentela*.' Sir F. Pollock and F. W. Maitland, *The History of English Law*, 2nd edn (2 vols., Cambridge, 1968), vol. II, p. 296.

18

He is my first cousin, he is one degree of relationship closer than you; but you bear my name, and for that reason you are at least his equal in relation to me.'[15]

Consanguinity, matrimonial alliance, spiritual kinship and clienteles

The great dictionaries of the seventeenth and eighteenth centuries, in common with the civil law, held the notions of *kinship* and consanguinity to be absolutely synonymous. A kinsman is 'a person who is united to us by blood', wrote Richelet in 1680. And the Academy, in 1694, defined kinship in one word: 'consanguinity'. Nevertheless, the matter is debatable. After asserting that 'all kinship comes from birth and derives from the fact that persons descend from the same stock', the *Encyclopédie* had to admit: 'It is only those who are born of a legitimate marriage who are kin to their father and mother; for bastards have no kinsfolk, except for their children born in legitimate wedlock.'[16] Logically, it could have gone further: the consanguinity of kinsfolk was not always evident in a society which recognized affiliation through men as well as through women. The reference to blood, however, was part of the ideology of kinship.

Moreover, canon law, in condemning marriages between kinsfolk as incestuous, held a much more complex view of kinship. In addition to consanguinity, whether legitimate or otherwise, which it termed *natural kinship*, it took cognizance of *legal kinship*, created by adoption and deemed to exist between the adopted person and the entire family of his foster-father; *legitimate affinity*, which marriage caused to exist between each of the spouses and the family of the other; *illegitimate affinity*, which resulted from all illicit carnal relations; and, finally, *spiritual kinship*, which united the baptized child and his parents with the godfathers and godmothers and their close relatives, and even the confessor with the penitent and the catechist with the catechumen. If one admits, therefore, that kinship is a social convention characteristic of each culture, and not a gift of nature, we should examine this ecclesiastical view of kinship – a maximizing one – with as much attention as the restrictive interpretation given by the civil law.

One cannot, in fact, explain this multiplication of impediments to marriage as simply the result of an incest-psychosis: it reveals the existence of ties of kinship other than those of blood, *race* or household, and particularly the solidarity which marriage established between two families, even after the death of one of the spouses. In linguistic terms, the analogy between 'allies' and kinsfolk was more clearly recognized in England than in France: the word *kin*, if one is to believe Abel Boyer, meant affinal as well as consanguineous relations. 'Are you any kin to him?' was translated as 'Etes-vous son parent?', whereas 'He is no kin to me' was rendered as 'Il ne m'est point allié'.

However, the strength of ties of kinship formed by matrimonial alliances was equally firmly established in France as well. In order to prevent certain families from dominating the royal law-courts, Louis XIV decided in August 1669 to 'stipulate by law the degrees of kinship which are incompatible with the holding of office in the same place'. He was mistrustful not only of the 'kinsmen of the first, second and third degrees of relationship, that is to say, fathers and sons, brothers, uncles and nephews', but also of 'affinal kin as far as the second degree, such as fathers-in-law, sons-in-law and brothers-in-law', going as far as to forbid – in that society in which homogamy was customary – 'that the permanent officers accepted and at present serving in our said courts and seats of government shall hereafter contract alliances of the first degree of father-in-law or son-in-law'.

In the history of France and England in the sixteenth and seventeenth centuries, one finds a very great number of examples of this solidarity of cognatic and affinal kinsfolk in the conquest or the exercise of power. At the court of Henri II, for example, two great families contended for power: on the one hand, the Guises, who sprang from the house of Lorraine and could count on its unfailing friendship; and, on the other hand, the Montmorencys, led by the old Constable and his three nephews, Admiral de Coligny, Colonel-General d'Andelot and Cardinal de Châtillon. The accession to the throne of François II, the husband of Mary Stuart, who was the niece of the Guises, was enough to destroy the equilibrium existing between the two factions: the Guises took complete possession of power and drove out all their rivals, who inclined, along with Coligny and the other malcontents, towards Protestantism.

In the age of Louis XIV, families played almost as important a part in political life: throughout his reign, the Colberts contended for power with the Le Telliers, of whom Louvois was the most celebrated representative, while some less eminent *races*, such as the Phelypeaux, made efforts to retain some offices.

Less is known, perhaps, of the part played by family politics in the conquest and exercise of power by Richelieu. All the members of his family – the Du Plessis and the La Portes – were raised through his influence to positions of power or prestige: his brother became a cardinal, his niece a duchess, his cousin La Meilleraye a Marshal of France, his nephew Du Pont de Courley General of the Galleys, while his more distant relatives occupied innumerable other offices. He owed these favours to them, according to the moral ideas of the age, and he owed them to his own glory. These promotions, however, also served another purpose: even though some of his relations left something to be desired as regards their intelligence or their reliability, he appointed them to important posts because they were 'naturally' attached to him and he could therefore count on their fidelity.

In addition, Richelieu established, outside the ranks of his kinsfolk, a network of trustworthy clients: Father Joseph and Mazarin are the best known, but there were plenty of others. Many of these clients were attached to him by family tradition: the best example is that of the Bouthilliers. The ancestor, Denis Bouthillier, lord of Fouilletourte, had been clerk to François de la Porte, Richelieu's maternal grandfather. At his death, François de la Porte had left him his professional practice, commending to his care 'his grandchildren who had lost their parents', according to Saint-Simon. In fact, their mother was still alive, and did not die until 1616, but that did not matter: 'Bouthillier took care of them as of his own children, and that is the origin of the fortune of the Bouthilliers.' Richelieu installed Claude Bouthillier, who was a Counsellor of the *Parlement*, in a post under Marie de Medici, as 'executive secretary to the Queen Mother', and then had him appointed, ten years later, Secretary of State. His brother, Denis Bouthillier, lord of Rancé, was also secretary to the Queen Mother, which made it possible for him to keep Richelieu informed as to her intrigues and changes of mood. Victor Bouthillier was appointed Bishop of Boulogne, and later coadjutor to the Archbishop of Tours; in these posts, he could keep Richelieu informed of the activities of the clergy. In return for this collaboration, the Minister obtained for him all sorts of favours and benefices, particularly the post of Almoner to 'Monsieur', which made it easier to keep a watch on the activities of the intriguer Gaston d'Orléans. The fourth brother, Sébastien Bouthillier, was Bishop of Aire and Prior of Le Cochère. It was he who, in 1619, together with Father Joseph, obtained from Marie de Médici the recall of Richelieu from his exile in Avignon. Finally, Léon Bouthillier, Count of Chavigny, the only son of Claude, took over the appointment of Secretary of State for Foreign Affairs when his father left it to become Superintendent of Finance. He, too, in accordance with family tradition, was a faithful client of the Cardinal, and one of the most partisan.[17]

When one examines the part played by ties of kinship in the establishment of clienteles in the sixteenth and seventeenth centuries – a sociopolitical phenomenon deserving of a study as systematic as that devoted to the feudal system – one must, therefore, take into consideration the consanguineous and affinal kin of the clients as well as the kinsfolk of the patron. One should also, probably, take into consideration the ties of 'spiritual kinship', which made it possible, to a greater extent than matrimonial alliances, to institutionalize the ties of solidarity between the client and the family of his patron or between the patron and the family of his client.

It is, in any case, clear that at an equivalent social level these ties of fidelity, which might arise out of sympathy or interest, had to be consecrated by marriage, or otherwise they would incur the risk of remaining changeable and insecure. Saint-Simon gives us a glimpse of this when he recounts his first steps towards matrimony.

> Though maintaining a considerable establishment, I felt myself extremely isolated in a country where credit and consideration were more important than anything else. Being the son of a favourite of Louis XIII and of a mother who had lived only for him, whom he had married although she was no younger than he, without uncles or aunts, or first cousins, or close relations, or influential friends of my father and my mother – so cut off from everything on account of their age – I found myself very much alone...The Duke of Beauvillier had always remembered that my father and his had been friends, and that he himself had been on the same footing with my father...His valour, his gentleness, his polished manners, all made him stand high in my esteem. His enjoyment of official favour was then at its zenith: he was Minister of State after the death of M. de Louvois, he had as a very young man succeeded the Marshal of Villeroy in the appointment of head of the council of finance, and he had followed his father in the post of first gentleman of the bedchamber.[18]

In short, for this young duke without relatives and without the sovereign's favour, it was absolutely necessary to find powerful affinal kin. This was more important than marrying a rich heiress, which, however, he also needed very much to do, because his patrimony was saddled with debts. He said so frankly to his well-wisher the Duke of Beauvillier, asking him for the hand of any of his daughters of marriageable age. Unfortunately, the eldest wished to become a nun, the second daughter was forced into that estate by her physical deformity, and the others were too young. The marriage could not, therefore, take place, to the great regret of the two men:

> I expressed my regret, in replying to him that the needs of my business affairs [that is to say, his need for a dowry to settle his debts] did not allow me to wait until I could marry his youngest daughter, for perhaps not all of them would become nuns; and this was, in fact, my view of the matter. At the end of the conversation, there were the most tender protestations on both sides of an intimate and eternal mutual interest and friendship, and he promised to assist me in every way with his advice, in both small and great matters, and said that we would look on each other from thenceforth, and for all time, as father-in-law and son-in-law in the most indissoluble union...He told me that his only consolation

was the hope that his children and mine might some day be married.[19]

2. THE DIMENSIONS OF KINSHIP

After having thus considered the different ways of being a kinsman and having observed the strength of each of these modes, we must now describe more precisely the dimensions of kinship. Let us first examine the civil law – that is, the rules of inheritance and of 'lineal repurchase'.[20]

In the Nivernais and the Bourbonnais, the rules recognized kinship only as far as the sixth degree. These were the most restrictive customs. More often, inheritance and lineal repurchase applied to those of the seventh degree of relationship. This was the case, for example, according to the ancient custom of Beauvaisis described in the eighteenth century by Beaumanoir, and it still survived, in the sixteenth and seventeenth centuries, in the customary law of Normandy, Sens, the Duchy of Bar, and the Bassigny. The *Très ancienne coutume de Bretagne* placed the limits of the *lignage* at the ninth degree; and most of the other compilations of customary laws did not establish any limits. As time went on, this tendency became more generalized, probably because the advent and the improved accuracy of registers of baptisms, marriages and burials made the proof of distant relationship easier. 'In accordance with the civil law observed in France', asserted the *Encyclopédie*, 'one succeeds *ad infinitum*, both directly and collaterally, as long as one can prove kinship, even when one cannot describe the exact degree.'[21] Moreover, the jurist Pothier quotes, in the eighteenth century, cases of lineal repurchase by relations of the twentieth and even the thirtieth degree. It may well be doubted whether ties of lineal solidarity, and even the knowledge of the relationship, ever in fact extended so far.

This discrepancy between the unlimited character of legal kinship and the very limited character of the ties of lineal solidarity is, moreover, demonstrated by surviving wills. In these one often finds, in fact, particularly in Provence and the region of Lyons,[22] a clause directed against known or unknown relatives who might try to lay claim to a part of the inheritance on the basis of the customary rules. For example, in 1559, in the will of Bernard Salomon, a painter of Lyons: 'Item, he gives, and by right of appointment of heirs, to his relatives and friends claiming rights, to each one five *sous*. . .' Or, in that of Louise Labbé, of 8 April 1565: 'Item, the said testatrix has given and bequeaths by right of appointment of heirs to all other claimants against her aforesaid property the sum of five *sous* of Tours currency. . .without their being able to claim or demand any other part of her aforesaid property.' This clause, which was quite customary, cannot be explained by any particular enmity which certain testators might entertain towards any of their kinsfolk. It constitutes evidence both of the rights which the law recognized as being possessed by the kinsfolk, however distant, with regard to the property of a deceased person, and of the refusal of a testator to concede such claims to the detriment of heirs who were nearer or dearer.

Did canon law, then, provide a more realistic definition of kinship? It had given extremely variable definitions in the course of the early Middle Ages. At first the Church had forbidden marriage only as far as the fourth degree of consanguinity according to the Roman computation; between the tenth and the twelfth centuries it had gradually come to forbid marriages as far as the seventh degree according to the Germanic computation, which was the equivalent of approximately the fourteenth degree according to the Roman computation (Figure 1). This bordered on the absurd: supposing that in each generation each couple had brought up and given in marriage one boy and one girl – which was lower than the real average, taking into account the increase of population in the eleventh and twelfth centuries – a marriageable youth would be forbidden to marry 2,731 cousins of his own generation, without counting their ancestors or descendants of marriageable age. In other words, whether he were a great lord marrying into his own class, or a peasant bound to the soil, he would be unable to marry all the marriageable girls he could possibly know and a great many more besides.

Without taking into account the impediments arising from spiritual kinship, which had multiplied, and those deriving from affinity, which had also been extended as far as the seventh degree, it is evident that the majority of young people had to remain celibate or defy the prohibitions. The constant infringements led to an extreme instability of the matrimonial tie, whether this was the result of the 'incestuous' spouses being denounced by some jealous person, or of one of the spouses, tiring of the other, demanding the annulment of the marriage. This was the reason why, in 1215, the Fourth Lateran Council limited the impediments on the grounds of consanguinity and legitimate affinity to the fourth degree of relationship, and that based on illicit affinity to the second degree.

These facts are a clear demonstration of the unrealistic nature of the prohibitions of the early Middle Ages, and hardly testify to the realism of subsequent canonical decrees. Moreover, the Protestants curtailed still further the impediments on the grounds of kinship, and the Catholic Church came to a similar decision in 1917, with the publication of the new code of canon law. It appears that canon lawyers and theologians did not, for the most part, comprehend the social utility of the impediments on the grounds of kinship, and that the majority of them were, above all, obsessed with the sin of incest.

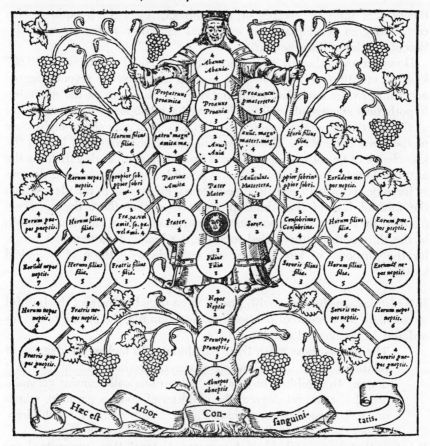

1. The tree of consanguinity. In each circle, the upper figure indicates the degree of kinship according to the Germanic (or canonical) computation, and the lower figure the degree according to the Roman (or civil) computation. From *Decretum Gratiani* (Paris, 1561), folio, col. 1939–40.

Nevertheless, it is impossible not to be impressed by the analogy between the evolution of the impediments and what we can observe of the evolution of the ties of lineal solidarity. The latter appear to have reached their zenith between the tenth and the twelfth centuries, and it was precisely during that era that the impediments were extended so excessively. When, on the other hand, from the thirteenth century onwards, the *lignage* became more narrowly based under the influence of the patrilinear tendencies which preceded the introduction of patronymic surnames, and when, paradoxically, the ties of lineal solidarity became weaker – as regards both vengeance and rights to landed property – the impediments were severely reduced in scope. One cannot, therefore, in the present state of research on this subject, reject the hypothesis of a certain degree of adaptation of canonical legislation to the actual evolution of the ties of lineal solidarity.

However, even though it is obvious that one could not know the 10,687 kinsfolk constituting the system of kinship as far as the seventh degree according to the canonical computation – on the basis of the minimum hypothetical average of fertility which we have adopted – reckoning as far as the fourth degree there were only 188, of whom only eighty-eight were of the same generation. This is few enough, if one compares it with the knowledge of ties of kinship possessed by certain peoples described by the anthropologists. It is, therefore, quite possible that the canonical decrees in force between 1215 and 1917 gave formal expression to the ideas which the faithful had of their kinship systems, or that those decrees were inspired by such ideas. It was not without some reason that Beaumanoir, in the thirteenth century, tried to make the limits of customary kinship, for the purposes of judicial 'rescue', coincide with those of canonical kinship.[23]

It is also known that the parish priests were urged to instruct the faithful to calculate the degrees of relationship. For example, the Bishop of Troyes ordered, in the synodal statutes of 1374:

> The priests must teach their parishioners to reckon the degrees of relationship in the following manner: brothers are of the first degree; the children of brothers, whom one calls cousins germain, are of the second degree; the children of cousins germain, whom one calls second cousins, are of the third degree; and their children, whom the people call third cousins, are of the fourth degree.[24]

It is true that it was probably not necessary to teach these peasants about their ties of kinship – the popular terms to which the text alludes suggest that they knew them well enough. It was rather a question of familiarizing them with the canonical computation. It must be observed, finally, that canon law attributed to kinship limitations similar to those attributed to it by customs of inheritance and of lineal repurchase, since the fourth degree according to the canonical computation corresponds to the seventh and eighth degrees according to the civil computation.

All these theoretical indications, however, need to be verified. Memoirs, journals and family record books provide the materials for this, particularly as regards the bourgeoisie. Before utilizing these sources, however, let us examine a more exceptional document, emanating from a nobleman: 'Nominal roll of my nephews, great-nephews and great-great-nephews, according to the custom of Brittany, which I, Brantôme, may have, and which I have made today, the 5th November 1603'. The interest of this document lies in the fact that the author attempted to compile a list of *all* his nephews. This was not usually the case. The authors of the family record books did not mention all the kinsfolk that they doubtless knew, and genealogies usually make only scant mention of collateral relations.

Disregarding repetitions, and without taking account of the common ancestors whom he does not name, Brantôme's list mentions 185 kinsfolk – which is not far short of the 188 that we calculated above – and is able to name seventy-three of their spouses. As a total, therefore, he would have 258 consanguineous or affinal kinsfolk. However large this number may appear, this total of kinsfolk lies more or less within the canonical limitations: Brantôme names only exceptionally – and because they belong to princely houses – his kinsmen of the fourth degree. In fact, he only had, in practice, relations of kinship as far as the third degree according to the Germanic computation.

It is also necessary to emphasize that he is not always capable of informing us whether a particular one of his male or female cousins had children, and if so how many and what their names were. In most cases, this can be explained by the very young age of the children concerned. Of Messieurs de Saint-Aulaire, de La Renaudie and des Estres – his nephews of the fifth degree according to the civil computation – he merely says that 'they have had a large number of children who are still very young today'. Why take them into account, since some died during the nursing stage and others were born? Moreover, since first names were not used, it was difficult to name these children individually before they received a title. This might happen early in the case of the boys. Thus, perhaps, 'the little M. de Coutures, who is today a young man'. The girls, on the other hand, often remained without any identity until their marriage: of M. de Saint-Aulaire, his first cousin, Brantôme writes that 'he had many daughters: the eldest was married at Borz-Saunier, and the second at Fradeaux. . .; and there were many other sisters whose names I do not know'. This is not due to lack of recent news, since he already knows that the second daughter, married at Fradeaux, 'has had many children'. The reason was, therefore, that there was not yet any interest in knowing them, their number – there were eight of them, counting the two eldest – condemning the youngest ones to obscurity. By way of a further example, he knows that his 'niece' of the fifth degree according to the civil computation, Madame de Charlus, had a son married to a daughter of the Count du Lude. Suspecting that she has had other children, and not knowing them, he takes it for granted that they are girls. In short, he mentions the unmarried girls only when they become known at court, e.g. 'Mademoiselle du Lude who died unmarried at court', or 'the beautiful and agreeable Maumont, brought up at court, who was the mistress of Monsieur the Dauphin', or when they are rich heiresses. Examples of this were the children of the two marriages of one of his 'nieces' of the seventh degree: 'The eldest is now married to

Monsieur the Duke of Usez, and the other is still unmarried, and both of them are very rich heiresses of the house of Saint-Sulpice; as also that of Montluc...[who] must still be only twelve or thirteen years old.' If he identifies them, even when they are young, despite their unmarried state and the fact that they bear only the eighth degree of relationship to him, it is because they are destined to form splendid matrimonial alliances and found new stocks.

However, Brantôme has not simply compiled a *Who's Who*: the knowledge that he possesses of his kinsfolk appears to imply – except in the case of the princely houses – effective relations of kinship. A proof of this is his ignorance, in cases where geographical separation has prevented continuous contacts: 'Monsieur de La Rochandry married, and his daughter was Madame the Countess of La Chambre, who was married in Savoy... and I have seen her brought up as a daughter of Madame de Savoye at her court, where Monsieur the Count of La Chambre married her. I do not know if there have been children of the marriage.' He could meet his other kinsfolk at the court of France, when he lived there, or receive news of them after he had left it. On the other hand, the geographical distance, and the strained relations between France and Savoy at that time, isolated him from that particular kinswoman.

This leads one to suppose that other examples of his ignorance – the most significant for our purposes – may be attributed to the distance of his relationship with the persons of whom he is speaking. Of Madame de Pescels and her sister the Viscountess of Panas he writes, 'They have children, but I am unable to name them, and yet we are closely related.' Paradoxically, this comment supports our interpretation: it is not the age or sex of the persons concerned that he considers, but the distance in genealogical terms. In fact, however close Brantôme may consider his kinship with these 'nieces' and their children – because they are descended from one of his great-grandfathers – it is nevertheless the most distant that one can find in his compilation. According to the civil law these ladies were of the eighth degree of relationship, and their children of the ninth degree, that is, beyond that seventh degree at which the majority of the customs established the limits of the *lignage*. According to the Germanic computation, his relationship to them was of the third to the fifth degree, and to their children of the third to the sixth, therefore canon law did not establish between them impediments to marriage on the grounds of kinship.

It was because he wrote this memoir towards the end of his life that Brantôme was able to know 'nephews, great-nephews and great-great-nephews, according to the custom of Brittany', who were distant by four or five degrees from their common stocks. However, with the exception of those stocks that connected him with princely houses, Brantôme himself is never at a distance of more than three degrees from these stocks. In other words, he remains within the theoretical limits of his kinship. If this was the case with a nobleman, so attached to his genealogy, what can one expect of the bourgeoisie and the peasantry?

In order to evaluate bourgeois kinship systems in France, we will examine in detail two private journals written in the early sixteenth century: that of Jehan de Gennes, a prosperous merchant of Vitré, which was kept from 1490 onwards;[25] and that of Nicolas Versoris, a Parisian lawyer, which covers the period 1519–30.[26] The kinsfolk concerned are living – or actually die – at the moment when they are mentioned, whereas, in order to explain his ties of kinship with living people, Brantôme took into consideration the existence of kinsfolk long since dead. This artificially reduces the relative importance of these bourgeois kinship systems. On the other hand, whereas Brantôme was a bachelor and therefore had no affinal kin, our two bourgeois diarists were married, and the kinsfolk of their wives have almost as important a place in the journals as do their own. In addition, the strength of kinship based on matrimonial alliances is emphasized by the appellations 'brother' and 'sister' which designate brothers-in-law and sisters-in-law as well as full brothers and sisters. It often happens, indeed, that the reader is incapable of distinguishing between a brother-in-law and a brother sprung from the same womb. Furthermore, the two journals are written from a different approach, which makes comparison between them difficult. Nicolas Versoris notes, day by day and as they happen, the events which have appeared to him to be 'notable' – in particular, for our purposes, births, marriages and deaths. Jean de Gennes, on the other hand, has included, in what is as much an account book as a journal, details of his closest kinsfolk. The inventory of these details would have been instructive if the 'journal' had been published in its entirety. Since its publication was interrupted, the most interesting procedure is to make an inventory of the consanguineous and affinal kin whose presence he mentions at the betrothals and weddings of his closest relations.

Jean de Gennes mentions thirty-five consanguineous relations, twelve affinal kin of these relations, and eighteen kinsfolk of these affinal kin. One must add fifteen relations of his wife, and seven affinal kin of these affinal kin, making a total of eighty-seven cognatic and affinal kin. More significant than this number is the genealogical proximity of his thirty-five consanguineous relations. These consisted of seven children, his father, his mother, eight brothers and half-brothers, two sisters, nine nephews, three uncles or cousins on his mother's side and four uncles or cousins on his father's side. That is to say, they extended as far as the second degree of relationship according to the canonical reckoning. Similarly, the relations of his wife, or those of the wives of his brothers, do not include those farther removed than uncles and first cousins. As far as kinship is concerned, the bourgeois had a short memory, which most certainly did not preclude – quite the contrary – the existence of a family spirit.

Nicolas Versoris mentions only thirty-four consanguineous kinsfolk, including eight children, six brothers and sisters, fifteen nephews and nieces, one maternal uncle and four cousins. To these are added fourteen affinal kin of these blood-relations, and twenty-three cognatic and affinal kin of his two successive wives – a total of seventy-one cognatic and affinal kin. Even though four of the children died within fifteen days of their birth, and some of his nephews may have met the same fate without his recording it, this still amounts to a considerable total of kinsfolk. Moreover, this is a record of only part of them: those who have been born, or have died, or have been married, or have even been godfathers and godmothers to his children and nephews, between 1519 and 1530.

The godparents, in both the Gennes and the Versoris families, were generally chosen from among the cognatic and affinal kinsfolk. Thus, spiritual kinship, by coinciding so often with consanguinity and legitimate affinity, did not cause complications with regard to future marriages. During the lifetime of the people concerned, there is no doubt that this custom had the additional advantage of making family ties closer. One extreme example seems to constitute evidence of this: when Nicolas Versoris chose, as godmother to his daughter Anne, the second wife of Pierre Herbert – of whom he does not even tell us the surname and Christian names – it was no doubt with the object of retaining within the kinship system of the Versoris Pierre Herbert, whose first wife, Marguerite Versoris, niece of Nicolas, had died six months previously. It also happened that a person was invited to stand as godfather in order to establish ties which one could not form by marriage because of a difference in social status. Perhaps the nobleman Guyon de la Charonnière, Constable of Vitré, and the wife of the chatelain of Vitré, who stood as godparents to the second daughter of Jean de Gennes, were a degree above him in the social hierarchy. This is by no means certain: it may have been simply a very short-term political manoeuvre. However, when he took as 'little godfather' to his eldest son, and as godmother to his second son, Pierre Tirel and Perrine Tirel, the children or close relatives of his trusted employee, it is evident that he was thus seeking to institutionalize a bond of fidelity which could not be institutionalized by marriage.

In the fascinating work of historical anthropology which he has devoted to the family life of Ralph Josselin, Alan Macfarlane has emphasized the few contacts which this rector of an Essex village had with his kinsfolk.[27]

30

Neither christenings nor funerals provided him with an opportunity of meeting them. We regard these ceremonies as essentially family occasions; but they were not so, to such an extent, in past times. When Bodynays de Gennes, a prosperous merchant of Vitré and one of the principal attorneys of the town, died on Thursday, 15 August 1521, around four o'clock in the morning, in his home at La Brosse, few family members were present at his funeral.

> On the said day after vespers his said body was carried to his house in the Rue de la Poterie [his town and business residence]..., and later the guilds and religious confraternities of this town and its suburbs came to fetch it, and his said body was carried by four merchants of note to the Church of Our Lady...and afterwards escorted by the said guilds and carried by the said merchants to the cemetery of Saint Martin, where it was buried close to and at the end of the tomb and sepulchre of my late father.

The family, in this account, is represented only by its dead members.

Occasionally the living relatives were present, in the more ostentatious funeral ceremonies, but discreetly so. An example of this occurred in April of the same year, when they buried the father-in-law of Jean de Gennes, André Cholet, lord of La Mereyaye, who died at midday on 8 March.

> And on Wednesday, the ninth day of the said month, members of the guilds of Our Lady and of Saint Mary Magdalene and of the Augustinians came to fetch the body, and they carried it, to wit: the lord of the Hayrie Jehan de la Reaulté, lieutenant-governor of Vitré, Maître Jullien Dargentré, attorney, and François de la Mue, lord of the Chederie, and the pall was carried by Guillaume Dollier, lord of the Caillere, Maître Guillaume de Grasmenil, lord of the Meix, Maître Pierre Brocquet, lord of the Feu, and Gile Gaulay, lord of the Mesnil Morel.

Apart from Giles Gaulay, there is no mention of these persons as being kinsmen: they are the most notable men of the town, and it is in that capacity that they are present. They were followed by crowds of poor people dressed for the occasion in 'robes of very good frieze' and carrying torches, candles or flares in honour of the deceased. These, too, were part of the ostentation. The family, as such, appeared only at the moment of interment, the body then being carried by four of the grandchildren of the dead man. All four of them, however, were accompanied and guided by two men and two women from among the most notable citizens of the town, who thus associated the participation of the body politic with that of the family. Finally, the closest relations were distinguished by their being dressed in mourning: 'And mourning was worn by the said lord of the Neuptumières and his brother (the two grandchildren of the deceased), representing the men. And, representing the women, Jacquine Cholet,

Briande Cholet and Gilete Cholet, all three of them unmarried girls and the sole heiresses of the said late lord of the Mereyaye.' The unobtrusiveness of the immediate family, on this occasion, was not, therefore, complete. Furthermore, Jean de Gennes observed in conclusion that at this funeral service 'there were present many gentlemen who were kinsmen of the said deceased man, and most of the people of the better class of the town and the suburbs of that place, both men and women, and most of them dined at the house'. However, these kinsfolk, whether close or distant, were not the only ones concerned in the event, nor did they occupy the most prominent place at the ceremony. At the other funerals of the Gennes family, which were less ostentatious, they did not appear at all. Nevertheless, the journal of Jean de Gennes leaves us in no doubt as to the closeness of the ties that he maintained with his cognatic and affinal kin.

The consanguineous kin of whom Macfarlane has made an inventory, based on the journal kept by Josselin, are not, however, less numerous than those that we have found in the journals of the two French bourgeois: thirty-three, as against thirty-five and thirty-four. This total does not include either the four children who died in infancy, or the grandchildren, of whom one at least brought great joy to Josselin, or the nephews whom his four sisters might have given him. Moreover, there are cited by name in this kinship system seven uncles and fourteen cousins, whereas uncles and cousins totalled no more than seven in the entire journal of Jean de Gennes and five in that of Nicolas Versoris, the essential core of the kinship systems of the two bourgeois being constituted by their brothers and sisters and their nephews. It is true that, with the exception of two of them whom he visited four or five times, Josselin never, or hardly ever, saw his cousins. This is not surprising, however, when one considers the distance that separated them. What must be emphasized, in the case of these kinsfolk of Josselin, is their geographical dispersion. In that respect, they bear a resemblance to kinship systems in developed industrial societies. Was this, however, in the seventeenth century, a habitual characteristic of bourgeois kinship systems?

As compared with forty-three family events, Nicolas Versoris noted, between 1519 and 1530, sixty-three deaths or marriages occurring among the lawyers and physicians of Paris. One should not, however, conclude from this that the professional or social milieu enjoyed, among his preoccupations, a higher place than the family milieu. His family milieu was quite indistinguishable from his social milieu: it was more restricted than the Parisian professional bourgeoisie, and it did not reach the summit of that class, but it was entirely included within it. The same can be said of the de Gennes family and their affinal kin in relation to the bourgeoisie of Vitré, subject to some differentiating factors – such as their residences in the country and their matrimonial alliances formed in Nantes or Alençon.

As a country parson, Josselin was in a very different situation. Like the nobleman in his feudal domain, the country clergyman was of a status different from that of his parishioners. Even though he succeeded in forming relations of friendship with certain neighbours of his own social and educational level, he could not usually convert these into relations of kinship: ecclesiastical benefices were not hereditary in the way that feudal domains were, and the children of the clergy were not destined to possess the same social status in the same locality. Furthermore, the nobles, by reason of their leisurely lives, enjoyed living in the company of their kinsfolk and friends; they had the means to offer them hospitality; and when they were as distinguished as Brantôme was, they regularly met them at court. The clergyman, on the other hand, lived in principle a life of austerity, little calculated to attract his kinsfolk, and he hardly possessed the means to entertain them. Like the village *curé* in France, he was condemned to live far away from them, and, with a wife and children, he had less interest than the *curé* in his nephews and nieces, and thus lived more enclosed in his own household. In short, the family life of Josselin was probably typical of that of many clergymen, but it is by no means certain that it provides us with an accurate portrayal of kinship solidarities among the propertied classes in England in the seventeenth century.

Another noteworthy English example is that of Simon Forman, a London astrologer of Shakespeare's time.[28] Coming from a good family living in the neighbourhood of Salisbury, he kept in touch with his brothers and sisters who occasionally came to consult or assist him, but he paid most attention to his wife's family, after a late marriage which ensured his fortune and his social standing.

Samuel Pepys,[29] on the contrary, situated in the uppermost sector of the bourgeoisie, lacked affinal kin, because he married the daughter of a French *émigré*. However, he mentions in his diary over eighty living relations – for the most part quite distant, since we often have difficulty in understanding his relationship to them – and he had regular contacts with a large proportion of them. Moreover, he owed his education at Cambridge, and his brilliant career, to the patronage of Lord Sandwich, who was his second cousin, even though Pepys never had the impudence to remind him of this relationship. The son of a poor tailor, he had thus become one of the most eminent representatives of the Pepys family, and one can understand that his close or distant relations should have wished to cultivate his acquaintance.

3. KINSHIP AND NEIGHBOURHOOD AMONG THE PEASANTRY

The co-terminous nature of the social milieu and the kinship system, which we have emphasized in the cases of Jean de Gennes and Nicolas Versoris, as an element favouring solidarity between kinsfolk, was just as universal among the French peasantry. The census held at Brueil-en-Vexin, at the beginning of the seventeenth century, demonstrates that, whatever the differences in material fortune between heads of households, the circle of matrimonial alliances included all the 'lines of descent'. All of them, even the most recently established, had cognatic or affinal kin in the village.

The reason for this is that it was customary, among the peasants, to take a wife from the same parish. In the eighteenth century, at Saint-Méen-le-Grand (Ille-et-Vilaine), the proportion of endogamous marriages within the parish was 71.6 per cent; at Bilhères d'Ossau (Pyrénées-Atlantiques) it was 74.2 per cent; at Vineuil (Loire-et-Cher), it was 80.2 per cent; and at Roziers-sur-Loire (Maine-et-Loire) it reached a level of 93 per cent between 1661 and 1700. The proportion was even more impressive in some villages in mountainous areas, such as Caillac (Hautes-Alpes), where almost all marriages had to take place with dispensations from the impediments on the grounds of kinship. Elsewhere, dispensation was not customarily given, and the endogamic tendency was then curbed by the prohibitions of the Church. There were, it is true, some villages where the frequency of marriages among two young people of the same parish was much less marked than in the examples previously given: the proportion was 34 per cent at Rumont, in the Gâtinais; 33.3 per cent at Saint-Agnan, in the Morvan; 31 per cent at Rouvray, in the Vallage (Champagne). These were, however, generally small villages where the network of kinship was already too all-embracing for a young man to find a wife without infringing the prohibitions: Rumont had only 260 inhabitants, and Rouvray 216. The correlation between the size of villages and the degree of endogamy within the same parish is clearly shown in the Vallage, which has recently been the object of an excellent demographic survey:[30]

At Rouvray (216 inhabitants): 31% of the marriages were endogamous
At Donjeux (305 inhabitants): 46%
At Blécourt (442 inhabitants): 55%
At Mussey (511 inhabitants): 68%

In short, the ties of kinship reinforced neighbourhood solidarities both in the larger villages – where the high rate of marriages between people of the same parish continually made the ties closer – and in the smaller ones, where endogamy was rare on account of the density of their networks of kinship.

It remains to be ascertained how far ties of solidarity within the village were based on kinship and how far on the simple fact of neighbourhood. Ethnologists have observed that in certain villages of present-day France one considers systematically as kinsfolk the other inhabitants of the village, even when one does not have any known tie of kinship with them, for the mere reason that they are from the same village.[31] It is as though the concept of kinship were founded on the fact of belonging to the village community more than on ties of blood and affinity. This, however, might be because the peasant has been accustomed for centuries to being related to all the inhabitants of his village; for if one wished to emphasize only the fact of belonging to the village community, why make use of the terms of kinship? Such a custom, paradoxically, is evidence of the importance of ties of kinship in the ideology of the peasantry.

However, the customs which regulated the peasant life – whether in the extremely community-oriented regions of the north-east of France and the Paris Basin, or in the other regions – were related to membership of the village and the neighbourhood rather than to kinship. This was the case not only as far as political and agricultural life was concerned, but also as regards what we refer to as 'private life' and 'family life'.

The young people of the village, as a group, regulated the meetings between lovers and intervened, again as a group, in the nuptial cere-monies, particularly by means of the rite of the 'barrier', when the young bride married an 'outsider', and by the mock serenade, when the marriage was not to their liking. These two types of intervention expressed, more or less consciously, the girl's membership of the village, and the rights over her which that conferred on the marriageable young men of the parish. Moreover, their right of supervision of the relations between the sexes did not cease after the wedding: women who were unfaithful to their husbands and, worse still, complaisant cuckolds and husbands who suffered chastisement from their wives were called to order by the mock serenade and the 'azouade', i.e. the punishment of being promenaded on a donkey. Whereas among the nobility or the bourgeoisie such lapses in behaviour often led to the meeting of a family council, among the peasants and even among the town-dwellers it was the people of the village or of the suburb who intervened. It is of particular significance that in the 'azouade' the principal role was customarily played by the nearest neighbour of the couple that had caused the scandal, whether he led the donkey which the husband was forced to ride in a ridiculous posture, or, as happened more frequently in the period with which we are concerned, he himself had to ride the donkey and play the role of the husband who had suffered chastisement. This was a way of emphasizing his duty of surveillance and, in consequence, his responsibility for the misconduct of his neighbours.

Neighbourhood solidarities were particularly strong in the case of the women, who were more attached than their husbands to the house, at least in the peasant environment. Every day they would go to borrow a cooking utensil from one woman neighbour, to ask the advice of another, and they would gossip on the doorsteps of their houses, or meet in those traditional meeting-places of the womenfolk – the well and the washing-place: 'Two women make a dispute, three make a great chatter, four make a complete market.' The peasant men, on the other hand, spent the entire day dispersed throughout the area of the parish – except in winter and during the summer months, when collective help was needed for the major tasks – and, when they met in the tavern in the evenings, it might be among friends or men of their own age-group as often as among neighbours.

It is possible that in the towns the men were more closely associated with their immediate neighbourhood. This was true in the case of the craftsmen of Lyons in the eighteenth century.[32] They all lived in houses of from eight to twelve, and sometimes more, apartments, and they were subject, under the authority of the proprietor and of the municipality, to certain collective obligations under the supervision of a 'principal occupant': to maintain the latrines, and sweep the stairways, the corridors and the pavement in front of the building. This was, one suspects, the source of frequent conflicts. Their solidarity, however, often manifested itself in a more salutary way. When there was the slightest incident, everybody appeared at the windows, and everybody kept silent when the police made enquiries. When a trial took place, the neighbours provided the accused with certificates attesting to his upright life and conduct. And when the bailiffs or the police arrived with the intention of dealing severely with an occupant, the neighbours spontaneously offered their assistance. To quote one example among thousands: a man named Carra, a shoemaker working at his home in the Rue Puitspalu, was involved in a dispute with his guild, and the masters of the guild came one day to his house to deliver a summons. At once the occupant of the ground floor, a confectioner, recognized them, and from his back-shop he shouted to Carra to lock himself up in his apartment. At the same time, the women of the house who were in the street shouted to the shoemaker 'Carra! Carra! Shut your door, the master-shoemakers are coming up to see you!' This assistance was effective because, finding the door barricaded, the delegates postponed their visit until another day.

Everywhere, woman neighbours lent their assistance on the occasion of confinements, baptisms and funerals. In the Pyrenees, custom even prescribed in detail the obligations of each man and woman neighbour in these circumstances. In the case of a death, for example, it was the duty of the closest neighbours to hurry and inform the kinsfolk and friends of the deceased person, and to prepare the house, while the second neighbour cooked the meal and attended to the livestock. The closest woman neighbour stood, in church, at the side of the bereaved; and it was often the four closest neighbours who carried the coffin.[33] They were taken into account even in the regulations which attempted to limit the ostentation of funerals. Thus, Article 19 of the statutes of the Val d'Azun prescribed that: 'In order to remedy the abuses and the great expenses that take place on the days of the burial of the dead, which ruin families of limited fortunes, only the two neighbours and the four closest relatives of the bereaved person may enter the house of the heirs of the deceased, except for people from another village.'[34] This article, however, also demonstrates that neighbourhood solidarity did not supplant kinship solidarity, whether the kinsfolk were from the village or from elsewhere.

In the relationships which a peasant had with his kinsfolk living in the same village, did he take account of their kinship? This question has hardly been studied at all, but the following dialogue, reported by Rétif de la Bretonne, suggests that he did:

> We were joined by a man who was coming out of his vineyard, with his basket on his back; it was Jean Piôt, the weaver, the maternal cousin of the Abbé Thomas. He says to this man: 'Good day, cousin. Have they not said that you come from Paris?' 'That is true, cousin.' 'Do you know that your cousin Jean Piôt, son [of] Jean Le Maréchal, [who lived] opposite your grandfather, is dead?' 'No, cousin.'[35]

If, among the inhabitants of the village, kinsmen were thus identified, we may suppose that kinship did not fail to have certain specific effects.

When one had kinsfolk outside the village, one occasionally visited them. Nicolas Rétif recalled how, in his childhood, 'the two Rétifs from Joux, Jean and Bénigne, often came to the house. . .They brought news of what had been happening to the east of my village.'[36] The village referred to was Sacy, at six or seven kilometres' distance from Joux-la-Ville. More exceptional was the visit of 'my two Gautherin girl cousins', who came from Aigremont, situated a dozen kilometres from Sacy.[37] 'They were the daughters of a sister of my father's mother. Marie, the fair-haired eldest girl, was to be married; she came to tell her uncle of this.' Young Nicolas, who was then about ten years old, appears to have been seeing them for the first time. As an infant, he had also been shown once to Jean Rétif – an attorney at Noyers, at about fifteen kilometres' distance from Sacy – and to 'my cousin Droin, from the villages on the river-bank'.[38] These were two old men, of whom the former was first cousin to Pierre Rétif, the grandfather of Nicolas. He had often shown an interest in his peasant cousins, and particularly in Edme, the father of Nicolas. However, even though there is frequent mention, in the journal of Nicolas, of the Rétifs of Grenoble, the children of that judicious and well-to-do kinsman of Noyers, he does not seem to have ever met them.

Much closer, in terms of both kinship and distance, were the full sisters of Edme, who remained at Nitry, which their brother had left when he married. Marie, the youngest, who died when Nicolas was a small child, had spent some days at her brother's house, shortly after her second marriage.[39] As for the eldest, his aunt Madelon, she must sometimes have travelled the five kilometres to Sacy, because Nicolas asserts that he has known her well and loved her from his earliest years. Not having had any children by her two successive marriages,

> she loved those of her brother as if they had been her own; I, above all, was the object of her endearments and of her tender and sincere affection; thus, whenever they spoke of me of going to see my aunt Madelon, I was beside myself with joy. It was a highly esteemed favour which my father did me, in taking me to the patronal festival at Nitry.[40]

It appears, however, that he was over ten years old when he went there for the first time: 'I had in Nitry another uncle-by-marriage, the husband of my [deceased] aunt Marie, the younger sister of my father, named Pierre Leclere. My aunt [Madelon] took me to his house for me to pay him my respects...; he had with him a son, one or two years older than I. We became acquainted.'[41] It was on that same day that he also made the acquaintance of all his other kinsfolk in Nitry, beginning with the beautiful Edmée Boissart.

> We were approaching the church...when I saw coming out of a nearby house a girl...who was bringing home some small ducklings with their mother. Her beauty struck me like a flash of lightning... 'Edmée?' said my aunt to her, 'this is your cousin Nicolas, from Sacy, and are you not going to kiss him?' Edmée ran towards them; but when she got near me, she blushed and became all bashful. My aunt made us kiss one another. Thereupon we went to the church...I felt in my heart of hearts my natural timidity, which would have been very much more marked if my father had not been greatly respected in Nitry, if I had not been so well dressed and if I had not been among kinsfolk who had the highest opinion of me...[42]

When they reached the church, Nicolas discovered the exclusive rights conferred by residence and the privileges of kinship.

> My uncle, who was following us, took charge of me and led me to the choir, where his stall was; he, for his part, was going to sing bass in the choir. My father, ever since he had abandoned the place in church of the honourable Pierre, would never accept that which

his kinsmen or friends offered him; 'I am no longer anybody in Nitry!' he would say. And he would go and sit, as though in exile, by the door of the church, under the belfry, behind the poorest people. . .[43]

However, outside a public place such as the church, the ties of kinship could manifest themselves to the full. Edme Rétif

had brought with him his genealogy; he read it to his two brothers-in-law, who were hearing it for the first time. They were enchanted with it, and I heard the praises of my grandfather re-echo. They did speak, however, of some of his defects. . .After dinner, all our kinsfolk of both sexes came to call on my father, the only descendant with a respected name; for each one of them wanted to invite him for tea or supper. Then there arrived Edmée Boissard, Ursule Simon, Catin Doré, Georgette Lemour, Catiche Touslesjours, Dodiche Gautherin, Ursule Lamas and other girls of my family, the most agreeable girls in the district. They took me to their cottage gardens, to make bouquets to give me, while their fathers and mothers chatted with my father, my aunt and my uncles.[44]

This exceptional appearance of Edme Rétif and his son in the birthplace of their family demonstrates, therefore, the abundance of kinsfolk in the surrounding countryside more effectively than do the day-to-day tasks, christenings, funerals, and even weddings, for on those occasions not all the kinsfolk from outside the village made their appearance, and those within the village were inextricably intermingled with the neighbours and friends. Nevertheless, one should not conclude, from the exceptional character of the family reunion in Nitry, that relations of kinship were a luxury for the peasantry. They were often useful, and even possessed, in peasant life, quasi-specific functions.

Uncles, aunts and grandparents, not to mention more distant relations, felt a sense of responsibility towards their nephews, nieces, grandchildren and young cousins, and public opinion did indeed hold them responsible. This was especially evident on the occasion of weddings, not only among the higher nobility,[45] but also in the lowest social circles. When her father was ruined as a result of the burning down of his house, Barbe Ferlet, the future mother of Rétif, went to live in the house of a wealthy kinswoman, Madame Pandevant, in Auxerre and later in Paris. It was there that she made the acquaintance of M. Boujat, who proposed marriage to her. The girl 'asked him to apply for permission to Madame Pandevant. Enchanted by the gifts that this man bestowed on his intended wife, this lady accepted the suitor. The wedding took place within eight days.' Unfortunately, Boujat was a bigamist. His legal wife, when she found out about this second marriage, went to Barbe and asked her: 'Have you been married for long?' 'Eighteen months, Madame.' 'How did you make the acquaintance of M.B.?' 'It was in the house of my cousin Madame Pandevant, Madame: it was she who arranged our marriage.' 'Ah!. . . it was with the authorization of a kinswoman?. . .That makes things different.'[46] If the young wife had got married on her own initiative, she would have been culpable. But she could not be reproached on any grounds, since the marriage had taken place under the authority of that kinswoman with whom she was living.

Another example was that of Elisabeth Bernard who, in 1666, wished to have her betrothal annulled by the officiality of Troyes. She maintained that she had become engaged only 'out of respect for her mother, her grandmother and her relations, and that she had never had. . .any affection for the said Gross', her fiancé. The latter approached the question from another viewpoint, without contradicting her as to the facts: he maintained that 'the said promises of marriage had been made with the free and untrammelled consent of her aforesaid kinsfolk', that is to say the mother, the grandmother, the uncle, the aunt and other kinsfolk and friends of Elisabeth Bernard.[47]

The intervention of the kinsfolk, which on this occasion took place to the detriment of the feelings of the girl concerned, might, on the other hand, be requested by young people who desired to escape from the tyranny of a father, a mother or a guardian. Furthermore, the law itself suggested such a course: 'The young person may complain to the Judge of the tyranny to which an unjust and barbarous father or mother may try to subject him; the father and mother of the young person are then called in evidence, and sometimes the kinsfolk are called: in this latter case, their decisions have judicial effect.'[48] This procedure was employed particularly in disputes arising between an orphan and his guardian. Thus, when Marie Guillier requested the officiality of Troyes to permit her to marry Jean Dauvert, despite the opposition of her guardian, the court ordered 'that fourteen of the closest kinsfolk of the said Guillier, that is to say seven on the father's side and seven on the mother's side, shall be called as witnesses regarding the said promises'.[49] Moreover, it is probable that this recourse to the kinsfolk did not always take place through the mediation of the courts.

In this society, in which widowhood and remarriage were much more frequent than today, it was accepted that the close kinsfolk should intervene to protect orphans from ill-treatment at the hands of a stepmother. This stereotype of family relations appears clearly in one of the children's games described by Rétif, the game of the stepmother, which was particu-

40

larly dramatic. It required four principal actors: the father, the stepmother, the orphaned girl and the 'maternal aunt, sister of the dead
mother'.

The aunt arrived from a neighbouring village. As she approached
the place where the stepmother was sitting with the stepdaughter,
whom she was forcing to work without ever raising her head, she
sought information on every side as to how her niece was treated
by her stepmother. Some said, 'She only gives her mouldy bread.'
Others said, 'She only gives her half-rotten wild apples to eat.'
The aunt, every time, would answer 'Oh! my poor niece! daughter
of my poor sister whom I loved so much!' She reached the house of
stepmother, who assumed a kindly expression. 'Good day, sister...
Now then, my little girl, leave your work; you have done enough.'
The stepdaughter stood up, but she had had her head bent down
for so long, toiling at her work, that she could not lift it. 'Hold your
head up, then, my niece!' 'Alas, I do not know how to. My neck is
bent, it will never be straightened!' The aunt turned her head away
to hide her tears, and the stepmother made the stepdaughter
straighten herself up by two sharp blows before and behind. 'Come,
sister,' went on the evil woman, 'you have come from far; you would
like a bite to eat. I am going to lay out the tablecloth.' The stepdaughter brought her the tablecloth, in which was wrapped some
black mouldy bread which fell to the ground. The stepmother said
in a whisper, 'Bitch, pick up your bread.' And out loud, 'there is no
lack of bread here; for one lets it get mouldy.' They all sat down
at the table, and the stepmother served eggs and cheese. The aunt
said to her niece, 'Eat, now, my girl!' But while she was not looking, the stepmother took away what she had on her plate, and
gave it to her own children, by the father's second marriage, who
were standing round the table. The stepdaughter got up, without
having eaten anything. She surreptitiously picked up a piece of
mouldy bread, which she devoured. 'What is that you are eating,
my child?' said the aunt. 'It is some dainty that she has filched from
me,' said the stepmother, 'for she is fond of delicacies and I spoil
her somewhat.' But the aunt had seen everything, without showing
that she had, and she flew into a rage, taking from her niece the
piece of mouldy bread, which she showed to the father as he
entered the house. Then she repeated to him the rigmarole of words
which they had addressed to her when she arrived. The father beat
the stepmother and gave the stepdaughter to the aunt, who took
her away and kept her in her house. When she went out, she told
the two rows of people who stood in her way all that she was going
to give her: 'I shall feed her with white bread, fresh eggs and

cheese made from cream. I shall dress her in fine linen and striped Siamese cloth; her under-petticoats shall be of soft flannel, and her outer garments of fine cotton embroidered with flowers; her corsets of dimity; her stockings of white wool with red clocks; her shoes shall have high heels, and her coifs shall be of muslin with neatly pleated lace.' The object of this game was to discourage remarriage by widowers with grown-up children.[50]

There are numerous historical instances of orphans who really did suffer persecution at the hands of a stepmother. One of the best known and the most tragic is that of Captain Coignet.[51] However, the oversimplified picture which this game represented of the wickedness of a stepmother and of the hopes that an orphan girl could place in her maternal aunt constitutes, fundamentally, a more sound historical document, more revealing of the stereotypes of the society concerned, and it does not necessitate any reflection as regards the personal character of each of the actors in the drama, or the situation of the person narrating it. It is evident that the situation of the second wife – though less tragic than that of the orphan – was by no means easy, either. Rétif de la Bretonne provides evidence of this, when he recounts the disputes of his own mother, Barbe Ferlet, with her five stepdaughters. 'As was the custom, she was not loved by her stepchildren, and there was no one to take her part in the village, because she was an outsider.'[52] It was not by mere chance that she had this status: in the case of a second marriage, the impediments on the grounds of affinity combined with those on the grounds of kinship, and made it more difficult to find a wife in the village.

> She wanted to exercise authority over her stepdaughters, who were already grown up and accustomed to being independent; she was unsuccessful in this, and suffered on this occasion from the defects of her personal upbringing; never having been contradicted, she doubtless went too far, but it was when one had overstepped the limits with her. Nevertheless, the husband never noticed these domestic disputes. His wife became all serene in her demeanour as soon as he appeared, and only rarely complained. It was another person who informed the father of the family of what was happening in his house.

This other person was, once again, an aunt, but this time the sister of the father, which might serve as a guarantee of impartiality.

> A sister of my father had occasion to spend some days in the house; on the first and second days, everyone kept their feelings in check, but the older girls lost their patience on the third day, in the morning. They were in the wrong; and the aunt, surprised by this outburst, took the part of her sister-in-law against her nieces. But

this was not the way to restore peace. The girls cried, and said that they had been abandoned by everybody ever since that beautiful lady had come to steal away their father's heart from them. On the following days, the same scene was repeated. Then the aunt, now quite convinced that people so ill-suited to live together were making each other miserable, spoke of the matter to her brother. 'It is what I had foreseen', he replied, 'and I had congratulated myself too soon on being happily deceived.'[53]

Everyone was aware of the fact that a stepmother and stepdaughters inevitably made one another unhappy. For this reason the maternal grandfather of the five girls, when his son-in-law came to speak to him of the possibility of remarrying, was violently opposed to it. 'Thomas Dondaine took fright at the very idea of this marriage. He fulminated against it and, on the following day, made an inventory of the property of his daughter and his son-in-law in favour of his grandchildren.'[54] However, once the second marriage had taken place, the only solution to the inevitable conflict was for the children of the first marriage to leave the house. In the case of Captain Coignet, of whom no kinsman had been willing to take charge, this departure took place in the worst possible circumstances: he fled, wandered from place to place, and was brought up in the house of strangers from his early childhood. The daughters of Marie Dondaine, because they had kinsfolk on their mother's side, had more good fortune in their plight.

'It is the older girls who cause all the trouble', Edme Rétif had asserted, to justify their expulsion from the house.

I have been asked to give the eldest in marriage; the match is advantageous, but I hesitated; yet I will marry her off. The second girl wants to go to the town to serve an apprenticeship: she shall go. My father-in-law Dondaine has asked for the third one; I will give her to him. He already has the fourth; therefore I shall keep here only the youngest, who is of an amiable character and, besides, is but a child. . .These are all natural arrangements. But, believe me, sister, if I were in a different position, I would have been able to speak as a father and master and bring all these little people to their senses.[55]

This recourse to the maternal grandfather was due to the fact that he lived to an exceptionally great age and he still possessed the patrimony of the Dondaines. He did not die until the age of eighty-eight, when Marie-Anne Rétif was twenty-six and Marie-Madeleine twenty-one. The former was by then married to a wet cooper of Joux-la-Ville, and the latter was housekeeper to her brother, the parish priest of Courgis. Usually, however, it was an uncle who had inherited the patrimony and who took charge of the boy and girl orphans.

There are innumerable examples in the registers of dispensations for marriage of this recourse on the part of orphans to their uncle. A farmer of the diocese of Meaux, whose son and niece, both aged twenty-three, had fallen in love with each other, thus causing a scandal in the entire district, declared

> that it is only too true that the petitioners have been together often, the said female petitioner having lived in the house of him, the witness, for about six years with the said male petitioner, to which the witness was obliged to consent by reason of the fact that he was her guardian and that she could not conveniently live in another place; that the public had often spoken of their association, for which reason he, the witness, had sent the said female petitioner to the house of her uncle, living at Lumigny, but she had not been able to stay there, owing to the ill-treatment she received from the wife of the said uncle.[56]

Similarly, Madeleine Millet, aged eighteen, the daughter of a farmer, and in love with her first cousin Joseph Bertin, explained 'that they had been in each other's company for a long time, the said female petitioner having lived since the age of nine years in the house of the mother of the said male petitioner'.[57] It is clear that this situation, even though it facilitated 'incestuous' love-affairs, did not inevitably lead to them, and that there were many more orphans brought up by uncles and aunts than these registers of marriage dispensations indicate.

Moreover, it was not necessary to have lost one's father and mother to go and live in the house of a kinsman. The better-off farmers, who always had work to be done, frequently offered a place as a domestic worker to their poor relations. Thus, the man named Lange, who had made a girl pregnant, in the bailiwick of Provins, was a 'carter working for Lange, his uncle, a farmer at Fontaine-Argent'.[58] Another example was the man called Touslesjours – in fact a Rétif – 'a ploughboy, and kinsman of the house', whom Edme Rétif, when he was still living with his father, 'had himself brought up', and whose conduct had so satisfied him that they 'struck up a warm friendship'.[59] Yet another example was Nicolas Siot, that young saddler of the village of Saint-Jean-de-Rebès, in the diocese of Meaux, whom his cousin Marie Varié summoned on the death of her husband, who had also been a saddler, to take over the shop and marry the eldest girl who was to inherit it in due course.[60]

In this type of arrangement between a kinsman who possessed a means of production and a proletarian kinsman, the position of a son-in-law, which gave rights over the inheritance, was in principle better than that of a nephew or of a young cousin employed as a servant. Not all sons-in-law, however, were satisfied with the situation. Edme Rétif, who lived and worked for seventeen years in the house of Thomas Dondaine, 'suffered much on account of the harsh temper of Thomas'; 'his servitude – for it really was such – terminated at the death of the respectable Marie. . . As soon as Edme was made a widower, discretion and his obligations towards his young family did not permit him to live any longer with his father-in-law. He left him, and went to work on his own account.'[61] This idealized account – which pictures the association of Edme and his father-in-law as similar to the seven years of slavery that Jacob underwent for the love of Rachel – unfortunately gives no details of the provisions of the marriage contract nor of the actual possibility or impossibility of Edme's establishing himself on his own account earlier. It has some value, however, in making clear to us the psychological problems to which these family arrangements might lead. The resentment of Edme found an echo, at the other extremity of France, in the Basque or Béarnais proverbs emphasizing the misfortune of being a son-in-law – or describing the misfortune of having only sons-in-law instead of sons – and the Provençal proverbs portraying the cupidity of nephews.[62] In these arrangements between kinsfolk, each one was under the impression that he was assisting the other on account of their kinship, and was being duped by him. However, notwithstanding the obsessive repetitiveness of the proverbs on the subject, people generally preferred to serve their kinsfolk – or be served by them – rather than have recourse to strangers. An extreme example was that of the young Coignet. After spending many miserable years in the service of strangers, he entered the service of one of his half-sisters who was married to an innkeeper, concealing from them his identity, and he spent in her house some years which were happier than the preceding ones. Was it by mere chance that he had recourse to her, or was it because he preferred, in his heart of hearts, to serve a sister and a brother-in-law rather than strangers? Nevertheless, he bore a deep grudge against her for having engaged his services without recognizing him and for not having, as a sister, taken him away from his father's house, where his stepmother was ill-treating him: he was to create a considerable scandal, in front of the whole village, when he left her service.[63] Rather than sentiments of affection – which might be aroused, but rather as a result of esteem and personal sympathy, as between Edme Rétif and Touslesjours – kinship established obligations, and a moral and legal bond, considered as 'natural'.

The father of a family, even if well-to-do, often turned to kinsfolk for the education of his children. On two occasions Edme Rétif sent his son Nicolas to live in Vermonton, in the house of his son-in-law Michel

Linard, the husband of Anne, the eldest daughter by the first marriage and godmother of Nicolas. Later he sent him to study at Bicêtre, under the tutelage of Thomas, the second son of the first marriage; and, when Nicolas arrived in Paris, he quite naturally went to stay at the house of another half-sister by the first marriage who had married there. Finally, he was entrusted to the parish priest of Courgis, the eldest son by the first marriage, who was to look after him for two years. All the kinsfolk who took charge of Nicolas were, it is true, very close relations. However, there was no hesitation in approaching more distant relations: it was to his cousin, the attorney in Noyers, that Pierre Rétif had sent Edme, when he resolved to 'take some care' over his education.

The lawyer did not assume this responsibility for Edme out of an unsatisfied need for paternity. 'There lived with this kinsman, in addition to his two children, a first cousin...named Daiguesmortes', as we have observed. He appears to have been impelled by two sentiments which are both evident in the brief speech which he addressed to Edme to explain his preference for Daiguesmortes. The first was his sense of obligation, which was all the stronger because the relationship was closer: 'He is my first cousin, and the son of an aunt who has been like a mother to me... He is one degree of kinship closer than you...' Besides this, however, he also expected a tangible benefit from this kinship:

> He has great intelligence, and my object is to support his natural talent as far as I can, for I am persuaded that this young man can make a name for himself and bring honour to us all...As for you, to try to treat you as I treat him would be a waste of time and trouble: he has wit, and you have none.[64]

In the society of former times, whether one wished it or not, one shared in the glory of one's kinsmen as in their dishonour, and the closer the relationship the more this was so.

This was true of the peasants almost as much as of the bourgeois and the nobles. More so, one might say, when it was a question of dishonour. In 1751 Louise Thomas, a girl of twenty-four, had been made pregnant by Michel Maury, a farmer of forty, in whose house she was a servant. The dishonour seems to have been even more irremediable by reason of the fact that the seducer, being the godfather of his servant and mistress, could not marry her without a dispensation from the Church. Who felt themselves to be affected by this scandal? Maury declared that he 'had heard it said by the kinsmen of the said Thomas that if he did not make reparation for her honour they would handle him roughly and his life would no longer be safe'. And the innkeeper of the village confirmed that he himself 'had heard...a kinsman of the said Thomas, talking with other persons of the dishonour of the said Thomas,...and saying feelingly that if the said Maury did not marry her whom he had thus dishonoured, he would take his life or Maury would take his'.[65] Such a scandal was intolerable to the honour of the kinsfolk, especially if they lived in the same or a neighbouring village.

Distance attenuated the seriousness of such problems, but it did not sever kinship ties. Even if, for years, one had had no contact with kinsfolk living far away, they constituted so many islets of familiarity in an external world looked upon as 'alien'. In so far as kinship created a solidarity of honour – and also of fortune, by virtue of the customs governing inheritance – one could place one's trust in one's kinsfolk; it was to them that one turned 'naturally' when one was without protection in an unfamiliar and hostile world. Conversely, when an outsider arrived in the village, he was no longer exactly an outsider, seeing that he could count on his kinship with one or more 'inhabitants' of the parish. Since his behaviour towards the villagers involved the honour of his kinsfolk, they could be counted on to remind him of his obligations, whereas, in the case of an outsider lacking any ties of attachment to the village community, one could expect anything.

The only way to prevent these village communities constituting so many closed societies, hostile towards one another, was to multiply the relations of kinship existing between villages, and, with this end in view, to encourage exogamous marriages. The greatest theologians – Saint Augustine and Saint Thomas Aquinas — seem to have understood that this was the reason for the prohibition of incest. However, the day-to-day practice of the peasantry ran counter to the exogamic policy of the Church. In many villages, if not in all, the 'big boys', grouped together as an institution, made efforts to establish their monopoly over the marriageable girls of the parish.[66] Every girl married to an outsider represented, in fact, for the less fortunate among them, an increased probability of remaining a bachelor and a servant in the house of another. Thus it was that with cudgel-blows, if one is to believe Rétif and some other observers, they dissuaded outsiders from associating with the village girls. Furthermore, they proclaimed the dishonour of such girls as became interested in others than themselves. This attitude on the part of the village youths met with the approval of their parents, who were always perturbed if they saw a girl take away as her dowry a fraction of the patrimony of the village, to bestow it on a stranger who would not pay his share of the fiscal obligations of the parish. In short, the village community as such had all sorts of methods of preventing the marriages of girls with men from outside the village. This was the reason for the proportion of endogamous marriages, which was often startlingly high, and for the recourse to dispensations from the impediments on the grounds of kinship.

Not all the dispensations, however, were granted to betrothed couples from the same parish: quite the contrary. For example, in Saint-Agnan, in the Morvan, the four marriages which, between 1730 and 1794, required dispensations from the impediment on the grounds of kinship, all took place with someone from outside the village. The fact was that kinship – an impediment to marriage according to the Church – really encouraged marriages between young people of different parishes. This was not so much because consanguineous marriages made it possible to join together again plots of land which had previously been divided – this was true, primarily, in the case of cousins belonging to the same parish – but rather because having kinsfolk in another village was the best means of introducing oneself into that community. Furthermore, kinship with a girl made it possible to associate with her under the pretext of cousinhood; and if one succeeded, as a result of such association, in arousing feelings of love, the youths of the village were no longer in a position to prevent the marriage. This was the origin of the ambiguity of cousinhood with a pretty girl, and the character of the cousin in love stories.

Finally, how do the ties of kinship in the society of former times compare with those in our society? It has for long been asserted that they were stronger, and this seems to be undeniable in the legal sphere. To take only three examples, the possibility of the right of lineal repurchase, the rights which kinsfolk could claim with regard to an inheritance, and the help that young people could secure from a family council against the abuse of authority not only of a guardian but even of a father or a mother, are sufficient evidence of this.

As far as mental outlook and behaviour were concerned, the strength of the ties was especially evident among the nobles, who were obsessed with their ancestors, their descendants, and their cognatic and affinal kin, because these ties of blood or of affinity were the foundation of their honour, their privileges, their power, in short, their place at the summit of society. Moreover, even if there is no justification for identifying the great clienteles of the sixteenth and seventeenth centuries with the traditional medieval *lignages*, it is nonetheless true that family solidarities formed the thread of those clienteles which, in their struggles for power, formed the structure of political life as do the parties today.

It has been asserted in recent years by certain French and, above all, British historians that among the peasantry, on the other hand, family attachments were less solid than in the present time. And we have, in fact, observed that not only in day-to-day activities and in agricultural labour, but also on the occasion of the important family events — births, christenings, funerals, perhaps even weddings — the kinsfolk were less prominent than the neighbours, the guild associations, the notable citizens of the locality, etc. This evidence is not, however, decisive. It shows, above all, the abundance of ties of solidarity in society in past times, in comparison with our society, where the majority of services are bought or sold, or are provided free by the State. Amid the general collapse of the older ties of solidarity, those of family solidarity have survived best, and therefore appear in certain respects to be more fundamental than before. In many circumstances, however, they were more necessary and more effective in former times than today. This was so, for example, in the case of the orphans, who were much more numerous than in our time, or of the poor peasants who did not know what to do with their children, or of the rich man looking for a trustworthy servant, or, in more general terms, of all those who had business to do outside their village, in an unfamiliar and hostile world.

2. The household:
size, structure and material life

It is not the relations of kinship, which have hardly been studied except in connection with the medieval period, it is the structures and dimensions of households which nowadays give rise to controversies among historians who study the sixteenth, seventeenth and eighteenth centuries. Until the last few years, those who were interested in the history of the family – primarily the sociologists – still accepted, to a greater or lesser extent, the image of it presented by Frédéric Le Play. It is this image which has recently been questioned by a group of historians, chiefly British, led by Peter Laslett.

According to Le Play, one of the most lamentable characteristics of industrial society is what he terms the *unstable family*, a family composed of a married couple and their unmarried children, since when they marry the children leave the house and found new households. The family has all the less opportunity of perpetuating itself, in this industrial society, as it is not firmly rooted in one house, but rents its accommodation, changes frequently and adapts it to the varying number of its members. When all the children have left the house of their parents and the parents die, nothing any longer remains of this contemporary family.

As a contrast to this system of the unstable family, Le Play described that of the *stem family*, which was characteristic of western society in former times, and of which he found traces in certain parts of Europe that had undergone comparatively little transformation by industrialization. The stem family was firmly implanted in one house, of which it enjoyed the full ownership and which it transmitted from one generation to another. This house symbolized the family and guaranteed its perennial character. The father of the family transmitted it at his death to his eldest son, the 'heir'. During his lifetime, however, he already involved this heir in the management of the family business, instructed him in the secrets of his profession, arranged his marriage 'within the house' and thus saw his descendants increase and multiply.

The girls who, when they married, entered other houses, and the younger sons who wished to leave home, were given an income from the revenues of the family, and not from the capital constituted by landed property, which passed to the heir in its entirety. Whereas the heir was tied to the house and to his father's occupation, the younger sons, who enjoyed greater freedom, could launch out into major enterprises and, being assisted on their departure by their family, the more fortunate among them could found stocks in their turn. As for the girls who remained unmarried and the less enterprising younger sons, instead of being abandoned by all and leading miserable existences as in our industrial society, they stayed quietly at home, accepting 'naturally' the authority of their elders (whereas that of an 'alien' employer, which is less natural, is today only grudgingly accepted), and they worked for the common good of the family, feeling ties of affection towards their nephews, to whom they gladly gave guidance during their lifetime and to whom, at their deaths, they would leave their meagre savings.

When there were not enough younger brothers and children for the tasks involved in the family business, one engaged servants who, instead of being looked down on as they are today, became part of the family, were totally devoted to it, and did not seek to lead their lives elsewhere, but accepted almost as 'naturally' as did the younger sons the authority of the head of the family. At their deaths they, too, often bequeathed their small savings to the children of the house. It must, of course, be emphasized that the younger sons and the servants benefited from this enviable situation only on condition of their practising a meritorious celibacy, for only the heir was able to beget children in the house.

This economic system, which guaranteed social peace by means of system-atic alienation, was spontaneously linked with a specific system of educa-tion. It was in the house that the children were educated by the father, the mother, the uncles and aunts, the elder brothers and sisters, and even the grandfather and grandmother. They were not taught useless knowledge – which, in any case, only those of exceptional intelligence could compre-hend, Le Play maintained – but they were given a solidly based moral and professional education which the school of today is quite incapable of giving them. The differences in age accustomed the younger sons to respect their elders, and the elders to acquire a sense of their responsi-bilities. Respect for the hierarchies within the bosom of the family, inculcated by practice from early childhood, guaranteed respect for the 'natural and inevitable' hierarchies of society. Today, on the other hand, school education cannot control the spirit of mischief (another term for 'original sin') which exists in the child, and incarceration in school, the

51

authority without love of a strange schoolteacher, and antagonism with schoolfellows of the same age, all encourage the spirit of revolt and individualism.

This organization of society on the basis of the family was destroyed, according to this theory, primarily in France, by the rule of obligatory partition among heirs imposed by the legislation of the Revolution. Thenceforth, knowing that his business was destined to perish with him, the father of the family lost interest in it after a certain age. The younger sons, in the expectation of receiving a part of the inheritance, were impelled into idleness. The elder sons, like their brothers, left the house before the death of their father, and thus no longer ensured the continuity of the family. One no longer waited to be the owner of a house before getting married, and the rented house was no longer a real home. Everything became unstable. Nothing was assured of survival. There was no longer any tie between brothers and sisters. Finally, to avoid these misfortunes, married couples came to limit their fertility, and there was a decline in population.

To give concrete form to his ideas, Le Play proposed a typical example of a stem family, resulting, he affirmed, from taking an average from among families which he had actually been able to observe in the few parts of Europe where the old system had survived, principally in the Pyrenees. He considered this typical family 'at the moment when the heir-associate chosen by the father had just contracted the marriage which was destined to perpetuate the *race*'. It then comprised eighteen persons:

> The heir and his wife, aged twenty-five and twenty; the father and mother, the heads of the household, married for twenty-seven years and now aged fifty-two and forty-seven; a grandfather aged eighty; two unmarried kinsfolk – brothers or sisters of the head of the family; nine children, of whom the eldest are nearly as old as the brother who is the heir, and the youngest is a baby, often still at the breast; finally, two servants living on terms of complete equality with the other members of the family.[1]

It is well-known that Le Play devoted his life to the establishment of social peace by means of the social sciences, and it can be observed that his approach was decidedly reactionary – at least in the etymological sense of the word – even though he personally defined himself as 'reformist' and denied being 'retrograde'. This political intention implied in Le Play's work is the part that historians have most often reflected in their own work. However, sociologists who have studied the family, even when they have been politically opposed to Le Play, have been receptive to the value of his analysis and the coherence of his system: it was, in fact, the system of the stem family that Pierre Bourdieu was to discover in Béarn, in connection with his excellent study of celibacy among the peasantry.[2]

The size of households

In more general terms, it has become a commonplace to contrast our present-day family, small in size and 'conjugal' in its structure, with the families of the pre-industrial era, more numerous both because of their 'natural fertility' and because of their being 'broadened' or 'extended' to include persons other than the father, mother and their children.

However, the historians who met at Cambridge in 1969 under the chairmanship of Peter Laslett, after analysing with the aid of a computer the data derived from about one hundred house-by-house censuses, reached the conclusion that the families of former times were small in size – from four to six persons, on average – and that this was true not only of England but of Europe as a whole. Moreover, they concluded that most of these families were of the 'conjugal' type, that 'extended' families were even less common than in our day, and that the stem family and other types of 'multinuclear' family hardly ever existed.[3] Should one, therefore, as some have hastened to argue, relegate these 'extended families' to the museum of sociological myths?

1. THE SIZE OF HOUSEHOLDS

The size of families in former times had already been disputed by French demographers. Le Play thought that in former society 'mothers, over a period of twenty-five years, brought into the world between fifteen and twenty-four children'. For a long time everybody was convinced, like him, that 'this fecundity was common, in the seventeenth century, in all parts of France, among both the bourgeois and the peasants'. 'It would be easy', he added, 'to quote many examples of this, in families of which the memory has been preserved in written documents.' However, the examples quoted usually concerned aristocratic and bourgeois circles, and it was not possible to make generalizations on the basis of these. By reconstituting families on the basis of records of christenings, wedding and funerals, it has been demonstrated that the 'child per year' was definitely exceptional, at least in the families in which the mothers themselves breast-fed their children. On the average, the interval between two births was two years or more. Furthermore, there were very few women who had twenty-five years of fertile conjugal life; women married, on the average, at around twenty-four years of age, rather than twenty; a considerable number of them died in childbirth, and many others, lacking medical care, became sterile before the normal age of the menopause. Thus, instead of having an average of from fifteen to twenty-four children, the woman had, rather, six or eight. Finally, mortality caused some tragic reductions among this offspring: between 200 and 300 children out of every thousand died in their first year, and often less than half survived to the age of twenty.

The household

All this has been emphasized, since 1960, by Pierre Goubert. Neverthe-less, the 'family record cards' which the French demographers have com-piled on the basis of parish registers, in accordance with the method of Louis Henry,[4] do not permit one to ascertain the size of the households of a parish at a given moment in time. When the bride and the bridegroom came from different parishes, they were often married in the parish of the bride and thereafter lived in that of the bridegroom, so that in neither parish had there been registered all the data needed for the compilation of their family record card. Furthermore, these record cards did not keep a total of the children whom a man might have by several successive wives, or a woman by different husbands. They recorded the deaths of children – if they died in the parish – but not their departure from the house, nor even their marriage when it took place in another village. In short, the method known as 'the reconstitution of families' makes it possible to study the fertility of couples in former times, but not the real size of households. Moreover, in France in the 1960s there was hardly any interest in pursuing this question: when one had the good fortune to find a house-by-house census, one drew from it 'demographic' conclusions regarding distribution by age or celibacy, rather than any reflection as to the dimensions and structure of households.[5]

It has been the British demographic historians who have studied these data from this perspective, not only because they have paid more attention to the results of anthropological research, but doubtless also because they possess more numerous and more accurate censuses than the French. (The opposite is the case with parish registers, which are better in France than in England.) The Cambridge researchers have been able to compile a sample of one hundred censuses, taken between 1574 and 1821, of which five were taken between 1574 and 1645, forty-five between 1662 and 1749, and fifty between 1750 and 1821. This sample includes urban as well as rural parishes, and covers all the counties of England.

Computer analysis of this sample gave the following results. The average size of households in each of the hundred parishes was calculated, and then the median of these averages was established, which gave a figure of 4.73 persons per household. This does not differ appreciably from the average size of households in England at the end of the nine-teenth century: 4.60 in 1891.[6]

One might, it is true, enquire as to the significance of this median, and ask whether it does not conceal considerable deviations between one parish and another of the sample. In fact, the average size of households was only 3.63 persons in the village of Little Strickland (Westmorland) in 1781, whereas it was as high as 7.22 persons in the London parish of St Mildred Poultry in 1695. However, a frequency diagram shows that the average size of households fell below four persons in only 6 per cent of the parishes, and rose above 5.75 persons in only 5 per cent. In other words, the average was between four and six persons in 89 per cent of the parishes in the sample. This figure is very far removed from the eighteen persons in the average stem family portrayed by Le Play.

Pursuing this line of enquiry further, the British historians obtained from research workers from other countries, as a result of a colloquium held in Cambridge in 1969, some data for the purposes of comparison. One could not, clearly, expect from these researchers studies as momentous and as costly as the studies of England carried out by Peter Laslett and his group: each one submitted an analysis of a single parish in his country, and these parishes are not necessarily typical of the national averages. Nevertheless, this comparison is instructive because of the similarity of the results obtained in different regions of Europe (Table 1). Between these parishes of different countries, indeed, the average size of households varies even less than between the hundred English parishes. One is, apparently, obliged to conclude that it was not only in England but throughout Europe that the average size of families was between four and six persons.

Table 1. *Average size of households in various localities of Europe*

Country	Community and region	Date	Number of households	Average number of persons per household
Scotland	Aross-in-Mull (Western Isles)	1779	211	5.25
Colonial America	Bristol (Rhode Island)	1689	72	5.85
Germany	Löffingen (Württemberg)	1687	121	5.77
Poland	Lesnica (Silesia)	1720	311	5.40
France	Longuenesse (Pas-de-Calais)	1778	66	5.05
Italy	Colorno (Duchy of Parma)	1782	66	4.16
Serbia	Belgrade	1733–4	273	4.95

Source: P. Laslett, *Household and Family in Past Time* (Cambridge, 1972), p. 61.

The theory that this family of reduced size was a phenomenon characteristic of the west, in the sixteenth, seventeenth and eighteenth centuries, is supported by the fact that the only example of deviation that has been found is from outside Europe, in the Japanese village of Yokouchi (in the county of Suwa), where the custom of annual house-by-house censuses has provided abundant documentation: 7 persons per household in 1676; 5.5 in 1746; 5.1 in 1823; and 4.4 in 1846. It is, therefore, possible that the transition from a feudal economy to a market economy brought about a clearly perceptible reduction in the size of households. However, either this reduction as a result of the economic transition had taken place in Europe before the sixteenth century, or the small household had always been a characteristic trait of the west, ever since the Middle Ages. Such is the conclusion one inevitably reaches if one admits the relevance of the statistical enquiry carried out by the Cambridge historians and their associates.

Is it relevant, however, to the analysis of society, to carry out these researches into the average size of households in each parish? Is it true that, within the parishes, the margin of variation in the size of actual families is as insignificant as the variation in the 'average size of households' from one parish to another and from one country to another? Rather than using the abstract data provided by variations from the mean, with which the statisticians generally answer this question, let us borrow a specific example from Peter Laslett's well-known study, *The World We Have Lost*.[7]

In 1676, the village of Goodnestone-next-Wingham, in Kent, contained 277 inhabitants, whom the clergyman responsible for taking the census presents to us as grouped in sixty-two households (Table 2): three households of the gentry, twenty-six of yeomen, nine of tradesmen, twelve of labourers, and twelve of poor men. The category of 'tradesmen' includes

Table 2. *Size and composition of households in Goodnestone-next-Wingham (Kent) in 1676*

	Gentry	Yeomen	Trades-men	Labourers	Poor men	Total
Number of persons	28	151	35	38	25	277
Number of households	3	26	9	12	12	62
Persons per household	9.3	5.8	3.9	3.2	2.1	4.47
Number of servants	16	34	2	0	0	52
Percentage of persons	57.1	22.5	5.7	0	0	19
Number per household	5.3	1.3	0.2	0	0	0.8
Number of children	7	64	16	15	11	113
Percentage of persons (excluding servants)	58.3	54.7	48.5	39.4	44	50
Number per household	2.3	2.5	1.8	1.2	0.9	1.8

Source: P. Laslett, *The World We Have Lost* (London, 1965), p. 64.

two families of carpenters – of which one had a servant – two families of masons, two families of weavers, the family of a shoemaker, that of a tailor, and a woman living on her own who described herself as a grocer. These trades were those commonly found in English villages. On the other hand, since there is no mention of the blacksmith, nor of shepherds, cow-herds or thatchers, other trades commonly found in the country areas, those who pursued them were probably classified among the labourers.

The average size of households, in this village, was 4.47, that is, lower than the national average at that time. This is understandable, when one observes that the households of the tradesmen comprised, on the average, 3.9 persons, those of the labourers 3.2, and those of the poor 2.1. These households of the lower social categories clearly form the majority – thirty-three out of sixty-two – and their average size is under three persons.

However, they comprised only just over one-third of the population: ninety-nine persons out of 277, or 35 per cent. The rest lived in the larger households of the yeomen and of the gentry, that is, in households which comprised, on average, over six persons (6.2). In other words, 65 per cent of the population lived in households of which the average size was exceptionally large, in terms of what we have concluded regarding the average sizes in the hundred English parishes. However, these averages calculated on the basis of social categories are still liable to give a distorted picture of the real situation.

Of the three households of the gentry, one comprised twenty-three persons – Sir Edward Hall and his wife, their six children and their fifteen domestic servants – while the two others were of extraordinarily limited dimensions: one was a bachelor living with one servant and the other, a couple with one child and no servant. Either these gentry lived like poor peasants, or they lived in the manor-house with Sir Edward Hall and did not, therefore, constitute real independent households.

Of the twenty-six households of the yeomen, there were twelve large ones which accommodated about a hundred people. Among them were two families by the name of Neame, comprising fourteen and twelve persons, three families of the name of Wanstall, of which two comprised eight persons, the family of William Tucker which comprised ten, those of Richard Fuller and Stephen Church which comprised nine each, and that of John Pet which comprised eight. The lord of the manor and these dozen yeomen – who owned almost all the land, gave employment to other families and were the political as well as the economic leaders of the village – accommodated in their great households over half the population of the village. Can it be said, in these circumstances, that large households were non-existent or without importance?

The household

Peter Laslett has demonstrated why – in contrast to what was formerly believed and to what even the French demographers were prepared to admit – the households of the poor were so small in size. In Goodnestone-next-Wingham, out of 277 inhabitants, there were fifty-two domestic servants, of whom fifty worked in the manor-house or in the houses of the yeomen, only two in the houses of the tradesmen, and none at all, of course, in the houses of the labourers and the poor. This information is in no way surprising. It is, however, only half of the explanation: the other factor is that the households of the poor had considerably fewer children than those of the rich. In Goodnestone, out of 113 children, seventy-one belonged to the twenty-nine households of the gentry and the yeomen, whereas only forty-two were to be found in the thirty-three households of the lower classes. The proportion of children in the house-hold – after deducting the total of domestic servants, of whom many were probably children – increased and decreased regularly according to social status (Table 2, above). At the lowest level of society the poor, it is true, appear to upset this neat correlation: out of twenty-five people, eleven, i.e. 44 per cent, were children. Among the poor of Goodnestone, however, there were only 0.9 children per household, as compared with 1.2 in the case of the labourers. What inflates their proportion in relation to the adults is the astonishingly small number of adults: only fourteen, in twelve households. This suggests that, in these twelve households, there were, at the most, two couples: the households of the poor were generally former households of labourers which had sunk into poverty on the death of the father of the family.

Why, then, did these poor households contain fewer children than the rich ones? There may be two explanations of this problem: the first is demographic, and the second socio-economic.

The later a woman married, the shorter was her period of fertility. Poor girls were often prevented from marrying as young as rich girls, because they had to earn their dowry by working for ten or fifteen years as domestic servants. This was, apparently, the case in Tourouvre-au-Perche (Orne) and in Nottinghamshire. However, there were instances where, for other reasons, the average age at marriage was higher among rich girls than among poor girls; this was true in Amiens.

Many French researchers have observed that the fertility of the poor was lower – at the same age – than that of the rich. The explanation of this appears to be the longer interval between births in the case of poor women. For example, in Tourouvre-au-Perche, the average interval between the first and second births was 23.6 months in the case of the farmers, merchants and craftsmen, and 27.6 months in that of the labourers and makers of sabots. The reason seems to be that the poor women breast-

58

fed their children and sometimes those of others, which suspended their fertility for a time, whereas among rich women a certain number put their children out to nurse, and for this reason had a much shorter interruption of their fertility. This was particularly perceptible in France, where mercenary wet-nursing was more widespread than in England.

Poverty inevitably increased infant mortality – other things being equal – as is demonstrated in the case of Argenteuil: in the 'upper class' it was 193 per thousand, in the 'middle class' 226, and in the 'lower class' 258.

These three demographic reasons for the smaller number of children in poor households than in rich ones are supported by evidence principally from France, and it is not certain that they have been such important determining factors in England. In England, however, the increased concentration of landed property was accompanied by the creation of large agricultural holdings and the proletarianization of the smaller peasants, so that the poor, lacking the means to support their children – at least beyond a certain age – sent them to work in the houses of the rich as domestic servants. It is unfortunate that Peter Laslett has not been able to provide evidence of this phenomenon at Goodnestone-next-Wingham, by means of an analysis of the ages of the children in the poor households and of the servants. There seems no doubt, however, that this is what really happened.

In France, an old proverb asserted that 'children are the wealth of poor people'. In other words, those who have neither land nor money nevertheless have children: the poor man, in this case, means the proletarian. However, in both France and England, as the poor lacked the means to make profit from this wealth, they were obliged to give it to the possessors of the land. Ultimately, as regards their children, they knew only the trouble of bearing them and of ensuring their survival until adolescence.

Large households connected with large agricultural holdings, which were to be found in most parts of England, also existed in many parts of France. From the sixteenth century onwards, in fact, the nobles and bourgeois had taken steps to deprive the peasantry of possession of the land, which had generally been achieved by the latter during the last two centuries of the Middle Ages. Subsequently, with a success that varied from one region to another, the nobles and bourgeois had established large agricultural holdings: the big farms of the Paris Basin, and the big share-cropping holdings of the Gâtine, in Poitou,[8] or in Sologne.[9] In Sologne, where they were the masters of the land from the beginning of the eighteenth century, they generally permitted smallholdings of a few hectares to survive alongside the share-cropping holdings of from seventy-five to a hundred hectares and sometimes more. These smallholdings, *locatures*, also belonged to the nobles and bourgeois, and could provide a labour force to supplement that of the share-croppers. Here too, however, as in

Poitou, the concentration of property was accompanied by a transformation of the agrarian scene, with a decrease in sown arable land and an increase in pasturage – to reduce the costs of labour, which was unprofitable in these poor lands – and the destruction of buildings no longer in use, in order to reduce the burden of taxation and the expense of their upkeep. Thus, in Tremblevif, according to the record of grievances compiled in 1789, two-thirds of the *locatures* and the share-cropping holdings disappeared in the course of the eighteenth century. As a result of this process, some share-cropping holdings reached a size of from 100 to 200 hectares, e.g. in Vouzon, and there was even one of 450 hectares.

Despite the importance attained by stockbreeding, such holdings required a comparatively large labour force. In 1754, the share-cropping holding of Villeneuve, in Brinon, permanently employed twenty workers in the household: two farm-boys, two cowherds, three servant-girls, two male servants, seven shepherds and shepherdesses, that is a total of sixteen adults, in addition to which there were four children, of whom one tended the cows, two the pigs and one the turkeys. Besides these twenty workers in the holding one must, of course, count the share-cropper himself, his wife and their children. There was a similar situation in Sennely where, in 1775, the biggest share-cropping holding employed twelve workers in addition to the family of the share-cropper. In the usual type of share-cropping holding, there lived about ten people, including the share-cropper, his wife, their two or three children, three or four adult and one or two child workers, often orphans of whom the share-cropper had assumed the guardianship in order that they should cost him nothing.

This economic development, therefore, resulted in an increase in the number of large households, not only in Sologne but also in the Gâtine, in Poitou, the cereal-growing plains of the Paris Basin and probably, to a lesser degree, in most of the other regions. In the places where there had been, in the fourteenth and fifteenth centuries, small peasant families working smallholdings, one discovers in the eighteenth century large 'families' on big farms or big share-cropping holdings.

This does not imply, however, that the large family has been a characteristic of modernization in western Europe. Firstly, not all the large households had as the reason for their existence the need for labour on a large agricultural holding. Secondly, the tendency towards the concentration of capital and the enlargement of units of production has led to the enlargement of households only in societies in which the unit of production has been co-terminous with that of consumption – in other words, through the employment of a domestically based labour force – and in our society this no longer happens. We can therefore consider this phenomenon as a characteristic of archaism.

Up to now we have not taken into consideration the important fact that large households, in the seventeenth and eighteenth centuries, were probably more numerous in the big towns – or at least in certain districts of the big towns – than in the country: of the five parishes of the English sample in which the average size of households exceeded six persons, three were in London. The reason is that the big towns, which had been the centres of decision-making and social meeting-places since the seventeenth century, attracted the powerful and their 'families', which were as abundant as they were unproductive. In their town houses, as in their castles, the members of the upper aristocracy maintained, in fact, dozens of servitors, sometimes even hundreds of them.[10] At the end of the seventeenth century, Gregory King estimated an average of forty persons in each family of the Lords Temporal, of whom there were 160 in the realm. Implying an almost exact correlation between the size of the families and the social status of their heads, he estimated an average of twenty persons for the families of the bishops, sixteen for those of the baronets, thirteen for those of the knights, ten for those of the squires, and eight for those of the ordinary gentry. On the whole, the 17,000 families of the aristocracy and gentry comprised from eight to forty persons, and the 100,000 families of the upper and middle bourgeoisie from five to eight persons. Even though these estimates are debatable – as they certainly are, since the figures vary in different editions of this table compiled by Gregory King – the exactness of the correlation between social status and the size of the household merits our close attention. Why did the élites of that time maintain such a large number of unproductive domestic servants, when in our day even the richest men are content with only a few, apart from engaging extra help for big social receptions?

One can, to a certain extent, explain this reduction in the domestic staffs of the leisured rich by the increase in wages and the multiplication of domestic mechanical appliances. There is, however, another factor – a change in the attitude of the rich towards the servant problem. The present-day attitude is eminently practical: one engages a domestic servant only if one considers that one 'needs' one, and if one cannot find any cheaper or more convenient solution. It is not that wealth today is no longer ostentatious: people will buy for pleasure or for ostentation new cars – to say nothing of electronic microscopes and computers in the context of their professional life – but there will be a tendency to engage or keep on a servant only if he or she is 'profitable'. In former times, the aristocracy had a different attitude. Impelled by a taste for luxury and a desire for ostentation, they multiplied their domestic servants as well as their carriages. This practice was not, however, motivated only by vanity; it was also a duty. Indeed, avarice – that is to say, the inclination to hoard one's wealth rather than distribute it among one's close associates – was thought to be 'ignoble', and therefore the urge to maximize the profit from one's domestic household could not be developed to the same extent as today. Above all, a great man had obligations towards his clients: he had to take in as a servant the daughter of the tenant-farmer, or engage as secretary the godson of a kinsman, etc. One did not set out to ask oneself whether or not one needed the person concerned; one asked oneself, rather, whether or not one wished to come to the assistance of one's clients, and, perhaps, whether one could afford to. The higher one was placed in the social hierarchy, the more clients one had, and the more one was reputed to possess the means to come to their assistance. What made it even less possible to escape from the logic of this situation was the fact that the power of a great man was, above all, calculated on the basis of the number and fidelity of his clients.

If one accepts the views of those eighteenth-century writers who protested at the proliferation of domestic servants, the servants were all parasites. This is evidently an exaggeration, even when one considers the matter from the point of view of the interests of society. The two domestic servants who, in Goodnestone-next-Wingham, worked for the tradesmen, certainly contributed to the national production. The same is true of the thirty-four employed by the farmers, and probably of most of the sixteen who worked in the manor-house. However, from the economic point of view, the function of the domestic servant was ambiguous. Whereas nowadays an industrialist draws a clear distinction among those on his payroll between the hundred or so workers employed in his factory and the few servants who work in his house, this distinction was not made in former times, either terminologically or in real life. Some domestic servants concerned themselves only with the house and the well-being of their masters, others assisted him only in his professional activities, while still others worked in both sectors at the same time. This would happen, for example, in the case of girls working on a farm, who helped their mistress with the housework, but also worked in the farmyard and the kitchen garden and, during the season of the major farm tasks, might go to help their master.

If a distinction has become established today between the worker and the domestic servant, the reason is that, with the exception of some 'agricultural workers', the worker today is no longer accommodated in the house of his employer. The co-terminous character of the unit of production and that of consumption, which was formerly customary, has become exceptional. This should not be attributed to the development of capitalism because, in former times, in the big households, the domestic servants had no more rights over the capital than does the worker today. Moreover, it is known that the workers on collective farms, who, by contrast, do have rights over the land which they work in common, nevertheless live in small households. Nor is it the gigantic size of present-day business concerns that has made this separation necessary. In former times there existed gigantic families, of a hundred or more persons, in the entourage of certain great lords: one might, therefore, imagine a factory manager similarly living with his workers in a family household. The coincidence between the unit of production and that of consumption had, moreover, certain advantages which have by no means disappeared: a proof of this is the multiplication of works canteens, crèches, cooperatives for purchases, residential estates for the workers close to their place of work, all managed by the firm itself. However, it also had drawbacks which former society accepted more readily than our own, for example the celibacy of domestic servants. We must investigate the reason for this.

The large family, with a sizeable domestic household, is not a creation of the period with which we are concerned, nor even of the Middle Ages: it is merely a continuation of the family based on slavery of the ancient world. Its characteristics can be explained by no better a reason than the continuity of a tradition. All that appears unfamiliar to us, in the status of the domestic servant, was already characteristic of that of the slave. In the first place, the slave was a domestic servant in the sense that he never lived in his own house but always in the house – or one of the houses – of his master. Being a servant under compulsion, he could only, in fact, live as part of the 'family', and under constant surveillance. Like the domestic servant, the slave could be employed on all sorts of tasks, domestic or productive, without his social status being thereby modified. The range of these tasks was very great in the case of the slaves of antiquity, and it was still great in the case of the domestic servants of the seventeenth and eighteenth centuries. Finally, marriage, which implied the right to dispose freely of oneself and the possibility of leading an independent life, was incompatible with the status of a slave, and also with that of a domestic servant. The domestic servitor of the sixth to the eighth centuries – the *servant* – had inherited the status of the *servus* of antiquity. His condition was different only in that he had the right to abandon his status in order to contract marriage and establish himself in his own house, whereas the slave of ancient times could do this only after being freed by his master. However, this right of the domestic servant was often more theoretical than real: to establish himself, and to get married, he needed a small amount of capital, which it took him a long time to accumulate. Also, his wages were often not paid to him at regular intervals, but accumulated in the hands of his master, who finally gave him the where-withal to establish himself when he thought fit.

The ancient philosophers compared the slave to a child: like the latter, he was totally dependent on the father of the family. The domestic servant, too, in the period with which we are concerned, found himself in the same situation with regard to his master as the child with regard to his father. In the ancient world, the father of the family had possessed the right of life and death over his children and his slaves; in the seventeenth and eighteenth centuries, he still had the right to chastise his children and servants. Similarly, the domestic servants were often young people, and their dependence was as transitory as that of the child. Conversely, the child, like the servant, had to learn to serve – a traditional form of educa-tion – before being able to establish himself and become, in his turn, the 'father of the family'. It is not surprising, in these circumstances, that words like 'maid', 'boy' and 'valet' should have been used to designate young people as well as domestic servants.

If the French use the word *domestique* rather than a word derived from the ancient linguistic root, this is probably because in the Middle Ages some of the 'serfs' lived outside the master's house. The system of agrarian organization of that time is well-known: the lord's reserved land, of which the produce fed the people of the castle, was cultivated by both domestic serfs and the *chasés* serfs, that is to say, those established in their own cottages and feeding their families there from a plot of land which had come to them as an inheritance to encourage them to procreate their species. In addition to the domestic servants there had been, since the early Middle Ages, dependent workers married and living outside the family household, like the day-labourers and journeymen of the sixteenth to eighteenth centuries or the workers of the nineteenth century.

It is true that, between the tenth and the eighteenth centuries, many things had changed. The lord's reserved land, partitioned during the last centuries of the Middle Ages, was granted to the peasants emancipated from serfdom, but subsequently, with a greater or lesser degree of com-pleteness depending on the region concerned, it was reconstituted between the sixteenth and the eighteenth centuries, and granted on short-term leases to big farmers or share-croppers. The servile labour force of the early Middle Ages was replaced in the seventeenth and eighteenth centuries by a labour force, paid more or less regular wages, consisting of the domestically based agricultural workers and the day-labourers who possessed a house but not sufficient land to feed their families. Neverthe-less, despite all these changes, the agrarian scene of the eighteenth century was characterized, like that of the tenth century, by the co-existence and complementarity of large holdings and small ones, which supplied the manual labour. From the tenth to the eighteenth centuries, without interruption, though in varying proportions, there existed in western Europe castles and thatched cottages, dominant large households and dependent small ones. It is this co-existence and this association that characterized western society in former times. The averages calculated on the basis of the parishes can give no indication of this.

2. THE STRUCTURE OF HOUSEHOLDS

The British historians have distinguished, in terms of ties of kinship, five principal types of household, subdivided into nineteen secondary types (Table 3). In conjunction with this typology, the Cambridge group has devised a system of graphic representation which makes it possible to see

Table 3. *Typology of households adopted by the Cambridge group*

1 Solitaries	(a) Widowed
	(b) Single, or of unknown marital status
2 No family	(a) Coresident siblings
	(b) Coresident relatives of other kinds
	(c) Persons not evidently related
3 Simple family households	(a) Married couples alone
	(b) Married couples with child(ren)
	(c) Widowers with child(ren)
	(d) Widows with child(ren)
4 Extended family households	(a) Extended upwards
	(b) Extended downwards*
	(c) Extended laterally
	(d) Combinations of 4a–4c
5 Multiple family households	(a) Secondary unit(s) UP†
	(b) Secondary unit(s) DOWN
	(c) Units all on one level
	(d) *Frérèches*
	(e) Other multiple families
6 Indeterminate	

'Stem families' ‡ $\begin{cases} 5b \\ 5b + 5a \\ 5b + 5a + 4a \end{cases}$

Frérèches, ‡
alternative definitions $\begin{cases} 5d \\ 5d + 5c \\ 5d + 5c + 4c \\ 5d + 5c + 4c + 2a \end{cases}$

Source: P. Laslett, *Household and Family in Past Time*, p. 31.
Note: All categories can be with or without servants.
* The descendants included in type 4b can only be grandchildren or great-grandchildren.
† The distinction between types 5a and 5b is generally arbitrary.
‡ Many research workers, rejecting these definitions, classify as 'stem families' households of type 5a or 4a, and as *frérèches* households of types 5c or 4c or even 2a.

The household

at a glance the general structure of the most complex households, the sex, age and status of each of their members, and the manner in which they were connected (Figure 2).

Statistical data

The analysis of certain villages – pending the computer analysis of the hundred parishes of the English sample – demonstrates quite clearly that, among the peasantry of pre-industrial England, the normal structure of households was the conjugal family. Here we are no longer concerned with averages, such as those of the size of households, but with frequency, which provides much more convincing proof. Households of type 3 constitute, in fact, between 69 and 85 per cent of the total (Table 4), or as much as from 76 to 85 per cent if one excludes the example of Bilston, where 7 per cent of the households are of undetermined structure. Extended households were considerably less numerous: six out of thirty-

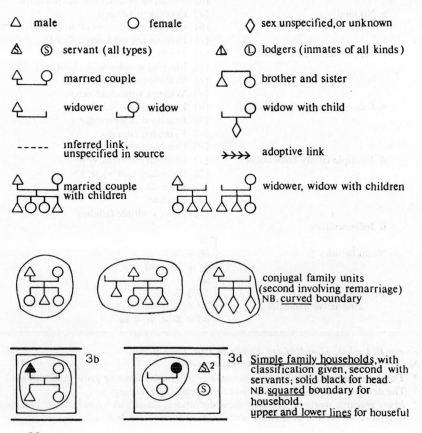

△ male	○ female	◇ sex unspecified, or unknown
▲ ⑤ servant (all types)		▲ ⓛ lodgers (inmates of all kinds)

married couple

widower   widow

brother and sister

widow with child

inferred link, unspecified in source

adoptive link

married couple with children

widower, widow with children

conjugal family units
(second involving remarriage)
NB. curved boundary

3b

3d Simple family households, with classification given, second with servants; solid black for head.
NB. squared boundary for household,
upper and lower lines for houseful

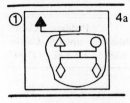

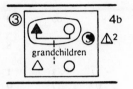

4d **Extended family households**

①Extension upwards.

②Extension upwards and laterally.

③Extension downwards with servant and lodgers.

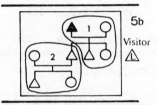

N B. Where source names relative(s) etc. and linkage cannot be fully specified, word describing relevant person(s) is reproduced and inferred linkage indicated.

Multiple family household
secondary unit DOWN, units numbered (secondaries all after 1), with lodger (inmate) specified in source as visitor

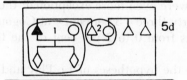

Frèrèche

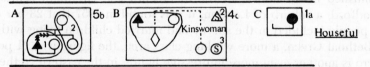

A. Multiple family household, secondary unit UP, with adoptive link.

B. Laterally extended family household, with 2 male and 3 female servants. Note that resident kinswoman not specified as to which spouse she is related to is shown as attached to conjugal link   C. Solitary widow

2. Ideographs representing domestic group structures. From *Household and Family in Past Time*, ed. Peter Laslett (Cambridge, 1972), pp. 41–2.

Table 4. *Household structures in England*

Type of household	Ealing 1599	Clay-worth 1676	Clay-worth 1688	Chilvers Coton 1684	Bilston 1695	Puddle-town 1724–5	Corfe Castle 1790
Percentage of households							
1 Solitaries	12	8	7	6	4	7	12
2 No family	2	0	1	4	7	4	4
3 Simple family households	78	83	85	81	69	79	76
4 Extended family households	6	9	7	8	11	8	8
5 Multiple family households	2	0	1	1	1	1	1
6 Indeterminate	0	0	0	0	7	0	0
4 + 5	8	9	8	9	12	9	9
Number of households	85	98	91	177	192	154	272
Average size	4.75	4.09	4.49	4.41	5.19	3.97	4.84

Source: P. Laslett, *Annales E.S.C.* (July–October 1972), pp. 866–7.

three, in the village of Cogenhoe (Northamptonshire) in 1628 – i.e. 18 per cent – is the highest proportion yet encountered in England.[11] Generally, however, their proportion varied between 6 and 11 per cent. Households comprising multiple family nuclei were even more exceptional: the maximum discovered was one out of thirty-three – 3 per cent – at Cogenhoe in 1620, but the usual proportion was from 0 to 2 per cent of the total of households.

What is even more damaging to the hypotheses of Le Play and to the customarily accepted ideas on the subject, is the fact that the proportion of extended or multiple households seems to have increased rather than diminished in the course of the nineteenth and twentieth centuries. In Woodford, a suburb of London, it was found in 1957 that 23 per cent of the people included in the survey had married children living with them. In Bethnal Green, a more working-class area, the figure was 21 per cent. There is another even more impressive figure: in the eastern Netherlands, around 1950, 25 per cent of the farms were managed by married couples living with their parents or parents-in-law.[12] These indications, however suggestive they may be, are not, it is true, directly comparable with the data of the sixteenth to the eighteenth centuries. However, the six English villages which had, during that period, only from 8 to 12 per cent of extended or multinuclear households, in 1850 had from 12 to 21 per cent

(Figure 3). So unequivocal an increase, in each of the six parishes considered, cannot be the result of chance. It seems to disprove, beyond question, the accepted notions regarding the supposed transition from the extended family to the nuclear family at the time of the Industrial Revolution.

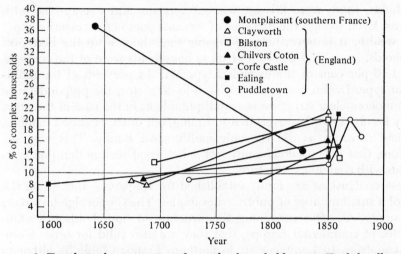

3. Trends in the proportion of complex households in six English villages and Montplaisant (Périgord). From Peter Laslett, *Annales E.S.C.* (July–October 1972), pp. 866–7.

It is unfortunate that the British historians have not indicated in which social sectors these different types of family were to be found. It may, however, be assumed that the families of the day-labourers and of the very poor, of which the average size was 3.5 persons according to Gregory King, only rarely had a complex structure. We know that these poor people could not support even their children for more than about ten years, so it is difficult to imagine them providing accommodation for an old uncle or even for their fathers and mothers. Although these households of the day-labourers and the very poor constituted, at the end of the seventeenth century, the great majority of households in England – 764,000, as compared with about 500,000 households of the well-to-do classes – they did not accommodate even half the population, according to Gregory King. One would, therefore, have liked to know whether among the propertied classes – and particularly among the aristocracy, the gentry, the bourgeoisie and the well-to-do farmers – the conjugal family was as preponderant, and extended and multinuclear households as uncommon. There is all the more reason to make this enquiry, because there is no lack of examples of aristocratic families accommodating different categories of kinsmen of the master of the household.[13] However, isolated examples do not suffice to contradict statistical results as definitive as those which we have just examined.

For lack of more complete information, let us consider once again some of the statistics published by Peter Laslett. In Ealing, out of eighty-five households, there were fifty-six without servants and twenty-nine with servants. Even though the presence of servants does not necessarily imply great wealth, it is nevertheless probable that these were the better-off households. Now, 72.4 per cent of these households were of the conjugal type, 13.6 per cent of the extended type and 3.4 per cent of the multi-nuclear type. In this comparatively well-to-do sector, the preponderance of the mononuclear structure is as indisputable as in the case of the poor. It may be observed, however, that in Ealing, out of six extended families, four had servants, as did the only multinuclear family. This suggests, therefore, that it is predominantly in the better-off sectors that one finds families with a complex structure.

These conclusions are firmly established for England – though on the basis of a small number of published examples. The Cambridge historians have suggested, after examining the structure of households in certain localities of continental Europe, that they are also valid for other European countries. In Longuenesse, in northern France (Table 5), although extended families accounted for 14 per cent of the total and multinuclear households for 3 per cent – slightly higher proportions than were generally found in the English villages – the conjugal structure is, nevertheless, as preponderant as in England, as it is found in 76 per cent of households. Moreover, the English model emerges even more emphatically from the analysis of the households of Brueil-en-Vexin, where, in 1625, 85 per cent of the households were of the mononuclear type, as compared with only 7 per cent of the extended type and none at all of the multinuclear type. All the villages of northern France so far studied reveal the same preponderance of the nuclear family. What is the reason for this?

To explain the rarity of extended families in England, Peter Laslett quotes as an example the story of a wet cooper of Clayworth, Nicholas Bacon. Unable to acquire by himself a house to accommodate his wife and children, he had to wait for the death of his father in order to marry. Then, being the sole heir to his father's property, in accordance with the English custom, he married, and evicted from the house his mother and his sister, abandoning them to public charity.[14] Such behaviour may have been habitual in England, and this may have some connection with the development of the poor laws from the late sixteenth century onwards. In northern France, however, even though late marriages took place to

Table 5. *Household structures in northern France*

Type of household	Longue-nesse (Pas-de-Calais) 1778	Villages around Valen-ciennes (Nord) 1693	Valen-ciennes (Nord) 1693	Rouen: Saint-Nicais quarter 1793	Breuil-en-Vexin 1625	Treil/Seine (Yvelines) 1817
Percentage of households						
1 Solitaries	1	1.5	12.9	39	7.3	17.9
2 No family	6	1.8	3.1	3.8	1.5	1.1
3 Simple family households	76	85.8	75.7	54.9	83.8	76.9
4 Extended family households	14	10.6	8.1	2.4	7.3	4.1
5 Multiple family households	3	0.3	0.2	0	0	0
4 + 5	17	10.9	8.3	2.4	7.3	4.1
Number of households	75	330	2,139	1,201	68	541

Sources:
Longuenesse: P. Laslett, *Household and Family in Past Time.*
Valenciennes and neighbouring villages: Unpublished research completed by the Laboratory of Historical Demography of the Ecole des Hautes Etudes.
Rouen: Unpublished research by J.-P. Bardet.
Breuil-en-Vexin: P. Lions and M. Lachiver, *Annales de démographie historique* (1967), pp. 511–20.
Triel-sur-Seine: Unpublished research by M. Lachiver.

almost the same extent as in England and for analogous reasons, it does not seem that widowed mothers, sisters and younger brothers were driven out of the house in this fashion. Even if one had wished to do so, one would not have been able to, because the customary laws governing inheritance did not permit it.

Let us consider, for example, the population of Brueil-en-Vexin, where the structure of households in 1625 was entirely comparable with that of the English households. In this population, there were five widowers and thirteen widows, which is a normal ratio, since men remarried more frequently than women. Of these eighteen widowers and widows, there was only one widow living alone; and she had no descendants in the village. Of the others, thirteen lived in 'incomplete conjugal family households', with unmarried children, and only four in extended family households with a married son or daughter. This scarcity of extended households cannot be explained, in this case, by the late marriages of the children: at twenty-four or twenty-five, all were already married, which is fairly exceptional. The

71

explanation is, rather, the prolonged fertility of the men and women and the small chance that they had of living for more than twenty or twenty-five years after the birth of their last child. In a society such as our own, in which it is exceptional to have children after the age of thirty-five or forty, and in which many women live beyond the age of sixty-five or seventy, the demographic conditions are much more favourable to the existence of extended households. Thus population trends probably provide a sufficient explanation of the increased number of complex families in the nineteenth century in the cases where this has been verified, as, for example, in the six English villages included in Figure 3.

However, although demographic conditions favourable to the nuclear family may have existed throughout France, as in England, it has been proved that in southern France the structure of households was quite different from that which we have observed above. In Limousin, Périgord, Rouergue, Provence, the County of Nice, Corsica, and apparently in most of the central and southern parts of the kingdom, there was a proportion of families with complex structures that was sufficiently large to cast doubts on whether the conjugal family was the norm.

To begin with, Corsica poses a problem:[15] the house-by-house censuses, covering entire sectors of the island between 1769 and 1771, have shown that in Corsica between 19 and 26 per cent of households were of the extended or multinuclear type (Table 6). The multinuclear type, in particular, which in England and northern France never constituted more than 3 per cent of the households, here constitutes between 13.5 and 18.5 per cent. Another original characteristic of Corsica was the existence of *frérèches*, that is to say, of households constituted by brothers and sisters, married or single, with or without children, but independent of their

Table 6. *Household structures in Corsica (1769–71)*

Type of household	Nebbio sector	Bastia sector	Ajaccio sector
Percentage of households			
1 Solitaries	2.0	2.5	2.1
2 No family	3.4	3.0	2.2
3 Simple family households	68.4	67.4	74.7
4 Extended family households	7.9	7.3	5.5
5 Multiple family households	17.5	18.5	13.5
With servants	0.9	1.4	1.9
4 + 5	25.4	25.8	19.0
Frérèches	10.9	11.3	7.8
Average size	4.2	4.4	4.3

Source: J. Dupaquier and L. Jadin, in *Household and Family in Past Time*, pp. 290–1.

ancestors. This family structure, which was practically unknown in England, is, moreover, inadequately revealed by the typology devised by the Cambridge historians, who disperse it among types 2a, 4c and 5d. When they are grouped together as a single category, these *frérèches* constitute, in Corsica, between 7.8 and 11.3 per cent of households.

Despite these specific characteristics – which one might ascribe to Corsica's marginal situation, in socio-cultural as well as geographical terms – the case of Corsica does not really contradict the thesis of the applicability of the English model to Europe as a whole: the conjugal structure is found there in between 67 and 75 per cent of households. However, its preponderance is noticeably more reduced in central and southern France (Table 7): it was found in 50.8 per cent of the households in Montplaisant (Périgord), 51 per cent in Mostuéjouls (Rouergue), 50.8 per cent in Mirabeau (Provence), and only 47.4 per cent in Saint-Martin-de-Vésubie (County of Nice). In these same regions, between 32 and 43 per cent of households were of the extended or multinuclear type. Researches, still

Table 7. *Household structures in southern France*

Type of household	Périgord	Rouergue		Prov-ence	County of Nice		Hautes-Pyrénées
					Saint-Martin-de-Vésubie		
	Mont-plaisant (1644)	Mostué jouls (1690)	Laguiole (1691)	Mira-beau (1745)	Vésubie (1718)	Péone (1787)	Bulan (1793)
Percentage of households							
1 Solitaries	11.0	3.2	7.0	6.7	11.2	NDA	3.7
2 No family	1.6	2.1	3.3	0.8			
3 Simple family households	50.8	51.0	56.0	50.8	47.4	NDA	54.7
4 Extended family households	15.9	42.6	32.2	19.2	41.4	41.7	32.0
5 Multiple family households	20.6			22.5			9.4
4 + 5	36.5	42.6	32.2	41.7	41.4	41.7	41.4
Number of households	63	94	214	120	152	259	53

Sources:
Montplaisant: J. N. Biraben, in *Annales de démographie historique* (1970), pp. 441–62.
Mostuéjouls: R. Noel, in *Hommage à Marcel Reinhard* (Paris, 1973), pp. 505–22.
Laguiole: R. Noel, in *Annales de démographie historique* (1967), pp. 197–223.
Mirabeau, Saint-Martin-de-Vésubie and Péone: A. Collomp, in *Annales E.S.C.* (May–June 1974), pp. 777–86.
For Bulan: Unpublished research by Mlle Antoinette Chamoux.

unpublished, carried out in the Pyrenean region of Baronnies and in Limousin, have confirmed these results,[16] and it was even found, in a group of seven parishes of Upper Limousin, where a census was held in 1831, that less than 40 per cent of families consisted of a simple conjugal nucleus.[17]

It must be observed that the statistical approach of the Cambridge group artificially reduces the importance of the complex structures. In the first place, in establishing the proportions in relation to the number of households one is giving one or two persons the same weighting as ten or twelve. At Bulan, in the Baronnies, out of fifty-three households there were only twenty-two – i.e. 41.4 per cent – of types 4 and 5, as against twenty-nine of type 3 and two of type 2; however, 240 persons lived in complex families, as compared with only 121 who lived in families with simple structures.[18] Furthermore, even if the cohabitation of a married child with the parents had been an absolute rule, there would have been a considerable proportion of nuclear families simply as a result of the mortality of the parents. At Saint-André-les-Alpes, out of 1,254 contracts of marriage drawn up between 1638 and 1792, only 568 envisaged the married couple living together with the parents of one of the spouses; but in the case of the 686 other couples, three-quarters of the bridegrooms had lost their father before the marriage took place and could not, therefore, live with him.[19] All these data, it is true, are of little importance in comparison with the overwhelming evidence of the preponderance of the conjugal family in England and northern France. However, these facts must be stated at this point, to emphasize that, in contrast with the France in which the conjugal family predominated, there was another France, where complex families were common. It now remains for us to explain this antithesis.

Customary laws governing inheritance and family structures

The explanation that first springs to mind is that these different family structures were connected with different rules governing inheritance. Le Play had already emphasized the connections existing between the stem family and the transmission of the patrimony to a sole heir, and between the conjugal family and the equal partition of the inheritance among the children. However, the egalitarian rule is not, as he implied, an invention of the Revolution: it existed traditionally, among the common people, throughout the northern half of France.[20] In southern France, on the other hand, the patrimony was bequeathed entirely, or almost entirely, to only one of the children. This was either because – in the regions where Roman Law prevailed – the father was free to dispose of the patrimony as he liked by making a will, after a sum had been set aside for the dowries of the daughters and the 'legitimate portion' of the younger sons, or because – in the central and western Pyrenees – he was obliged to bequeath it to an heir specifically designated by customary law. Until 1551, in Béarn, and throughout the Ancien Régime in Aure, in Lavedan, in the Barèges valley and in the Basque provinces, it was the eldest child, whether male or female, who was supposed to inherit the entire patrimony. 'The eldest, irrespective of whether they are males or females', declared the deputies of the Barèges valley in 1670, 'are, by a perpetual trust, the heirs of the houses from which they descend, and of the property of the stock or ancestral property, to the exclusion of all the other younger brothers and sisters, who each have only their "legitimate portion".' This last should be determined 'in accordance with the number of the children...their fathers and mothers...being able to dispose of or give one quarter of their property, including the expenses both of the funeral and of all legacies...'[21]

In these Pyrenean regions tradition was so strong that, as late as the twentieth century, families found ways of evading the Civil Code, either by playing tricks with the quarter of the inheritance which it left at the free disposal of the fathers, or by refusing to partition the inheritance and obliging the younger sons to live, unmarried, in the house of the eldest, or even by buying them out with a donation in money or chattels – which was rarely paid promptly – when they established themselves outside the house. This was the situation described by Pierre Bourdieu in Béarn at the beginning of this century.[22] This made it possible to preserve, or perhaps even to strengthen, the system of the stem family, with celibate younger sons living in the house.

In Limousin, around 1830, an observer described – in tones of disapproval – an analogous situation, deriving from 'a custom hallowed by the ancient laws of the region, and tolerated by certain provisions of our new Code'.

> In most of the houses of the well-to-do, the eldest of the male children, or the eldest of the girls if there are no boys, sets apart one quarter of the paternal inheritance and then receives, from what is left, a portion equal to that of each of the co-heirs. In addition, he has the privilege, when he marries, of occupying the family house and living there, he, his wife and his children, at the expense of the common fortune, until the moment when the death of his father delivers to him the greater part of it.

Already, however, the disintegrating effects of the Civil Code were beginning to make themselves felt in this region, if it is true that one could observe at that time 'a great number of families in Limousin embittered by lawsuits, and divided by hatreds. Brothers regard the eldest brother as a despoiler, as an enemy given to them by nature. The enmity of brothers is succeeded by that of their children towards one another. Thus the family spirit is lost.'[23]

In Périgord, the study of the family structures of Montplaisant makes it possible to measure the extent of this disintegration.[24] In 1644, in this village, 36.5 per cent of the households had a complex structure; in 1836 there remained only 14.6 per cent, while the proportion of conjugal families had increased from 50.8 to 74.4 per cent. One can make a useful comparison between this development and the doubling of the proportion of complex households which occurred at the same time in the six English villages proposed by way of example by Peter Laslett (see Figure 3 above). In both these cases the economic and demographic changes were analogous: it was apparently the introduction of the Civil Code which explains the development of the family structures in Montplaisant, and in particular the near-disappearance of multinuclear families, of which the proportion fell from 20.6 to 1.2 per cent. This suggests that the contrary development of family structures in the south of France and in England can be explained by the contrary evolution of the rules governing inheritance in each country.

In England, the rule of equal partition among heirs was derived, at one and the same time, from Celtic customs such as the Welsh *cyfran*, the Saxon *gavelkind*, and from Norman Law, both as it was in the time of William the Conqueror and as it was expounded a century later by Chief Justiciary Glanville. However, from the thirteenth century onwards, the requirements of the transmission of fiefs in their entirety had imposed the right of primogeniture on the 'common law' of the realm, at least as regards the men, for women – except in the case of succession to the throne – continued to have inheritance partitioned among them in the absence of male heirs. However, it is probable that this rule of the right of primogeniture, derived from the requirements of the feudal system, was not really applied among the peasants. It is known that as late as the sixteenth century partition among the sons of the deceased person survived in the mountainous areas of the north and west, which were archaic and imbued with Celtic traditions, and in the lowlands of Yorkshire, Norfolk and, above all, Kent, all regions attached to Saxon 'liberties'. It was, moreover, to this partitioning that the élites attributed, in the sixteenth and seventeenth centuries, the pauperization of the peasantry. It is true that these ancient rules of succession disappeared in the course of the seventeenth and eighteenth centuries, and had already been replaced, since the Middle Ages, in the other parts of the realm. However, had not the centuries-old practice of partition among heirs implanted in England a tradition of individualism – or, rather, was it not a manifestation of individualism – against which the new custom was powerless? The example of Nicholas Bacon evicting his mother and sister by virtue of his exclusive right to the inheritance seems to support this hypothesis.

This reflection regarding inheritance customs in England cannot be more than an exercise of the imagination, because the British historians have made no efforts to discover any connection between the history of the rules of succession and that of family structures, and have not discussed the spatial and temporal fluctuations, which are nonetheless perceptible, in the number of complex households. On the other hand, French statistical researches are not far enough advanced to make it possible to compile an accurate chart of family structures in France and to compare it with the comparatively well-known chart of the rules governing succession.

There were in fact some egalitarian regions in southern France. In the Bazadais, for example, the father could not, 'save by donation attested in writing, create inequality' between his children, or, at least, 'favour any one of them with more than a twelfth part of his property', although the Civil Code permits him to dispose freely of a quarter.[25] Similarly, in Mont-de-Marsan, 'the father cannot favour one son over another, by will or otherwise, as regards his patrimonial property'.[26] There was a still greater diversity of customs in northern France: Auvergne, the Bourbonnais, the Berri, the Nivernais and Burgundy formed, owing to their contacts with the written-law provinces, a transitional zone in which the father maintained a certain right to favour one of his heirs. However, although it is well known that this zone possessed a large number of multinuclear households, no statistical study – or hardly any[27] – gives any information regarding their proportion in relation to the simple-structure households. Neither is there any study of the areas of 'primogeniture among the common people', which extended from the mouth of the Seine as far as the Pas-de-Calais: Pays de Caux, Vimeu, Ponthieu and Boulenois. Furthermore, the proposed correlation between inheritance customs and family structures is somewhat upset by the existence of a zone of 'preciputary'* customs in the north of France, in Artois, Cambrésis, Hainault and French Flanders. It is known that in the Valenciennes region, which forms part of this zone, complex structures occurred in only between 8 and 11 per cent of households (see Table 5 above). Even more disquieting is the fact that in Longuenesse the proportion was 17 per cent, although Longuenesse is in the bailiwick of Saint-Omer, where customary laws were markedly more egalitarian.[28] It is true that in the most egalitarian regions

---

* The *preciput* (in French law) is the 'portion of an estate or an inheritance which falls to one of the co-heirs over and above his equal share with the rest, and which is to be taken out before partition is made'. *Black's Law Dictionary*, 4th edn revised (St Paul's, Minnesota, 1968).

– the French Vexin and, above all, Normandy – researchers have found the very lowest proportion of complex households. However, much remains to be done before the relationship between family structures and inheritance customs can be fully elucidated.

The problem has, perhaps, been badly expounded, both from the point of view of the preoccupations of jurists, and of those of historians and sociologists. With regard to the rules governing inheritance, what must be considered in relation to family structures is not so much the freedom granted to the father of the family to favour one or other of his children as the tendency to divide or not to divide the patrimony, and the obligations towards the other members of the 'house' which devolved upon the heir. The customary laws of the Pyrenean region, which did not allow any freedom to the father in the disposition of his property, were, nevertheless, more obsessively concerned for the indivisibility of the patrimony than was Roman Law, which granted him complete – or almost complete – freedom to bequeath his property to only one of his children. Furthermore, only under certain conditions did the right of primogeniture involve the establishment of households extended to include the mother and the collateral relations. In the Pyrenees, it demonstrated the existence of a 'house spirit', which imposed on the heir the duty of assuming responsibility for the future of his brothers and sisters. In England, on the other hand, where this rule had been imposed artificially on a population that was traditionally individualistic, it merely had the effect of abandoning to public charity the widows, daughters and younger sons who had not been able to set up a home before the death of the father. As for the freedom granted to the father to favour the heir of his choice, this encouraged his cohabitation with this heir rather than with the younger sons. However, customs varied greatly according to the region. In Saint-André-les-Alpes, the heir was most frequently a young man whose marriage had been arranged within the household, because Provençal customary law, agnatic in spirit like Roman Law, conferred privileges on the males.[29] In Messeix-en-Auvergne, on the other hand, a census held in the eighteenth century showed that, compared with sixteen parents cohabiting with a married son, there were fifteen cohabiting with a daughter and a son-in-law. It is as though the reduced freedom granted by the customary law of Auvergne to the fathers to favour one of their heirs had prevented them, in half the instances, from keeping a son in the household.

Finally, the bequest of the patrimony to one child alone was not the only method of maintaining its indivisibility; there were other means, such as communities of heirs, which might involve the constitution of households larger and more complex than the stem family. Examples of these were certain *sociétés de consorts* in the Auvergne, and *communautés taisibles* in the Nivernais, which we will consider at a later stage.

House, 'lignage' and household

Within the concept of the extended family, the *lignage*, the numerous or curtailed patriarchal family, and other communities based on egalitarian principles are often confused. However, these are three fundamentally different entities, inspired by different ideals, as the legal historians have frequently emphasized. *House spirit*, which existed subject to slight variations in the written-law provinces and in the Pyrenean region, implies the bequest of the patrimony to a sole heir, married within the household, while the other children are destined to celibacy or exile. This house spirit is quite different from *lineal spirit*: a proof of this is the refusal of these regions to accept 'lineal repurchase right'. There appears to have been a correlation between house spirit, the full ownership of the allod – much more effectively preserved in these parts of France than in the customary-law provinces – and what were described, in fiscal terms, as the *pays de taille réelle*, where the land rather than the man enjoyed the fiscal privileges of nobility. These regions where house spirit prevailed are those in which Le Play discovered his 'stem family'; but there were also to be found in these parts other types of patriarchal family, either more or less abundant.

At the opposite pole from this house spirit was *lineal spirit*, which is more clearly evident than anywhere else in the lands where strict equality among heirs prevailed, as in Normandy. In such regions the family, like taxation, had a 'personal' rather than a 'property' basis. In other words, it was based on 'ties of blood' rather than on the preservation of the ancestral patrimony. At the death of the father, each child took away his portion of the inheritance, and the rights which each one had to it were indefeasible, even if he had parted from the family years before, or even if a formal renunciation of the inheritance had been obtained from him, because such rights were derived strictly from consanguinity. Moreover, in Normandy community of property between spouses was unknown: the system of the dower – which the wife took away with her at the death of her husband – prevailed exclusively there. This is a further symptom of individualism. This Norman Law, both personal and 'lineal', was apparently imposed from above (according to Jean Yver who has a detailed knowledge of it), perhaps by the Norman invaders, who had already been familiar in Scandinavia with the exclusion of the daughters and the obsessive preoccupation with equality among the boys.[30]

In marked contrast to this distrustful individualism characteristic of the Normans was the confiding and communitarian customary law of the French peasantry. *Household spirit*, which characterizes it, stands like the third apex of a triangle in relation to both lineal spirit and house spirit.

The household

In common with southern customs, French peasant customs linked the family to the patrimony; like the customs of the west, they were egalitarian; but they stood in contrast to both these sets of customs in that, instead of considering the family over the course of time, in its successive generations, they considered it as a phenomenon of the present. The family was the household formed, at a particular moment, by the parents and those of their children who were still living with them. Only these children had a share in the inheritance at the moment of the dissolution of the community, the separately endowed children, who had set up house elsewhere, being excluded from it. Of course, one should not exaggerate this household spirit so far as to assert, as does Olivier-Martin, that 'the foundation of the rights of the child is not the tie of kinship but labour and life in common': [31] father and children, in the customary law of the Ile-de-France, are never placed on the same level, as they have been in other more communitarian regions; nor were the children and such domestic agricultural workers as there might be. It is true, however, that the fact of kinship alone did not suffice to make one an heir. Nevertheless, although the exclusion of the separately endowed children was disputed by the bourgeois jurists – who, from the fourteenth century onwards, have replaced it with the right of option between favours acquired during the lifetime of the father and participation in the inheritance – it appears that it often survived well into the sixteenth century in the customary practice of the peasantry.

The impress of serfdom

It is possible that this exclusion of the separately endowed children, which impelled adults to remain in the household of their parents, had seignorial, rather than spontaneously peasant, origins. In fact, by virtue of the right of mortmain, the lord in the Middle Ages took possession of the inheritance of the serf who, at the time of his death, was not living in community with his heirs. Perhaps, therefore, the mass enfranchisements of the thirteenth century explain the changes in the inheritance customs of the Orléans and Paris regions during that period, and perhaps this change had the effect of substituting the nuclear household for complex ones. It does appear certain, on the other hand, that mortmain survived for a long time in the central provinces of the kingdom: in the March, Auvergne, the Bourbonnais, the Nivernais, Burgundy and the Franche-Comté considerable family communities still existed from the sixteenth to the eighteenth centuries. For example, in western Burgundy villages subject to mortmain were still numerous in the eighteenth century.[32] Thus, in Thomirey, the inhabitants noted 'the precautions taken by those who are subject [to mortmain] to maintain communions' – that is, to live in community with their children or other heirs of their status – which was the only effective weapon to counter the avidity of the local lord.[33]

In the Franche-Comté, which was famous in the eighteenth century for the number of its properties subject to mortmain, 'communities' were even more common, which would appear to confirm the influence of mortmain on household structures. Complex households had, however, become customary in all social sectors, both in the towns – where property was not subject to mortmain – and in the rural areas. The legal historians have amply demonstrated this.[34] Like the marriage contracts of the carpenter Jean Martin or the vine-grower Melchior Chasne, those of the doctor of law Pierre Bichet or of the merchant Bonaventure Vuillard provided that the future married couples should live with the parents of the husband, having community of property with them.

Patriarchal families and egalitarian communities

These communities differed widely as regards the number of their members, the relations of kinship which existed between them, and the rights that the contract granted to each of them. When Antoine Billard got married, it was his uncle Denys Belin and his aunt Foy Vuillin who made him a gift of 300 francs on condition that the young married couple entered their community. The marriage contract of Nicolas Finot and his future wife Symone Jeunet provided that they should live in community not only with the young man's father and mother, but also with his brother and sister-in-law. More complicated still was the community into which Anne Morel was to enter with her son Claude Gonin, her daughter-in-law Guyotte Maguenet, and the brother, sister and mother of the latter.

Some contracts established a strict equality of rights among the members of the community. Thus, Nicolas Pinot and his wife were to have a one-third share in the community which they joined, while a further third accrued to his father and mother, and the remaining third to his brother and sister-in-law. This was an egalitarian community embracing three couples. Other contracts granted to some members of the community certain minor privileges. For example, Anne Morel – who seems to have contributed the essential part of the property brought into the common fund – recognized, for each of the members of the community, as for herself, a share of one-sixth, but she reserved eighty francs to use and dispose of at her pleasure. Also, other contracts established a fundamental inequality between the father and his children. Thus, Pierre Chasne the Elder, who received into his community his married son Melchior, and his unmarried sons Claude, Pierre and Jean, reserved to himself four parts, whereas each of his sons, single or married, was to have only one. It was,

81

moreover, understood that Melchior and his wife would work for the house and would contribute to the communal cooking-pot whatever they earned by working outside the house during the day; and, if they wished one day to set up house on their own, the father would give them only one-eighth of the property acquired since the date of the contract. This bears a strong resemblance to the leonine contracts into which fathers entered with their sons or their sons-in-law in the written-law provinces such as Languedoc.

Originally, in the Franche-Comté, children had tacitly lived in community with their parents, having rights equal to theirs over the patrimony. Towards the end of the thirteenth century, however, the introduction into the province of the principles of Roman Law regarding the *patria potestas* had destroyed this family 'community': henceforth the father was – in the absence of a contract stipulating the contrary – the sole master of the family patrimony and free to dispose of it as he liked without the authorization of his children.[35] In Languedoc, where the supremacy of the father was traditional, the contracts which he concluded with his married children were much more often leonine, at least in the fourteenth and fifteenth centuries.

The father customarily made the children a donation, which was fictitious in immediate terms, since he reserved to himself the usufruct of it during his lifetime. In return, the child undertook to remain in the house and to live with him, sharing the same hearth and cooking-pot. As for the dowry of the wife or the son-in-law – which generally consisted of goats or other chattels – it was actually given to the community and passed under the control of the head of the family. Furthermore, young and old undertook to live together without differentiation, eating and drinking 'the same bread and the same wine' and sharing the same cash-box, although the children and their spouses swore never to retain a sum greater than five *sous* without the consent, expressed in due form, of the father. Within the community the patriarch claimed for himself – at least according to the terms of the legal agreement – 'domination, governance, management, usufruct of all property', while the sons and sons-in-law promised him 'honour, reverence, service, obedience'. These households which incorporated the spouses of the children were, therefore, patriarchal – or gerontocratic, since, in the absence of the father, the mother often claimed the same rights – and are very far from possessing the egalitarian structures which characterized the juridical concept of community. Often, moreover, the contracts of the fourteenth and fifteenth centuries prohibited the young people from liberating themselves from this domination by terminating this communal life. Others provided for the dissolution of the union by the mere desire of the father: 'If it should happen that I expel you, you and your wife, from *my* house. . .'[36] As late as the eighteenth century, some contracts made the discontinuance subject to such arduous conditions that in practice it was impossible.[37]

It was because the power of the father was so great that, in these southern provinces, there was conceived, on a totally different basis, another type of communal life – the *frérèche*, or household constituted by brothers and sisters. It is true that this community had a head, whom the legal documents term the *gubernator*. However, this head was, in relation to the other parties to the contract, only a 'brother', that is to say, an equal. The communal funds were kept in a chest, of which each of the brothers had a key, and each one undertook not to spend more than a few *sous* of pocket-money without the consent of the others. In the fifteenth century, such *affrèrements* became increasingly common in the whole southern half of the Massif Central – in the Cévennes, Gévaudan, Velay, Rouergue, etc. The agreements might apply to brothers, brothers-in-law or other kinsmen, friends, and also a husband and his wife or even a daughter and her father. Whatever the relations of kinship of the contracting parties, the contracts established among them an egalitarian community, as in the provinces to the north of the Massif Central.[38]

Of particular interest are the *affrèrements* between spouses. In addition to the customary clauses, there were two special ones, providing for mutual respect for the duty of fidelity and the obligation on the part of the husband to dress his wife becomingly. In the fifteenth century, in this region, this was the most efficacious method of establishing community of property between spouses, who previously appear to have been simply members of the patriarchal family, enjoying exclusive communion with each other only sexually. It may be observed how, in Languedoc, the conjugal family derived, in law, from larger communities; and the legal historians have observed an analogous development in other regions of France, for example the Nivernais and the Franche-Comté.[39]

In Languedoc there was an increase, from 1350 onwards, of marriage contracts providing for cohabitation with parents, and *affrèrements* were much in vogue between 1400 and 1550. Do these trends signify that complex households became more numerous during that period? This is quite possible, especially as in many other regions of France it is also in the fourteenth and fifteenth centuries that the communities are first mentioned in legal documents.[40] This is generally explained as being due to two fundamental causes: firstly, because during that period of exceptional insecurity it was necessary to multiply ties of solidarity; and, secondly, because the demographic crisis created, for the peasants who owned their own land, a problem of shortage of labour, and such contracts were a means of solving it. Or, rather, the development occurred in two ways: an authoritarian one, based on keeping the married offspring in the paternal household, and a more liberal one, in the case of the contract of *affrèrement*, whereby the younger son could be associated with the possession of the patrimony, of which the eldest son was the sole heir. This second solution must have been particularly necessary in those harsh mountain regions which the young people were tempted to abandon in order to seek higher wages in the lowlands and the towns, which were depopulated but nonetheless active during this period.

It is, however, possible that the increased number of these contracts is merely a reflection of a sudden increase in notarial acts – which is evident from other sources – and that, even though they have left fewer written traces, egalitarian or patriarchal communities were not less numerous before the fourteenth century. It is, in fact, known that in the sixteenth, seventeenth and eighteenth centuries, in the provinces to the north of the Massif Central – particularly in Auvergne and the Nivernais – there still continued in existence a number of *communautés taisibles*, that is, *de facto* communities, without any written contract, which the law recognized as having been tacitly constituted after a year and a day. In its twenty-second chapter, the compilation of customary laws of the Nivernais dealt at length with this matter, and in the sixteenth century Guy Coquille published a celebrated commentary on this chapter. Some of these communities were, in fact, *frérèches*: 'Between two brothers aged over twenty years, being independent of the authority of their father, who have lived together for a year and a day, having their property in common and sharing their earnings, there is a *communauté taisible* contracted' (Article 2). Others were tacitly established between children who had reached the age of puberty and had lost their father or mother, and also between the surviving spouse and his or her 'common participants', whether the latter were a new spouse who arrived accompanied by the children of an earlier marriage, or kinsfolk, or all other old or new associates. In a liberal spirit, the Nivernais customary law considered orphans who had reached the age of puberty as full associates in the tacitly constituted community; this was, above all, a means of safeguarding their rights when they had neglected to define these by means of an inventory drawn up on the death of their father or mother.

It is also true that, in its first article, this customary law appears to have refused the privilege of constituting a *communauté taisible* to other persons living under the same roof, probably in order to prevent the domestic servants; and also kinsfolk taken in out of charity, from one day claiming rights over the patrimony: 'Community of goods is not contracted tacitly between persons living together, for however long a time, unless there is an express agreement.' However, in his extremely authoritative commentary, Guy Coquille took a different view:

The agreement may be explicit or tacit; for will and consent are

84

as well attested and witnessed by deeds as by words. . .Therefore,
if some are not of the status of those between whom customary law
establishes the tacit association, based on a year and a day, sharing
their profits, earnings and resources one with another uniformly
and without differences for a long period of time, such as six, eight
or ten years, I would assert that by tacit agreement they are
members of the community. . .

The reason is that it was, in fact, frequent, in the rural areas of the
Nivernais, for communities to be tacitly established between persons who
were not brothers, or married couples, or orphans who had reached the age
of puberty and surviving kinsfolk.

This can more readily and easily be presumed in the case of the
houses in the villages, in this region, in which societies are not only
frequent but also customary, and even necessary, owing to the
characteristics of the region, in so far as the labour of the rustic
household is not only tilling the soil, but also feeding the animals;
and this [system] requires a great number of people.[41]

Economic structures and domestic structures

By what he omits to mention as much as by his observations, Guy Coquille
provokes reflections as to the relations that may have existed between the
structure of households and the conditions of agricultural production.
In fact, in seeking to distinguish between mere cohabitation and association, he did not adopt as a criterion the contribution or non-contribution
of property to the community. The reason is, perhaps, that in those regions
– at least in the fifteenth and sixteenth centuries – possession of land was
not worth more than the labour required to make it productive. One might,
therefore, suggest as a preliminary hypothesis that the establishment of
communities was a means of procuring manual labour in provinces where
the soil was poor, particularly during periods of low rates of demographic
growth and high wages. Conversely, where the land was fertile, it was
profitable to employ wage-labour, particularly during periods of high rates
of demographic growth and low wages.

However, the quality of the soil and the price of labour do not provide
a full explanation. At Triel, in 1817, in the fertile lands of the Ile-de-
France and at a time when wage-labour had become customary, only 5 per
cent of households employed domestic labour – the lowest proportion so
far discovered. One must, it is true, add that in this locality there was an
even smaller proportion of complex families (see Table 5 above). The
reason is that the cultivation of the vine, which predominated almost
exclusively there, requires a labour force which is highly skilled but small
in numbers – the holdings being very small – except on the occasion of

The household

the grape-harvest. On the other hand, the combination of tillage and stock-raising which characterized agriculture in the Nivernais required a large labour force, according to Guy Coquille, and therefore recourse was taken either to wage-labour or to kinsfolk and other associates. One could probably say the same of the agriculture of Auvergne or that of other mountainous regions such as the Cévennes, the Velay, the mountainous fringe of the Quercy and of Périgord, Limousin, Upper Provence and the Dauphiné, where there was a widespread increase in *frérèche* contracts in the fifteenth century.[42]

It sometimes happened that in a region both poor and short of labour, like Sologne in the eighteenth century, communities were unknown, and the share-croppers employed numerous domestic agricultural workers. The reason is that, in this region, the nobility and bourgeoisie had taken possession of the land, and exploited it in the context of an economy based on profit. They had succeeded in making wage-labour profitable by turning over arable land to pasture, as many big English landowners had been doing since the sixteenth century.[43] The egalitarian partnership between the owner of the land and the workers was conceivable only in the regions where peasant proprietors predominated and there was a subsistence economy, which appears to have been the case in the mountainous provinces mentioned above.

However, even in the mountainous regions, the marked increase in population in the eighteenth century and the development of the money economy seem to have made complex households more rare, just as the circumstances of the fourteenth and fifteenth centuries had provoked their increase. This was the case in Auvergne, which was still celebrated in the eighteenth century for its very large *communautés taisibles* and *sociétés de consorts*. The jurist Chabrol observed in 1786: 'They are less common today, and one scarcely finds examples of them except among the villagers; it is chiefly in the area around the town of Thiers that the custom has been preserved.' Indeed, as early as 1746, the records of the tax of one-twentieth paid in Escoutoux showed only eighteen quotas payable by *sociétés de consorts* out of a total of 175 quotas, i.e. hardly more than 10 per cent; and in Messeix, in the Puy-de-Dôme, out of 198 households, only thirty-one included a married son or daughter living in the house, that is to say 15.6 per cent.[44]

Finally, it must be observed that the conditions which, in our view, were necessary for the establishment of true communities of the egalitarian type, were not needed for the continued existence of large patriarchal families in the written-law provinces. At Montplaisant, in Périgord, share-cropping holdings were numerous as early as 1644. Despite this, there were ten extended and thirteen multinuclear families, which together constituted 36.5 per cent of the households. It is true that wage-labour was not

86

unknown, since 17 per cent of the heads of families employed domestic workers. This, however, was only as a last resort: whenever it was possible, they preferred the family labour-force. A proof of this is that, out of twenty-three complex households, only six included domestic workers, in contrast to what we have observed in the case of Ealing. The share-cropper G. Vidal needed a servant-girl because he had no daughter and only one of his two sons was married; another man employed a manservant because, of four children, he had only one son, although he also had a nephew. Although Jean Mourlhiou, the paper-manufacturer, employed four wage-earning workers to whom he does not appear to have been related by any ties of kinship, this was because his wife, his three daughters, his two sons-in-law and two brothers of his sons-in-law were not enough for the work. More fortunate in this respect, Jean Gibert the Elder worked his large share-cropping holding with the help of his son and his daughter-in-law, his three as yet unmarried grandchildren, his two married grandsons and their two wives. Counting his baby great-grand-daughter, he was the head of a household of eleven persons, comprising four generations, and three married couples plus himself, a widower.

While there remained in Montplaisant only one *frérèche* – established, as is readily understandable, on a *borderie*, or land owned by peasants – share-cropping gave rise to the constitution of patriarchal families some-times larger than the stem families described by Le Play, which allowed for only one couple in each generation. Moreover, it is known that, in many other regions, those who offered themselves for employment as managers of a share-cropping holding, accompanied by a family which was numerous and included people of working age, had more chance of obtaining the concession than a married couple on their own. Large families were appreciated even in the regions with an egalitarian tradition where the conjugal family was preponderant, as in Sologne in the eighteenth century, if one is to believe this extract from a record of grievances: 'A leaseholder' – working a small leaseholding – 'who has a number of children whom his work does not suffice to rear, offers himself to take over a farm by halves' – that is, in present-day terms, a share-cropping contract:

> and by this arrangement he succeeds in bringing up his family, which, when they are of an age to establish themselves, get married in the house of their father, who grants them small privileges as domestic workers. The children of these newly married couples are brought up with the family which, having shared out the profits produced from a number of gardens sown with hemp, and four or six sheep which are granted to them from the flock, with twelve *livres* payment in cash, puts them in a position to succeed their father and mother in the usufruct of the domain in which they have

been brought up, and, in due course, their children serve them as domestic workers.[45]

When one recalls that the ancient philosophers compared slaves to children, this last phrase, 'serve them as domestic workers', is an indication of the normal status of wage-earning labour in Sologne in the eighteenth century. Family labour, is common in the southern regions where patriarchal tendencies were strong, was, in the regions with an egalitarian tradition, nothing more than a Utopian solution proposed to offset depopulation and the high cost of domestic labour.

Structure of households and social status

This analysis of the relations between the structure of households and judicial traditions and economic structures has been carried out in order to throw some light on the ambiguous correlation that historians have discovered between social status and the complexity of families. In fact, depending on the region and, perhaps, on the historical period, it has been predominantly among the rich or among the poor that complex families have been found.

In an attempt to explain how it was that in the fifteenth century, during a period of depopulation, *frérèches* became more common in Languedoc, Emmanuel Le Roy Ladurie has affirmed that 'in the case of the big farms in the mountainous regions', in the absence of wage-labour, it was necessary 'to abandon the land, or to have recourse. . .to the large family'. This is quite probable, in so far as there were big farms in these mountainous areas.[46] When, however, the situation as regards demographic growth and wage-rates was the reverse, it is the poor or middling peasants whom one finds still organized in communities and *sociétés de consorts*. According to Abel Poitrineau, in Auvergne in the eighteenth century, 'the greatest number of contracts of association are entered into by fairly poor wretches or, at the most, peasants of the middling sort'. In this condition, for example, were two day-labourers of Saint-Martin-des-Plaines, Etienne Marquet and Jean Riffard, who, sharing their poverty, formed an association on 20 March 1720. Also miserably poor, as is shown by the inventory of their property, were Henri Madeuf and Annet Villemin, living in Sachapt, who on 3 March 1779 entered into an association 'to share cooking-pot and fire' for three years.[47]

Of course, neither these examples nor these impressions of reputable historians are as valuable as good statistical information. One thing, however, appears evident: at all times these communities were typical of the peasantry rather than of the bourgeoisie. They survived for longer among the peasantry, and one finds no trace of them among the nobility, except the very poorest sector of it. The legal historians affirm this unanimously, and Jean Gaudemet has repeatedly emphasized it in the brief study which he has devoted to the communities.[48] We have seen, moreover, that this was also the opinion of contemporary observers, as regards both the Nivernais in the sixteenth century and Auvergne in the eighteenth. These observations only apply, however, to the egalitarian communities.

The cohabitation of the parents with their married heir was an entirely different matter in the regions where the 'house spirit' predominated. In Saint-André-les-Alpes, in Haute-Provence, a meticulous analysis of marriage contracts has proved that the richer the parents of one of the spouses were, the more frequently the young married couples cohabited with them (Table 8).[49] It was customary, in this region, to arrange the

Table 8. *Wealth and cohabitation with parents in Saint-André-les-Alpes*

Amount of dowry (livres)	Contracts providing for cohabitation		Contracts not providing for cohabitation		Number of contracts
	(No.)	(%)	(No.)	(%)	
Under 100	0	0	2	100	2
100–199	13	28	33	72	46
200–299	17	35	31	65	48
300–699	44	65	24	35	68
700–1,000	5	100	0	0	5

Source: A. Collomp, in *Annales E.S.C.* (July–October 1972), p. 972.

marriage of one of the children 'within the house' – in principle, the heir, or, when there were no male children, the heiress. This practice required a large enough house and a sufficient patrimony to provide a living for the two families. The parents could impose cohabitation only when they were in a position to offer their son or son-in-law the prospect of an attractive inheritance. The poorest people, however, usually lost their children at the onset of their adolescence, sending them off to work in the house of another person, in the manner described by Ariès and Laslett. Therefore, the heirs apparently waited for the parents' death to provide them with a house in which to accommodate a wife and children before they got married. Finally, some of the smallest dowries were probably given to younger daughters marrying younger sons, although these 'marriages of hunger with thirst' – as they were called in the south-west – were, in principle, exceptional. In any case, when they did occur, the

The household

'house spirit' militated against these young couples living with their parents.

At Ealing it is also in the comparatively well-to-do sectors that most of the extended families have been found, and for analogous reasons, even though, in these sectors as in the others, the conjugal family was the most usual arrangement. The same was true in northern France, as is shown by the still unpublished statistics recently submitted by Jean-Pierre Bardet,[50] relating to a quarter of Rouen, the town of Valenciennes and the neighbouring villages (Table 9). What is striking, in the case of Rouen, is the

Table 9. *Household structure and social status in northern France*

	Type of household						
	1	2	3 Simple family house-holds	4 Extended family house-holds	5 Multiple family house-holds	4 + 5	Number of house-holds
	Soli-taries (%)	No family (%)	(%)	(%)	(%)	(%)	holds
Rouen (Saint-Nicaise quarter)							
Bourgeois and master-craftsmen	25.0	15.2	52.4	7.5	0	7.5	956
Day-labourers and workmen	39.4	2.1	56.6	1.7	0	1.7	172
Villages around Valenciennes							
Farmers and censive tenants	1.9	3.8	81.1	13.2	0	13.2	106
Rural craftsmen	2.9	1.0	85.4	10.7	0	10.7	121
Day-labourers	0	0.8	90.1	9.1	0	9.1	103
Town of Valenciennes							
Nobles and 'sieurs'	25.0	7.4	58.3	9.3	0	9.3	108
Officials, etc.	12.8	5.1	61.5	17.9	2.6	20.5	39
Merchants	4.5	1.8	77.3	15.5	0.9	16.4	110
Minor officials	4.4	1.1	85.9	8.7	0	8.7	92
Food trades	3.6	3.6	82.1	9.8	0.9	10.7	224
Textile craftsmen	3.0	2.5	87.4	7.0	0	7.0	398
Other craftsmen	3.4	0.3	87.3	9.1	0	9.1	298
Day-labourers and carters	2.5	0.8	88.5	8.2	0	8.2	122
Miscellaneous (esp. widows)	28.0	4.7	60.7	6.5	0	6.5	695
Beggars	18.2	0	81.8	0	0	0	33

Sources:
Rouen: unpublished research by J.-P. Bardet.
Valenciennes and the neighbouring villages: unpublished research by J. Dupaquier, Mme Hamon and J.-P. Bardet, of the Laboratory of Historical Demography.

number of uprooted people, particularly among the workers and day-labourers, of whom nearly 40 per cent appear to have been living on their own. This factor reduces the proportion of conjugal families to a level similar to that of the south of France. It must be remembered, however, that if one calculates the proportion of these solitary dwellers in relation to the number of households, instead of in relation to the number of individuals, one artificially exaggerates their importance and thus diminishes that of the conjugal or extended families. In addition, as might be supposed, extended families were clearly less exceptional among the bourgeoisie and the master-craftsmen than among the workers and day-labourers.

The example of Valenciennes also merits closer attention because it is, for the moment, the only study that provides statistical information with regard to the family structures of the nobility. In this social sector, where the right of primogeniture prevailed, the proportion of conjugal families was almost as low as in the written-law provinces – 58.3 per cent. The reason for this was, apparently, that the younger sons remained single. However, these unmarried nobles did not usually remain in the house of their elder brothers, and even more rarely did they work as part of the domestic staff in the house of some grandee, at least in Valenciennes; most often they lived alone with a manservant, a housekeeper or even a con-cubine. As a result, the proportion of extended families, in these sectors of the nobility of Valenciennes, was as low as among the petty bourgeoisie or the peasants. This proportion was markedly higher than the average only among the officials and other members of the liberal or mercantile bourgeoisie. Was this because they were often more wealthy than the nobles, even though they were in principle below them in the social hierarchy? Or is it, rather, an indication that the urban nobility included a great number of uprooted individuals, who had come from other places – like the workers of the Saint-Nicaise quarter, in Rouen – whereas the bourgeois and the officials of Valenciennes were, on the contrary, firmly rooted in their home town? Both these hypotheses are, in fact, tenable.

If, in contrast to the line of argument followed up to now, one wished, in conclusion, to consider only the simplicity and complexity of family structures, one would have to observe that complexity was related not so much to wealth or dominant social position as to the degree of rootedness in the ancestral soil. Solid and systematic, in the ancient sedentary popula-tions of southern and central France, this deep-rootedness was able to manifest itself in either patriarchal or communitarian organizations. In England and northern France, on the other hand, where the Germanic, Breton and Scandinavian invaders had imposed the system of partitioning the inheritance among the sons, the conjugal family was the norm, and disequilibrium and movement were continuous. Demographic and military expansion, and economic and social upheavals, were the apparent results of this. If this is a characteristic of Europe as a whole, then the conjugal family is eminently European. It must not, however, be forgotten that, even in these latter regions, the bourgeois most firmly rooted in their towns and, probably, the nobles in their fiefs, also practised to a certain degree the system of the extended family, while the peasants who were in process of being uprooted in their villages, and the workers and the younger sons of noble houses who migrated to the towns, were condemned to live in someone else's house or alone, or, at best, in small conjugal households, unable to keep their children.

3. THE MATERIAL CONTEXT AND THE RITUAL OF DOMESTIC LIFE

The castle and the cottage have left on the European landscape the imprint of the contrast between large and small households. Is it possible, in the same way, to rediscover the characteristics of family life in former times on the basis of what is known of the material environment? Evidence regarding the material life of our forefathers is, indeed, not lacking. We have the remains of the buildings of former times (particularly of the most beautiful, it is true, and of their external architecture rather than of their interior appointments); furniture and utensils preserved in our museums; paintings of interiors (unfortunately less plentiful and less realistic in France and England than in the Low Countries); inventories compiled after death containing detailed descriptions of the material context of the life of the deceased person; the mention, in some marriage contracts, of items of the bride's trousseau; and, finally, fleeting yet irreplaceable observations in the memoirs and novels of the period.

Interior architecture

First of all, let us attempt to summarize the excellent observations already made on this subject by Philippe Ariès.[51] Both in the palaces and in the hovels, undifferentiation was formerly very much greater than today, and this hindered the development of modern family feeling. The poor were so uncomfortable in their own homes that they lived elsewhere as often as they could, and parents parted company with their offspring when the latter reached adolescence, sending them to work in someone else's house. As for the rich, their vast residences were crowded with domestic servants and visitors, which prevented them from living in privacy with their wives and children.

The changes in the internal organization of the great houses of the nobility or the bourgeoisie, which occurred in the course of the eighteenth century, provide evidence of a quest for comfort and privacy. In the seventeenth century there were still large rooms, with no precisely defined functions, opening onto each other: people slept, ate and lived in them amid the coming and going of servants, children and visitors, the servants not hesitating any more than the children to take part in the conversation of their masters and the latter's friends, if one is to believe the evidence of the *Caquets de l'Accouchée*[52] or the comedies of Molière. At night, the servants slept near their masters, often in the same room, ready to answer their summons. At all times, privacy was unknown; each person, according to Philippe Ariès, lived 'in state' as at the Court of Versailles. In the eighteenth century, however, corridors were introduced and had the effect of giving autonomy to the rooms, which became specialized, more numerous and individual. The ladies, during the day, could shut themselves up in their boudoirs, or receive their close friends in small drawing-rooms. The servants were driven back to the kitchen, the servants' hall and the antechambers, and attempts were made to prevent the children from being too familiar with them. Within the confines of the great households, the modern 'family' began to achieve its independence.

After describing this development in broad outline, we must turn to the analysis of behaviour and the chronology of its evolution. Let us consider an anecdote reported by Longchamp, who was secretary to Voltaire after being *valet de chambre* of the Marquise du Châtelet.[53]

He tells us of the embarrassment that he felt when the Marquise stripped naked in front of him before getting into the bathtub and, in contrast to this, the unconcerned tone in which she had reproved him for his lack of attentiveness and his clumsiness when sprinkling her with the hot water. This certainly proves that, despite the greater privacy made possible by eighteenth-century interior architecture, some traditional customs took a long time to disappear. But how had these habits actually developed? Most of the commentators on Longchamp's account emphasize the contempt which such scenes implied on the part of the aristocrats – even those who were closest in outlook to the *philosophes* – towards those demi-men such as servants and others of the common people.[54] This, perhaps, became true in the eighteenth century; but was it also contempt for those who were present at his getting up, at his going to bed, and at his sessions on the lavatory-seat, that explains this kind of exhibitionism on the part of Louis XIV and of most of the other sovereigns? The reason might simply be that Louis XIV on his lavatory-seat and Madame du Châtelet in her bath were not ashamed to carry out, in accordance with the ceremonial appropriate to their social status, the ordinary acts of human nature. When Philippe Ariès emphasizes the life 'in state' which was that of all the great nobles, he does so to contrast it with a need for privacy which cannot be proved to have existed before the eighteenth century, or with a sense of modesty which one might describe as neurotic had it not become, in the eighteenth and nineteenth centuries, normal social behaviour.

It is still not known exactly how and why this need for privacy developed. One can, however, discern two elements which, directly or indirectly, are derived from the distrustful severity of the moralists of the Catholic Reformation and, indeed, the Protestant one. The communal living of earlier times had been accompanied by extremely rigorous sexual taboos: incest, adultery within the household, and the seduction of the girls of the house were punishable by death. The judicial records of the sixteenth and seventeenth centuries provide abundant evidence of this.[55] They also bear witness to the fact that, despite the rigour of the prohibitions, there were still dangers, which the militant Catholic reformers exerted themselves in trying to avert: not only did it become indecent to show oneself naked in front of the servants, but it became indecent to be in the nude by oneself, because nudity, even in solitude, involved the risk of inducing one to sin. Marie-Antoinette, brought up in accordance with these strict principles, avoided the immodesty of Madame du Châtelet not by bathing without witnesses, but by taking her bath dressed in a long flannel robe buttoned up to the neck. Moreover, while her two bath-attendants were helping her to get out of the bath, she insisted on a sheet being held in front of her to hide her from her women servants.[56] It was also Christian morality of the seventeenth century which multiplied the warnings against the bad influence on the children that might result from excessive familiarity with the servants. Finally, even though it was not possible to dissuade the masters of households and their grown-up sons from indulging in ancillary love-affairs, it became obligatory, on pain of public scandal and excommunication, to expel servant-girls from the house as soon as they became pregnant. This was one more way of keeping them in their place.

The desire for privacy seems to have been, at first, a reaction on the part of the libertines against the severity of this morality. It appears to have begun towards the end of Louis XIV's reign, when this moral code had become stifling, and it was a manifestation of the desire to lead a free life in a society extremely sensitive to scandal. Even after he had attained power, Philippe d'Orléans could not permit himself to do in public what he had been accustomed to doing on the occasion of his small intimate suppers. It was not until later, in the second half of the eighteenth century, that this desire for privacy came to be associated with the bourgeois joys of family life or the pastoral scenes of the Trianon. Before the triumph of the Catholic reforms, Henri VI had had no need to conceal himself in order to play with his children, legitimate or otherwise.

In the case of the popular sectors, it was the smallness of the dwellings that forced people into a communal life-style which to us appears intolerable, and their lack of comfort probably discouraged family reunions.[57] This, of course, is still the case in part of our western societies – from the shantytowns of Nanterre to the Harlem ghetto – to say nothing of the rest of the world. In the lowest levels of society, the history of family life corresponds to that of the standard of living, whereas among the élites, even as regards the most material aspects, it is a part of the history of culture. It is not, therefore, only because of the details revealed in historical documents that Philippe Ariès has described noble and bourgeois houses at greater length than popular ones: the principal reason is the decisive role played by the nobility and the bourgeoisie in the origin of our sentiments involving the family. Let us attempt, however, from the less genetic perspective that we are employing in this study, to imagine the domestic life of the masses in former times on the basis of what is known today about their material environment.

We are, in fact, beginning to acquire a more detailed knowledge of their habitat. In Lyons, in the eighteenth century,[58] nearly half the dwellings of craftsmen and workers had only one room. For example, Philippe Chalumeau, a journeyman-mason who died in 1780, lived in one room which contained a bed and three couches. His widow explained to those who were compiling the inventory that these couches were let by the month to three journeymen-carpenters. Another example was that of François Gaillard, a master-tailor, who lived with his wife and two young children in a 'room' in which, at his death, there were his tailor's worktable, some shelves, a chest of drawers for his wife's clothes – he himself wore, according to her account, those of his customers – and a loft containing a bed and two couches. Such scantiness of furnishings was comparatively rare in the case of the master-craftsmen having their shops on the ground floor, but frequent among the workers living in the upper storeys. The silk-workers and most of the craftsmen of Lyons lived in two rooms, one being predominantly devoted to their occupation, and the other being used for living in and cooking. Often the shop, or the room devoted to the trade, included a loft where the beds were stowed away. Studies of Coutances,[59] Aix[60] and Marseilles[61] confirm the evidence obtained in the case of Lyons: the overwhelming majority of urban households in the seventeenth and eighteenth centuries had only one or two rooms for accommodation and professional activities. In such material conditions, it was necessary either to get rid of the children – that is to say, not to lead what we would call a family life – or to live with them in an intolerable proximity. Usually, the youngest ones were put out to nurse and the adolescents sent to serve apprenticeships, while those between these ages – who might be numerous when, by good fortune, few of them had died in the nursing stage – spent the day at school or in the street, and only returned to their parents' house to sleep.

In the rural areas, the house of the poor or relatively poor peasant varied in size and appearance according to the region: in some places, the walls were of stone – although men were scarce where stone was abundant – and in others, of planks and daub; the roofs were most commonly of thatch, except in certain regions (the houses of the rich had roofs of tiles or slate); the floor was nearly always of beaten earth – soiled with refuse, among which the chickens scratched about – which in winter provided only poor insulation from the cold of the ground. In general, only one room was occupied and, in certain regions, the people lived there in warm and malodorous proximity to the farm animals. The optimistic description which Noël du Fail has left us of the house of a worthy Breton peasant of the sixteenth century,[62] mentions only one inhabited room, separated from the stables – a 'roof for the cows' and a 'roof for the sheep' – by 'fine poles of hazelwood interlaced with subtle workmanship'. Similarly, the literary descriptions of the old-time English cottages, whether they are emphasizing their poverty or are couched in a facetious vein, mention only one inhabited room.[63]

Perhaps these literary descriptions give one a more accurate idea of the ordinary dwellings of the English cottagers and labourers than do the probate inventories, which were much more common among the rich than among the poor. Of a total of 3,600 rural inventories of the sixteenth and seventeenth centuries studied by a team of British historians,[64] only 300, i.e. 8 per cent, concern persons designated as *labourers* or *cottagers*, although these constituted 25 per cent of the population of England at the beginning of the sixteenth century, and 47 per cent at the end of the seventeenth century. This justifies the presumption that only the wealthiest fraction of this social category enjoyed the benefit of a probate inventory. An extreme example was that of Robert Wood, a 'peasant labourer' of Nuneaton – a parish in the forested part of the Midlands – whose 'farm' contained seven rooms and abundant, almost luxurious, furniture. This landless peasant was, in fact, a cheese-manufacturer on a large scale, and there must have been many others among those for whom an inventory of property was drawn up who were as unrepresentative of the typical condition of 'labourers'. Nevertheless, the fact remains that three-quarters of these inventories do not make any specific distinction between the rooms of the house, most probably because there was only one room.

These inventories also show how the value of the domestic property of these 'labourers' could vary in spatial and temporal terms: the average was £1-10s in the low-lying areas of the north of England, £3-10s in the rural parts of the Midlands, £4 in East Anglia, £4-10s in the forested parishes of the Midlands, £6 in Somerset and £7-10s in Hertfordshire. In the low-lying parts of the north domestic property, which constituted on an average, 18 per cent of the inheritance at the beginning of the sixteenth century, came to constitute 29 per cent in the seventeenth century. During the same period, the proportion increased from 35 to 46 per cent in the open rural areas of the Midlands, from 59 to 69 per cent in Hertfordshire, and from 40 to 50 per cent in England as a whole. This would appear to signify, among that fraction of the 'labourers' whose property made it worth while compiling a probate inventory, an undeniable improvement in terms of comfort. From other sources, however, the evidence leads one to suppose that the other 'labourers', whose number increased continually, experienced a decline in their standard of living.

In France, the probate inventories of the peasants have not yet been the subject of comparable statistical studies. However, the few that have been published provide similar instructive information with regard to the communal style of domestic life. Let us observe, for a change, those referring to the better-off peasants and the rural 'bourgeois'. The house of a cooper in the Mâconnais,[65] of which the inventory was compiled in 1674, contained only one room for living in, in which there were four beds in good condition and two not in use. That of a well-off farmer, described in 1723, consisted of a principal room, with a curtained bed, and a small adjoining room without a fireplace, with two uncurtained beds. At a still higher social level, one may observe as an example the house of the widow of an inspector of military finances, who died in 1780, leaving two unmarried daughters who had been living with her and three sons who had established themselves outside the house, one being a merchant in Lyons, the second a 'bourgeois' in Viviers and the third a master-surgeon. The house consisted of three inhabited rooms: one, which was a kitchen, dining-room and drawing-room, in which there were no beds although there were cupboards for clothes; one bedroom, with a curtained bed for the mistress of the house and a truckle-bed for the maidservant; and another bedroom for the two daughters, with two curtained beds. The specialization of the rooms is, therefore, more marked in this case than in the previous examples, and there is less communal living; this may be due to three reasons: perhaps the later date of the inventory; certainly, the higher social status; and, probably, the fact that the husband was already dead and the sons living outside the house when the inventory was compiled. Support for this last hypothesis is found in the fact that in the attic there were the pieces of a fifth bed. However, even in this well-to-do house, apparently almost emptied of people, the mistress of the house still shared her bedroom with the maidservant.

The household

Sleeping arrangements

In certain regions, it was common for families to sleep together. Thus, in the Queyras (Hautes-Alpes), according to an observer of about 1830: 'Families are large; all the individuals that compose them, without regard to age or sex, sleep all together in the cow-stables, on a rough bed covered with woollen sheets which are never washed.'[66] In the Loire-Inférieure, at the same period, an observer reported 'the well-nigh universal custom, in all families, of sleeping in the same room'. 'Six beds, hung with curtains of woollen serge and separated by only a narrow passageway, were in this room. When they told me that they were the beds of the boys and girls of the farm, I could not avoid showing my surprise.'[67]

In the homes of the peasantry in most regions of France, as in the houses of the great lords, the absence of privacy was partly offset by the enclosed character of the beds. Noël du Fail speaks of the bed, 'closed and shut, and standing fairly high', of the Breton peasant. The folklorists of the nineteenth century have also left us plentiful descriptions of such beds. Although they were perhaps less monumental in size in other regions, the beds of the peasantry – above all, the marital bed – were likewise closed. However, one should not too hastily abandon the hypothesis of communal sleeping: in the house of the Breton peasant, there was only one bed, and in such a curtained bed there often slept all the members of the household, including the servants, while sometimes passing guests were offered hospitality there. This appears to have been, at least, the customary situation in the Middle Ages.

'We forbid brothers and sisters or other kinsfolk of different sexes to sleep together after the age of seven years', wrote the Bishop of Saint-Brieuc in 1507; he was convinced that this practice 'gives rise to an infinite number of horrible sins, as has been reported to us by many confessors'. Despite the excommunication and the fine of ten *livres* with which he threatened those who infringed this ordinance, it may be doubted that this practice ceased abruptly. Until the end of the eighteenth century the synodal statutes in all regions continued to complain about it. They also denounced, and with equal persistence, the practice of parents sleeping with their children in the conjugal bed. For example, in 1681 Mgr Le Camus, Bishop of Grenoble, wrote,

> we have ascertained in the course of our visits that one of the means which the Devil most commonly uses to make children lose their purity of soul by depriving them of that of the body, is the custom of many fathers and mothers of having their children sleep in the same bed with them. . .when they are beginning to have the use of reason.

He therefore ordered the parish priests to make every effort 'to remedy an evil so prevalent and so detrimental to the salvation of souls'. Yet how many beds could a poor peasant, if he was the father of a large family, both afford to buy and find room for in his house?

The fact that, in these complaints, reference is always made to 'kinsfolk of different sexes' merits our closer attention. The emphasis placed on the differences between sexes indicates that the secular clergy was more obsessed with the danger of heterosexual relations than with that of homosexuality. Though more culpable, the latter was, apparently, less frequent in France – unless it was merely practised more secretly. Moreover, was it because it was not often customary to sleep with the servants or with passing visitors, that no reference to them was ever made? Or did the complaints refer only to the parents because of an obsession with the gravity of incest?

It seems to have been customary to put together in the same bed persons of the same sex, whether or not they were related. In the legal action brought in 1533 by Marguerite, widow of Jean Jacomart, against her seducer Pierre Pellart, nicknamed Mordienne, a girl of eighteen testified 'that one night, when she was in bed with Marguerite in the latter's room, the accused came there and had carnal knowledge of Marguerite. She knows this because she was lying beside Marguerite and was touching her.'[68]

Towards the end of the fifteenth century and the beginning of the sixteenth, it also happened that adults of different sexes shared the same bed without any of them thinking ill of it. Others, it is true, were perhaps scandalized by the practice. Jeanne Jacquet, a girl 'aged twenty years or thereabouts', was, it seems, in bed with her mother and stepfather, when three young men knocked loudly at the door, crying out:

> 'Odds death! Odds flesh!. . .open the door, you whore!' The mother, hearing this noise, made her daughter get up and go up into the attic. Meanwhile, the three companions broke open the door. . . They came into the house and set about looking for Jeanne. They looked in the [only] bed, in the kneading-trough, in the oven, and, seeing that they did not find her, they went up to the attic and there they found her.

It is just possible that the pretext for this attack followed by rape was, in fact, the cohabitation of the girl with her stepfather. However, the records of the trial make no reference to this.[69]

The allusions are more explicit in another case of rape, in 1516, where the victim was a woman called Perrette. She had gone to see her child, who was being nursed in the house of Jean Gauthier, a vine-grower at Barberey-aux-Moines, near Troyes. 'In the evening, after Jean Gauthier had already gone to bed, while his wife and Perrette were undressing in front of the fire' in order to go to bed too, two men knocked at the door on the pretext that they wished to buy larks. 'Boys', said Jean Gauthier to them, 'I have no larks.' Then one of them said, 'Jean Gauthier, you have two women, and you do not need two. There is your one, and we need this one.' 'You shall have neither this one nor me,' answered the wife of Jean Gauthier. Finally, they went away, saying, 'others of us will come soon'. Thereupon *the wife of Jean Gauthier and Perrette went to bed, in the same bed in which Jean Gauthier and his manservant already were.* One or two hours later, the accused returned, accompanied by several accomplices. They broke down the door, and dragged Perrette off into the fields 'having no other clothes but her nightdress'. There 'they made her put on her petticoat which one of them had brought with him', then they raped her after thrashing her soundly.[70]

Although the presence of a woman in the house of a man who was neither her father nor her husband may have served as a pretext for some of these violent incidents – which were, in any case, common in those days – on the other hand, their sharing the same bed did not usually lead to this. No one remarked on it in the course of the legal proceedings, and no one seems to have been surprised by the fact that, for example, Jean Gauthier and his wife habitually slept with their manservant. However, from the sixteenth century onwards, even before the Council of Trent, this communal sleeping was a thing of the past among the well-to-do. Evidence of this is this dialogue of Noël du Fail:

> Do you not remember those big beds in which everyone slept together without difficulty?. . .Ever since people have worn shoes in Poulaine. . .the faith plighted by the women to the men was inviolable. . .As a result of this marvellous trust, there slept together all the married people, or unmarried ones, in a big bed made for the purpose, three fathoms long and nine feet wide, without fear or danger or any unseemly thought, or serious consequence; for in those days men did not become aroused at the sight of naked women. . .However, since the world has become badly behaved, each one has his own separate bed, and with good reason. . .One makes, by common consent, smaller beds for the benefit of some married men. . .Cursed be the cat, if he finds the cooking-pot uncovered, and does not put his paw in. . .[71]

Like the clergy, who tirelessly inveighed against the practice of the communal bed, it is for the sake of chastity that Noël du Fail here, somewhat facetiously, extols it. We, on the other hand, reject the communal living of former times less out of virtue than by reason of an instinctive repugnance.

We admit sexual contact only with selected persons. The warmth and the odour of another person, when they do not attract us, provoke our aversion. Is this due to a refinement of our sensibility, or of our modesty, that is the integration, at the most profound level, of taboos of which we are hardly conscious? It is, in any case, remarkable that in tracing the history of family feeling it is usually only those aspects of the communal living of former times that might run counter to our own family sentiments – the throwing open of the house, the room and even the bed to strangers – that have been emphasized. It has not occurred to historians to see in this practice one of the bases of the cohesion of the family in past times. There is, in our present-day delicacy, a sort of neurotic individualism that militates against the spontaneity of our relations with other people and, perhaps, with the members of our own reduced family. In the countries which, in principle, put conjugal love in first place, does not this delicacy go so far as to make married couples sleep in separate beds? We should, at least, admit the possibility that communal sleeping has been, among the peasants and other poor people in former times, one of the most interesting manifestations of the communitarian spirit, with the communal bed as one of the privileged places of family life, until, in the course of three or more centuries, the moralists obsessed with the sins of the flesh succeeded in abolishing it.

In any case, the communal bed was often the only meeting-place for poor families. The house was, above all, a refuge from the beasts and demons of the night-time. In summer, for pleasure or for work, both in town and country, people spent the whole day out-of-doors. In winter the peasants, ill-clad in cold hempen tunics, still needed energetic physical activity out-of-doors in order to get warm.[72] Fuel was, in fact, scarce and expensive in many parts of France and England, where there had been excessive deforestation. In addition, apart from cooking-stoves and ranges, heating systems were defective throughout France and in all sectors of society. The rich, sitting in front of their fireplaces, were roasted on one side and frozen on the other; the poor, with their wretched fires, sometimes situated in the middle of the room, got more smoke than warmth. To retain the heat, therefore, there was a preference for low ceilings, and apertures were reduced to the minimum. Thus, in Sologne, 'the inhabitants like to be able to touch the roof-beams of their rooms with their heads, which is a dangerous inconvenience for people of my height', the Prior of Sennely, who was not from Sologne, wrote at the end of the seventeenth century. 'They should open up [their houses] with big windows to let some air in, instead of which they are dark and more fitted to serve as dungeons for criminals than as the dwellings of free men.' These low and murky houses were lit by resin candles with hempen wicks which gave off a nearly unbearable smell.[73] In these conditions, there was little to encourage family reunions.

In these hovels, however, the inhabitants of Sologne had 'good feather beds', consisting of a wooden bedstead, a palliasse, the 'bed' itself – that is to say, a feather mattress – goose-feather bolsters, a drugget counterpane, curtains, cushions and festoons. The beds of the leaseholders were worth, on an average, 200 *livres*, those of the share-croppers 300, and even the poorest day-labourers had beds worth about a hundred *livres*. In a sample of fifty day-labourers, whose probate inventories have been studied, the bed always represents at least 40 per cent of the total value of the property.[74] There was, in short, a logical correlation between the discomfort of the house and the comfort of the bed. In this region, where wood was particularly scarce at the time, the only way to get warm, when one was tired of energetic physical activity, was to get into bed and draw the curtains to keep in the warmth of the body. In this warm intimacy in bed, did there not originate, among the members of the peasant family, a relationship as vital and as worthy of our attention as the rituals connected with our bourgeois homes?

Eating

In our traditional paintings of bourgeois interiors one of the great moments of family life is the family meal. The times of day at which these occurred and their degree of sacredness have all varied according to the historical period and the region concerned. In the French bourgeoisie of the nineteenth century, the ritual of the family meal seems to have been particularly important, and this probably has some connection with the high standard attained by French cuisine at that time, and the prestige, among Frenchmen today, of 'bourgeois cuisine'. Was this ritual as important between the sixteenth and the eighteenth centuries, and in which social spheres? In other words, did the act of feeding imply during that period the ritual reunion of all the family around the 'table', in that centre of the cult of the family which the 'dining-room' has become?

Among the rich, as Philippe Ariès has emphasized, the dining-room made its appearance at a late date. For a long time the table was set up only at the last moment, on trestles, in a room not assigned to any particular purpose.[75] This instability of the fundamental piece of furniture of our family life appears symptomatic of the lack of ritual importance in the daily meals and of the instability of the group that took these meals together. Our bourgeois tables, on the other hand – even if they are extended to cater for special celebrations – are normally adapted to the dimensions of a stable family group, and they remind old couples afterwards of the departure of their offspring.

Among the poor, the lack of any distinction between the kitchen, the dining-room and the bedroom is much less significant. What remains to be ascertained is what place the table had in the interior of humble dwellings. The peasants painted by Le Nain are sharing bread and wine with a visitor, on a makeshift table, while an enormous and ornate bed can be seen at the back of the room. There are texts describing identical scenes.[76] The inventory of the property of a day-labourer of Thil, near Bar-sur-Aube, compiled in 1744, mentions only two chairs, a bench and no table, which is surprising, considering the relative comfort indicated by the rest of his property.[77] However, the typical heavy tables of the peasantry do not date from the nineteenth century. One may observe, in the house of the Breton peasant described by Noël du Fail, 'the table of good material, without affectation, without decoration, but smooth'; or, in the inventories of the Maconnais, 'the table of walnut wood with its two benches' that one finds in 1674 in the house of a cooper, and the 'big table of walnut wood, with drawers, and flanked by two benches' belonging to a farmer in 1723.

The ritual character of the family meal was intensified by the recital of a prayer, the *Benedicite*. However, it seems that this prayer was not customary in all social spheres from the Middle Ages onwards, but developed, like other forms of worship within the family circle, only after the Protestant Reformation and the subsequent Catholic reforms. Philippe Ariès has observed that, in paintings, the theme of the *Benedicite* did not become frequent until the end of the sixteenth century.[78]

Among the peasantry, at what time of day did the whole family meet all together around the table?

It had not been possible for Edme Rétif to impose a certain pattern in the day for prayers, or even for meals: the duties of the various persons employed were entirely different; it was only at breakfast, at five o'clock in the morning, that they were almost all gathered together; for in summer the cowherd and the shepherd had already gone off to the pastures. They said a brief prayer together, consisting only of the Lord's Prayer; then they went their ways, and did not meet together again until the evening. Then, however, everyone was present.[79]

Between these two meals, the workers made shift with a 'snack': 'they take bread, some nuts or a piece of white cheese for the snack'. And twice a week, when Barbe Ferlet, Rétif's mother, made bread, she 'made some very thin cakes, with butter and raised pastry, while the oven was getting warm, and she sent them, piping hot, to be taken by the servant-girls to the men who were at work'.[80]

For people to go from five in the morning until five in the evening with so little food, a substantial morning meal was needed.

> In the house of our master, before we went off to the plough, we
> had a soup made from boiled salt pork, cooked with cabbages or
> peas, together with a piece of salt pork and a plate of peas and
> cabbages; or a soup made with butter and onions, followed by an
> omelette, or hard-boiled eggs, or green vegetables or fairly good
> white cheese.[81]

How fortunate were the domestic workers in good houses! The poor
peasants in Burgundy usually ate only 'barley or rye bread, a soup made
from oil of nuts or even hempseed' and drank 'a bad beverage, that
is to say, water strained through marc, or just plain water'.[82] In other
regions, the men often went off to work before daybreak, without eating
anything. Then, after sunrise, they had a snack with what they had
brought with them, or what was brought to them by a girl from the house.
Sometimes they returned at midday. Elsewhere – or during other seasons
of the year – they stayed in the fields until the evening. Some observers
have reported that, in the Pyrenees, men and women, even when
assembled, did not eat together.[83] However, in almost all parts of France,
it seems that at least supper could be eaten together.

> Every evening, at supper, which was the only meal at which all the
> family could be gathered together, [Edme Rétif] found himself,
> like a venerable patriarch, at the head of a numerous household; for
> there were usually twenty-two sitting at the table, including the
> ploughboys and those who tended the vines, who in winter were
> threshers, the cowherd, the shepherd and two servant-girls, of
> whom one helped to tend the vines and the other looked after the
> cows and the dairy. All these people were seated at the same
> table.[84]

This figure of twenty-two table companions is perhaps exaggerated, since
six of the children of the first marriage had left Edme Rétif's house shortly
after his second marriage, and those of the second marriage could not, as
a rule, all be assembled together, but the interesting feature – because it
was quite customary in the big farmhouses at that time – is the presence of
the domestic servants at the family table.

Each person, however, knew his place.

> The father of the family was at the head, by the fire; beside him
> was his wife, ready to bring in the dishes to serve – for it was she
> alone who concerned herself with the cooking; the women servants,
> who had been working all day, were sitting and eating quietly;
> then there were the children of the house in the order of their ages,
> which alone determined their rank; then the oldest of the plough-
> boys and their companions; then those who tended the vines, after
> whom came the cowherd and the shepherd; finally, the two servant-
> girls concluded the number; they were at the foot of the table,

opposite their mistress, from whom they could not hide any of their movements.[85]

Blood, age, sex and the greater or lesser degree of honourability of occupations created among the members of the household distinctions and a hierarchy. There is no trace, however, of that gulf which, among the bourgeoisie of the nineteenth century, separated masters and servants.

It is true that it was customary in the eighteenth century to distinguish master and servants by the use of different bread and wine. In La Bretonne,

> everyone ate the same bread; the odious distinction between white and whole-meal bread had no place in that house; besides, it would not have effected any saving, fairly rich bran being needed for the horses, the dairy-cows, pigs which were being fattened, and even ewes when they had lambed. As for the wine, since the father of the family drank little and had only adopted the habit late in life, he drank only old wine. The mother of the family drank only water, which her husband had some difficulty in persuading her to redden by adding only a few drops of wine. The children all, without exception, drank water. The ploughboys and the vine-tenders drank a wine which was much more agreeable to them than that of their master would have seemed: it was wine of the second pressing strained through odd remnants of crushed grapes. Everybody knows that the peasants like a wine that scrapes one's gullet; and this widespread taste is considerably intensified in Sacy, where the human species is of a coarseness and massiveness of which one can find few parallels, even in Germany.[86]

In the evening

In addition to being present at the table, the domestic servants in the large peasant households also took part in family prayers and in the after-supper activities.

> It was...after supper that the father of the family read from the Holy Scriptures: he began with Genesis, and read with unction three or four chapters, depending on their length, also making certain observations, which were brief and infrequent but which he considered to be absolutely indispensable. I cannot recall without a feeling of emotion the attentiveness with which that reading was received; how it communicated to all that numerous family a spirit of good-heartedness and brotherhood.

'In the family', Rétif notes in an aside, 'I include the servants'; this interpolation shows that, to his readers, this was no longer taken for granted. In the rural areas, however, the servants were still the children of the master of the house, who was obliged to educate them like his real children. 'My father always began with these words: "Let us turn our thoughts to God, my children; it is the Holy Spirit that is going to speak." The following day, at work, the reading of the evening before formed the subject of conversation, especially among the ploughboys.' These social evenings after supper varied in length according to the season.

After the reading there was, in summer, a brief prayer together; then the children were made to recite a lesson from the diocesan catechism; then one went to bed in silence; for after the evening prayers, laughter and conversation aloud were strictly forbidden. In winter, when the evenings are longer in the country – for in town the time is always the same – after the reading and the lesson from the catechism, the father of the family told stories, both old and new; he introduced into them, at appropriate moments, the finest sayings of the ancient writers. This was our recreation. Everyone was eager to hear these instructive narrations, and since everyone could laugh and make comments, it was a delightful amusement for peasants and children who had never known more agreeable entertainments. These conversations and the reading must have pleased them greatly: we have often had in our house the sons of the best inhabitants as domestic workers; and when their parents asked them the reason for their eager desire to come to our house, the reason they gave was the reading and the conversations in the evenings.[87]

It must not be thought, however, that Edme Rétif's house was exceptional in this respect. According to all the moralists of the seventeenth and eighteenth centuries, both in England and in France, the master owed to his servants and his children together the moral and religious instruction which he gave them. This subject will be dealt with more fully later. The profane stories which he told were a traditional feature of these social evenings. As early as the sixteenth century these stories were being told on winter evenings, in the big farmhouses of the Rennes basin described by Noël du Fail;[88] or in the house of the Sire de Gouberville, in his manor in Mesnil-au-Val, near Cherbourg, where he lived with two bastard children of his father, his own three natural daughters, nine male domestic servants and some female ones: 'On that day, the 6 February 1554, it rained without ceasing. Our people went to the fields, but the rain drove them home again. Later, throughout the evening, we read in *Amadis of Gaul* about his victory over Dourdan.'[89] It would appear, therefore, that from the sixteenth to the eighteenth century social evenings in the winter were, together with the evening meal and family prayers, one of the principal rituals of family life in the rural areas.

Nevertheless, a great number of other sources of evidence demonstrate that, among the humbler peasants, social evenings were only rarely family reunions. They generally, though not always, had a characteristic which is disappearing today: that of assembling in the same place men and women, young and old. They offered unmarried young people an opportunity of associating together, under the watchful eye of their parents.[90] However, precisely because they were meeting-places for young men and girls who could marry one another, these gatherings must normally have consisted of individuals living in different houses and often even in different villages. Let us note what Noël du Fail says of these occasions: 'There were meetings for spinning, which they call *veillées*, sometimes in La Valée, sometimes in La Voisardière, in Souillas and other well-known places, where there met together from all the surrounding parts many young men and clownish youths, assembling there and playing an infinite number of games that Panurge never even thought of.'

In some mountainous parts of Auvergne these social evenings lasted almost the entire day, and their multi-family character stands in particularly clear contrast to the familial character of the meals and the sleeping arrangements. An observer at the beginning of the nineteenth century wrote, 'In the Planèse, where there is absolutely no wood, the peasant would be horribly miserable during the winter and could not live there, if he had not discovered the means to do without wood to get warm: he does it by living in the midst of his farm animals.' After explaining why and how, in winter, these peasants carry their pallets to the cowshed, and how the men sleep late in the mornings while the women go out to look for water in the snow, light the fire, and cook the soup which is drunk at ten in the morning and then again at five in the evening, the observer finally describes these 'social evenings' spent in the day-time.

> It is rare for a family to spend the winter alone and isolated in its cowshed; neighbouring families assemble together spontaneously, and choose for the purpose the biggest and warmest cowshed. In the morning, *after the soup*, everyone hastens to join the group: they sit in a circle on benches, they chatter, they laugh, they complain about the taxes and the tax-collectors, they repeat the gossip that is circulating about the girls and young men, or they just sit and meditate. *At five o'clock they part company to go and have their meal*, then they return and continue chatting for a while, and *then each one returns to his own home to sleep*.[91]

Most of the descriptions of social evenings portray the women and girls working, while the men play cards or chat and the boys lark about. In this part of Auvergne, segregation of the sexes was carried even further.

> In all this only the men take part. The women, by reason of the

inferiority of their species, are not admitted to the conversations of their lords and masters. However, as soon as the latter have gone, their reign commences, and the social evening, which for the men finishes at eight o'clock, does not end for the women until midnight or one o'clock in the morning; then they make up for lost time; but – and this is a detail characteristic of the thrift of this region – since it would not be just, when lending them a parlour, that the master of the house should provide lighting as well, they have, for their private social evenings, a lamp for which the oil is paid for by all, from the modest earnings derived from spinning. Others, more economically, do without lighting, and the darkness does not prevent them from spinning or from talking.

More concerned to denounce the barbarity of these peasants towards their womenfolk than to comprehend the differentiation of the male and female roles in these mountain households, our enlightened bourgeois nevertheless does not conceal the fact that men and women did have activities in common.

In pious families, they have *preserved* the custom, in these winter reunions, of saying the rosary and of singing canticles. Others, more addicted to worldly pleasures, spend the evenings dancing. The man reputed to be the best musician stands up and sings; the women who are not dancing accompany him with their high-pitched voices, and all the rest skip and caper about, while the cattle chew the cud to the rhythmic beat of the sabots. Triumphant on these occasions are the national dances, the simple and figure *bourrées*. We have been present at some of the dances, and have noted that they take place to the accompaniment of authentic songs which, for the most part, are extremely satirical and refer to some scandalous incident well known in the district. The man who sings beats the time by striking the earth with a stick. . .A stove maintained at great expense would not give the cowshed as much warmth as it derives from this multitude of people and animals crowded together; the air becomes transformed into thick smoke, which one sees seeping in the form of vapour out of the apertures in the building; it becomes stifling, foul and unhealthy; it is one of the principal causes of the illnesses of those who live in the mountains.

In other regions of central France, it was not only within family dwellings that individuals drawn from several families assembled in winter to 'pass the time' together and escape from the cold, but also in outside dwellings, known as *écreignes*. We know about those of Burgundy, described in the sixteenth century by Etienne Tabourot, lord of Les Accords.[92] They also existed in Champagne, particularly in the region of Troyes, as late as the eighteenth century. 'The *écreignes*', Grosley observes,

> are houses dug out below ground-level and covered with dung, where the women of the village assemble to spend a social evening and where work is seasoned with the delights of conversation. . . The interior is furnished with seats made of clods of earth, to seat all those present. In the middle there hangs a small lamp, which gives light to the whole building. . .This lamp is provided, in turn, by all the people who come to the *écreigne*. The village woman whose turn it is [to provide the lamp] makes sure to arrive first, so as to receive the others there. Each one arrives, carrying her distaff, with the spindle in the distaff, with her two hands on her sewing-kit and her apron over her hands, enters hurriedly and takes her seat without further ado. As soon as everyone is seated, the hands leave the sewing-kit, the latter is put in its proper place, *ad proprias sedes remeat*, the spindle is drawn from the distaff, the fibre is moistened with a bit of saliva, the agile fingers turn the spindle, and there is the work under way. . .One knows. . .that prattling. . .is the purpose and the principal object of the *écreigne*, and that work is merely the pretext. The conversation therefore becomes animated, always lively, always sparkling, and it continues without interruption until the time when the meeting breaks up.[93]

Besides being refuges from the cold, and places for work and conversation, the *écreignes* were also places for *rendez-vous*: 'In these assemblies of girls one finds a great number of young striplings and lovers', wrote Etienne Tabourot, in the sixteenth century. In the diocese of Troyes, the same practice continued until, in 1680, a synodal ordinance promulgated by Mgr Bouthillier decreed excommunication for men and boys who went into the *écreignes*, or waited for the girls at the door to take them home, and also for girls who admitted young men to their assemblies. In his pastoral letter of 1686 on the same subject, which included detailed instructions for the repression of these activities, the reforming bishop asserted that it no longer concerned anyone except 'certain contumacious persons'.[94]

It seems that it is not by mere chance that these social evenings organized among neighbours and friends – in the home of one of them, in his cow-shed or barn, or in an *écreigne* shared by the girls of a village or of an urban district – are reported especially in the democratic and communitarian regions of the east and centre, rather than in southern France where the 'house spirit' predominated. In the study that he has recently devoted to social relations in Languedoc, Yves Castan does not mention these customs at all. On the contrary, he emphasizes the reluctance of the country people to permit any stranger to enter their homes, unless formally invited by the master of the house.[95] In the Pyrenees, where the social evenings in winter brought together, round the fireplace, neighbours and members of the family, the presence of the master of the house could never be ignored. He sat in the place of honour, in a wooden armchair; on his left were the women and girls busy with their spinning, on his right the older members of the family, while the boys – here, too, the indispensable trouble makers – found places wherever they could. Some evenings, the company listened to tales or 'true histories', often told by the shepherds; afterwards, the boys proposed games – 'hot-hand', blindman's buff or all-in wrestling. On other evenings, at a signal from the master of the house, the assembled company turned round, with their backs to the fire: the evening was to be devoted to dancing.[96]

Long-term changes

Between the beginning of the sixteenth and the end of the eighteenth centuries, the material context and the ritual of family life changed. However, there were such great differences in the character of material existence and family ritual between the aristocracy, the urban and rural middle classes, and the peasants, and also such great differences from one region to another among the humbler peasants, that it is not easy to make an overall appreciation of these transformations. The segregation between servants and masters, which was far advanced in the towns at the end of the eighteenth century, was much less developed in the rural areas. It seems that it was first of all between parents and children – and, among the latter, between boys and girls – that the practice of sleeping in separate beds, or even separate rooms, became established, under the influence of the Catholic reforms, in so far as the standard of economic well-being made this possible.

This progress of individualism within the bosom of the family – of which one must not disregard the disintegrating effects, both among the peasantry[97] and among the aristocracy[98] – was, perhaps, offset by a development and an increased ritualization of family life which can also be attributed, in France at least, to the Catholic reforms. The religious education of the children by their parents, communal prayers, the more ceremonious character of the family meal, and the struggle waged by the Church against social evenings spent outside the home, became prevailing family concerns, until in the nineteenth and twentieth centuries religious events such as Christmas, the baptisms of new-born infants, or First Communions came to be family celebrations. Because it detected the odour of paganism and the grave risks of lapses from chastity in the old popular festivals and societies of young people, the Church seems to have preferred to abolish them, and to place the children more continuously than before under the watchful eye of their parents. One may observe, for example, the ferocity of the Church's battle against the apparently innocent meetings that took place in the *écreignes* and at other social evenings; its denunciation of carnivals, torchlight processions and the Feast of Fools; and the ever-increasing distrust which it displayed towards popular pilgrimages, until the middle of the nineteenth century. While the strengthening of the framework of the family was a deliberate intention on the part of the Protestants in their struggle against the clericalization of the Church and the paganism of the traditional ceremonies, this policy rather imposed itself, less evidently, on the leaders of the Catholic reforms. Did they realize, then, that economic and social developments would in any case destroy the traditional structures? Or did they simply adopt a strategy which the Protestants had shown to be efficacious? It should probably be emphasized above all that the Catholic reforms, like the Protestant Reformation, were at first an urban phenomenon; and that they were the work of clerics reared in a culture based on book-learning and basically hostile to the 'pagan' traditions of the countryside. However, in order to evaluate more accurately the influence of these clerics, whether Catholic or Protestant, on the formation of modern family feeling it is necessary to examine more closely their moral teachings with regard to domestic relations.

3. Domestic morality

1. DIVERSITY OF CUSTOMS AND DOMINANT MORALITY

Among the individuals constituting the household there were, in former times just as nowadays, extremely varied relationships of affection, fear, condescension, respect, etc., depending both on the character of each individual and on the particular circumstances, which are not our concern in this study. These relationships, however, were also dependent on specific models of behaviour prevailing in society in past times. One must begin by examining these models, in order to study the transformation of familial behaviour in the course of history.

It is true that these models differed according to the region and the social sectors concerned: foreign travellers or the bourgeois who, at the beginning of the nineteenth century, expressed their curiosity regarding peasant customs, have left abundant evidence of this variation. In Aveyron, these observers noted with amazement that 'in society as in church, the women...are always completely separated from the men',[1] whereas in Loire-Inférieure they were, by contrast, surprised to see together in one room 'the beds of the young men and girls of the farm' and noted that 'the mixing of the sexes does not lead to any of the vices so common in the towns'.[2] This is probably an indication of differences in customs based on very long-standing traditions. In the Basse-Alpes, where Roman Law had for long prevailed, it was observed around 1830 that 'the paternal authority has preserved...its entire vigour'; and that in families which had become numerous by reason of 'the longevity of the old people and the precocity of marriages, the grandfathers and fathers constitute a sort of magistracy, whose will and decisions are always respected'.[3] This was, most probably, not the case in such regions as Normandy, where the father had never been empowered to confer privileges at his death on any of his children. In any case, one finds traces, in the records of marriage dispensations in the eighteenth century in Normandy, of a frequently liberal attitude of fathers towards their children as regards their choice of marriage partners. Thus, a farmer of Courville asserted that he 'has always left [his daughter] free to choose such a husband as she may find agreeable'; and a pedlar of Muneville-le-Bingard wrote to his son: 'If it is your good pleasure and you have affection for her and she for you, if God has destined you to spend the rest of your lives together, I cannot go against His will.'[4]

In Limousin,

> the custom of considering only the eldest son has led people to look on the younger sons as of small account, and the daughters as of no account at all. If one asks a woman whether she has children, she replies quite seriously, 'No, I have none'; and a moment later she tells you that she has three daughters: for a daughter is merely a daughter, whereas only a boy has the privilege of being a child.[5]

Other differences in customs, sometimes occurring within the same province, are less easy to explain, given the present state of research on this topic.

> In other parts of Anjou, husbands and wives of all classes address one another as *tu* from the day after their wedding; in the Mauges, on the other hand, as soon as the wedding ceremony is over, the married couple, who the day before still addressed each other as *tu*, now use the *vous* form: the wife henceforth speaks to her husband only with deference and respect.[6]

One may well ask why, in the Allier, 'the women have an amiability and a remarkable gaiety, qualities which survive the passing of time, and which attract one even more than their beauty. Marriage, for them, is not a yoke, but an exchange of consideration, kindness and tenderness.'[7]

In the mountains of Auvergne, quite close to this region, and particularly in the Planèse, it was a different situation:

> The women are saddled with all the work of the household: they milk the cows, and make the butter and cheese; furthermore, they go to bed later and get up earlier than the men. When a fresh fall of snow has covered the path to the spring, the boldest of them undertakes to clear a new path. Then, protecting her legs with gaiters and thick clogs, tucking up her skirts as far as she can, she goes back and forth several times in succession, until she has smoothed a path for her companions. A man would think himself dishonoured if he went out just to fetch water. These rough countrymen have for their womenfolk that profound disdain and despotic contempt typical of all savage peoples; they regard them as their slaves; their own tasks are to feed the animals, to thresh the wheat, and to go, if necessary, to the local market; apart from these occupations, nothing will rouse them out of their natural idleness.[8]

It is obvious that in the early nineteenth century the attitude of the peasants towards their wives and daughters was, to these bourgeois observers, an evident symptom of their barbarity. In almost all regions, for

113

one reason or another, it shocked observers. In the Mayenne, the women 'are kept in a status of inferiority which often makes their situation miserable...Even in the attentions that a young man pays to his betrothed, one sees a protector rather than a submissive lover; and at parties the young men dance with their intended only after asking their permission.'[9] In the Creuse, the women do not drink wine: 'If they accompany their husbands or their kinsmen to the tavern, it is to wait on them respectfully, but not to share their refreshment. The subordination and submission of the women to their menfolk are extreme.'[10] In the rural areas of Lower Brittany, they have 'only an inferior status. They wait on their husband at table, and speak to him only with respect.'[11] It was the same in the Mauges, as we have noted above. In the Aveyron 'the condition of the women...especially among the inhabitants of the rural areas, is arduous and wretched...marriage, instead of being for them a time of happiness and freedom, is often that of a more harsh servitude'.[12]

Even more than this inferior status, what seems to shock the bourgeois of that age is the fact that the peasants make their women work in the fields. It is only rarely that, as in the Marne region, the observers envisage this situation as a form of companionship: 'In the vineyard the wife is really only the workmate of her husband: she shares in his labours; the housework, which elsewhere is seen as the task of the weaker sex, is here regarded merely as its recreation; the rest of the work females share with our sex.' Almost all the observers regard this as a symptom of brutality and barbarity. For example, they speak of the practice found in the Aveyron, where 'their parents treat them with a kind of barbarity, and force them, from the most tender age, to devote themselves entirely to heavy labour in the fields'. Speaking of Lower Brittany, it is immediately after portraying the wife waiting on her husband at table that the commentator adds: 'In the poorer families they work in the fields and undertake all the arduous tasks.' Quite clearly, these observations tell us as much about bourgeois customs as about peasant customs.

Because, among the élites, the woman's role is to be beautiful, all the observers emphasize the damage done by this heavy labour to the beauty of the peasant women. In Lower Brittany, the women subjected to arduous labour are not pretty, their features are without delicacy, and their clothing is heavy and conceals the shape of the body. To have a red and heightened colour is considered a sign of beauty. In some places coquettish girls put grease on their forehead to make it shiny. In the Aveyron, 'sunburn, sweat and continual fatigue impair their features and their figure. Before the age of eighteen, girls who elsewhere would have been pleasing and pretty have suntanned skins, horny hands and a stoop.' Despite his optimism, the observer of the vineyard-workers of the Marne was obliged to make similar remarks: 'The custom of being in the open air and leading a hard-working life gives the women a strength that one does not observe elsewhere: they are less delicate and are, for this very reason, less attractive; they are usually very sunburnt.'

How can one love them in such circumstances? Bourgeois ideology furnished a ready reply: they were lovable because of their virtues. Thus the womenfolk of the vineyard-workers of the Marne: 'Being good wives and good mothers, numerous qualities replace, in their case, within the bosom of the family, what is lacking in them as regards beauty.' Similarly, in the Allier, where their 'amiability' and their 'remarkable gaiety' are 'qualities that survive the passing of time and which attract one even more than beauty'. In the Creuse, the observer's attitude was more pragmatic: 'It is...neither graces nor beauty that constitute the merit of the country girls; they are sought after by the young men on the basis of their reputation as good labourers, as hard workers and as painstaking with regard to the interior of the house.' With these criteria for the choice of a marriage partner, our observers seem to have admitted its pragmatic value, because they felt able to designate it as 'love of virtue'. When the same domestic logic impelled a widower or widow to remarry immediately, they were, however, scandalized, as is evident in this observation on the peasants of the Cantal:

> When a husband loses his wife or a wife her husband, the surviving
> spouse at once invites everyone to a meal: this sometimes takes
> place in the house where the corpse is still lying, and the guests
> laugh, drink, sing and make arrangements for remarrying their host
> or hostess. The widower or widow receives proposals, and gives
> reasons for acceptance or rejection; it is only rarely that the party
> comes to an end before the arrangement has been concluded.[13]

What had happened is that it had become the decent thing, by the beginning of the nineteenth century, to mourn one's dead, and in particular one's spouse: the grief manifested on such occasions was evidence of the love one bore to the deceased person; and marriage was supposed to establish or sanctify a sentimental relationship between the partners. Nevertheless, rapidity of remarriages was customary in the seventeenth and eighteenth centuries in other regions of France. It is true that in Béarn, at Bilhères d'Ossau, among widowers who remarried, one finds only 6 per cent who did so within six months; but in the Perche, at Tourouvre, the figure was 22.6 per cent; in the Bas-Quercy, at Thézels and Saint-Sernin, 42 per cent; in Champagne, in the 'five parishes of the Vallage', about 55 per cent; in Bresse, at Pont-de-Vaux, about 60 per cent; and, finally, in Lyons, in the parish of Saint-Georges, 80 per cent. For the sake of comparison, one may observe that in France as a whole, in the 1950s, only 15 per cent of widowers remarried within a year of the death of their wives. In the seventeenth and eighteenth centuries, however, the proportion was 45.3 per cent at Tourouvre and 46.6 per cent at Crulai, in the Perche; 48.4 per cent at Thézels and Saint-Sernin and 52 per cent at Sérignan, in Lower Languedoc; 63.6 per cent at Sotteville-lés-Rouen; 63 per cent at Pont-de-Vaux; 75 per cent in the five parishes of the Vallage, and 90 per cent in the parish of Saint-Georges in Lyons. It is evident that the affective unfeelingness and the brutality of marital relationships, if one can measure them by the swiftness of remarriages, was not peculiar to the Auvergne peasants alone, but was a characteristic of marriages in former times in most, if not all, of the regions of France.

Was this also true of the inferior status of women? A young priest from Bologna, Locatelli, who travelled through France in the seventeenth century, was astonished at the liberty that women there were allowed. In Lyons, for example:

> We found in the streets, the suburbs and even in the alleys, fine shops in which everybody was working without interruption. There, women have the principal jobs, they do the double-entry bookkeeping, they sell, they invite the customers to buy, they politely show them the merchandise, they count the money, put it away and keep it. They generally keep the key of the place where it is deposited, attached with other keys to a belt made of leather or of silver chain. In short, the husbands and fathers serve as assistants and shop-boys.[14]

This text, in fact, tells us more about the condition of the women of Bologna than those of Lyons. Moreover, all these observations regarding the behaviour of the popular sectors, since they are made by nobles or bourgeois, are equally ambiguous, including the most apparently objective ones.

All the house-by-house censuses that we possess indicate, in the case of each house, a head of the house whose name precedes that of the other members of the household. The reason is that the civil or religious authorities taking the census had a monarchical image of the government of the family, or, more prosaically, they needed one person to be responsible for each household. This, however, does not give us any certain information regarding the actual government of these households or the relationships existing between their members. The head might be an elderly father ruling the household autocratically, with all or nearly all powers over its members and its property, like those fathers who figure in the marriage-contracts of Languedoc in the fourteenth and fifteenth centuries. He might, on the other hand, be simply the representative of a democratic community in which each of the adults had an equal share in the common property and an equal power of decision, as in the southern *frérèches* and in many of the communities in the northern part of the Massif Central.

Moreover, the civil and religious authorities sometimes designated as head of the household an individual who was in fact subject to the authority of another member of the household. In Brueil-en-Vexin, for example,[15] it seems unlikely that Gervaise Desnouelle, aged ninety-five, still exercised any sort of authority over the eight persons that she was supposed to govern: it was probably her son, Benoist Havart, aged fifty, who exercised the real power. Similarly, Jeanne Commissaire, aged seventy-five, probably could not lay down the law to her son-in-law, Jean Delanoue, aged forty-five; this, however, is less certain. Still less clear is the relationship of authority existing between Noël Havart, aged seventy-five, and his son-in-law Nicolas Jorre, aged twenty-five. All these censuses, which sometimes even artificially divided a household, or regrouped individuals in artificial households, reflect the mental structures of the census-taker as much as the family structures of the village concerned.

The imposition of models that were at variance with local traditions might either leave the real situation entirely unchanged, or provoke a categorical rejection. Although, in 1789, the electoral law provided for the election of deputies by all men over the age of twenty-five and by them alone,[16] it has been proved that in many places the electorate was composed, as usual, of the heads of households, whether they were men or women. In most of the regions where women voted, those who did so were apparently widows, who had become heads of their households on the death of their husbands. It was different in the Basque country and other Pyrenean towns, where the eldest daughters, who were the 'heiresses' of their houses, traditionally exercised authority over the husbands and younger brothers. Until 1794, they continued to vote on behalf of their families. Then, when an attempt was made to impose individualistic and phallocratic rules which had been accepted for a long time among the bourgeoisie of northern France, this provoked intense hostile reactions among the entire population.[17] Moreover, until the twentieth century the heiresses, though discriminated against in the electoral sphere, continued to exercise authority within their households.

Nevertheless, these models imposed from outside might also take root in the mentality of the villagers. This was the case, as we have observed, in the Franch-Comté, where the introduction by the jurists of the thirteenth century of the principles of Roman Law regarding the *patria potestas* seems to have brought about a profound transformation of the relationships within the family: a proof of this is the leonine conditions which a father sometimes imposed on his married or unmarried sons in the community-contracts of the sixteenth and seventeenth centuries. Similarly, the

117

introduction of the Civil Code in Limousin led to a revolt of the younger brothers against their elder brothers from the beginning of the nineteenth century. Moreover, in Périgord it has been observed that this resulted, from 1836 onwards, in the virtual disappearance of multinuclear households.

These observations concerning the models imposed by the civil law are also applicable to those transmitted by Christian morality. Everywhere they conflicted with other models, characteristic of a region or of a social sector. Moreover, neither among the clergy nor among the faithful were these conflicts understood as being a contradiction between different moralities: the former saw in them a transgression of morality on the part of their parishioners; and the latter saw them as an attack on tradition and on liberties on the part of the priests. Finally, however, most of the 'Christian' models – which it would be better to define as the outcome of the interpretation of Christian doctrine by the clergy of a particular historical period – did succeed in structuring the mentality of the faithful. It is known that those Frenchmen, numerous from the end of the eighteenth century, who have rejected the teachings of the Church, have nevertheless remained essentially attached to the principles of its morality, to which they refer, in absolute terms, as 'Morality'. What is less widely known is that some of the practices denounced as popular superstitions by the reforming clergy of the seventeenth and eighteenth centuries had been imposed on the peasants by the clergy of the early Middle Ages. This is all the more reason for studying Christian principles of domestic morality and their formulation by the clergy of the sixteenth, seventeenth and eighteenth centuries.

2. THE GOVERNMENT OF THE FAMILY

The monarchical model

The two fundamental texts of Christian doctrine in this sphere are the Fourth Commandment of the Decalogue – 'Honour thy father and mother, that thy days may be long' – which the Protestants consider as the Fifth Commandment, and the Epistle to the Ephesians (5.22 to 6.9), in which Saint Paul established the authority of the father of a family over his wife, children and servants, and his duties of love and correction with regard to them.

Wives, children and servants must, according to Saint Paul, obey the master of the house in the same way that Christians obey God: 'Wives, submit yourselves unto your own husbands, as unto the Lord. . .Children, obey your parents in the Lord. . .Servants, be obedient to them that are your masters. . .with fear and trembling. . .With good will doing service,

118

as to the Lord.' Since the origins of Christianity, the family has been considered as a monarchy based on Divine Right.

One must not underestimate the historical – and perhaps even essential – importance to Christianity of the authority of the father or lord. It is true that the world in which Christianity made its appearance had known for a long time this sovereignty of the father, of the husband, and of the master. Perhaps this was, however, a necessary condition for the implantation of Christianity: is there any monotheistic religion which has not been born and first triumphed in a patriarchal society? The first Christians made use of the relationships of subordination to the father, to the husband and to the master (*dominus*), which formed part of the most firmly established social reality in the societies in which they were preaching , to explain and win acceptance for the concept of absolute obedience to a unique God, envisaged as the universal Father and universal Lord (*Dominus*). It is understandable that thenceforth the Church has had difficulty in admitting that one can call oneself a Christian and yet question the rights of the father, the master or the king to the obedience of his children, servants or subjects. In this century, when many Christians reject slavery, monarchy, the paternalistic management of businesses, and even question the authority of parents over their children, it is paradoxical and tragic that one can still speak of God only by using the images of the Creator-Father and the Sovereign Master.

In addition, the Epistle to the Ephesians establishes a reciprocity of duties between the father of the family and his subjects: to his wife, the husband owes love and sanctification; to his children, he owes education; and to his servants, indulgence. This emphasis on reciprocity is particularly demonstrated by the formula 'And, ye masters, do the same things unto them' (6.9) – a curious injunction, since Saint Paul has just commanded servants to serve their master as though serving God, and later he only commands the master to refrain from threats against them. In the world in which Christianity took root, this insistence on the duties of the husband, of the father and of the master was probably more original than the enjoining of obedience on the wife, the children and the servants. Furthermore, in order to establish the authority of God and of Christian morality in the patriarchal and slave-owning societies that did not know them, it was necessary to restrict the power of the husband, the father and the master, if only to safeguard the possibility of the conversion of the wife, the child and the slave. From antiquity until our own day – and particularly between the sixteenth and eighteenth centuries, as we shall see – the Church has often denounced the 'excesses' of marital, paternal and seigneurial power, thus sowing the seeds of a questioning of the traditional relationship of subordination.

119

The authority of the father of the family and the authority of God not only legitimized one another: they served to legitimize all other authorities. Kings, lords, patrons and ecclesiastics have all represented themselves as fathers and as the representatives of God. These images are not always understood, because that of the father has been perceptibly modified. Nowadays – and as early as the time of Louis XVI – to say that an authority is 'paternal' is to claim that it is benevolent, even indulgent; that its possessor loves, protects and only corrects for their own good those who are subject to him. In former times, and as late as the age of Louis XIV, to say that an authority was 'paternal' was above all to proclaim its legitimacy and the absolute duty of obedience on the part of those subject to it. When theologians and moralists justified the authority of these powerful men, they did so by reference to the Fourth Commandment of the Decalogue. 'Those who violate the laws and just commands of their superiors', wrote Benedicti, for example,[18]

> believing and saying that men are by nature equal and of the same condition, without some having authority over others, are heretics. For even if Adam had never offended,[19] there would have been, nonetheless, some superiority among men, just as there is among the angels: otherwise there would never have been a Church, which is a hierarchical order. For this reason, therefore, he who infringes the precepts of either ecclesiastical or secular Prelates, sins: for the conclusion of the Theologians and Canonists implies that they can oblige their subjects to keep their laws provided they are just, on pain of mortal sin. . .By this precept also we are commanded to honour Prelates, Kings, Princes and other superiors, who with good reason are also called fathers.

This social, political and ecclesiastical scope given to the Fourth Commandment is evidence of the fundamental importance of the parent–children relationship in western society in former times. However, it is also evidence of the scant interest in domestic affairs manifested by the Church for a long time.

When, in the early fifteenth century, Jean Gerson commented on the Fourth Commandment in his *Instruction pour les curez*, he referred to domestic relationships only in these words: 'Wicked heirs often desire the death of their parents, in order to possess their inheritance and have their property.'[20] This occupies three lines out of the fifty-two of the commentary. He devotes eight lines to 'those who show too much disregard for the ordinances of earthly Princes and what they do'; and all the rest of the commentary, i.e. forty-one lines, is devoted to what laymen owe to the Church and to the person of ecclesiastics.

The study of some other manuals for confessors published in different epochs, which also comment on the Fourth Commandment, suggest that from the beginning of the fifteenth century to the beginning of the eighteenth century, the Church's interest in domestic life increased considerably and continuously (Table 10). Like the Protestant churches – though in a more ambiguous manner and for different reasons – the Church of the Counter-Reformation made the family one of the privileged places of Christian life. Perhaps this was because the Reformation had helped it to take cognizance of the strength of domestic ties and of the possibilities that they offered of surveilling and educating the mass of the faithful. The Bishop of Milan, Saint Charles Borromeo, who was one of the earliest and most prominent Catholic reformers, wrote, for example: 'It would be desirable that, on all the first Sundays or other solemn days of the month, the heads of families should assemble in their parishes with the parish priest, to discuss together the measures which must be taken to regulate properly and govern their families.'[21] Even though this desire has scarcely been fulfilled, at least in France, it is significant of the new interest

Table 10. *Growth of interest in domestic relationships demonstrated in some Catholic manuals for confessors (fifteenth–eighteenth centuries)*

Author	Work	Date	References to domestic relationships in the chapter on the Fourth Commandment		
			Lines or articles with references	Total lines or articles	Percentage
Gerson	*Instruction pour les curez*	Early fifteenth century	3	52	6
Masurier	*Instruction à bien se confesser*	c. 1550			33
Perronnet	*Instruction des curez*	1574	14	28	50
Benedicti	*La somme des pechez*	1584	40	50	80
Toledo (translated by Goffar)	*Instruction des prêtres*	1599 (trans. 1628)	9	11	82
Fernandes de Moure	*Examen de la théologie morale*	1616 (trans. 1638)	8	9	89
Antoine Blanchard	*Examen général sur tous les commandements*	1713	154	154	100

In the first six manuals, only the relations between parents and children are included in domestic relationships, because in these works no distinction is made between domestic servants and other 'inferiors'. The last manual cited devotes twenty-seven articles, i.e. 17 per cent of the chapter, to the relations between the domestic servants and the master and mistress of the house.

of the Church in the familial context. This interest has often resulted in our obtaining precise information, in the manuals for confessors published after the Council of Trent, regarding what should be and what in reality often were the relationships between the members of the household.

The authority of the husband over his wife

In the government of the household, husband and wife tried to get the better of one another. Even on the wedding-day, when the bridegroom put the ring on the bride's finger, the latter tried to stop it at the first joint, to affirm her pre-eminence. An old proverb stated that:[22]

> A woman wants at all times
> To be mistress in her house
>
> (Gruther, sixteenth century)

Popular wisdom, however, in so far as we can know it from proverbs, assigned to the man the duty of imposing his authority.

> Suffer not your wife, for any reason,
> To put her foot on yours
> For tomorrow the silly whore
> Will want to put it on your head
>
> (G. Meurier, sixteenth century)

Women tried to impose their will by words, tears and cries:

> At all times
> Dogs piss and women weep
>
> (Meurier, sixteenth century)

> Where woman is, silence is not
>
> (Meurier, sixteenth century)

The man should make them keep silent in his presence:

> Woman in her turn should speak when the hen goes to urinate
>
> (Meurier, sixteenth century)

> A woman who talks like a man and a hen
> that crows like a cock are not worth keeping
>
> (Prov. Gallic., fifteenth century)

And the best way to achieve this, according to the ancient wisdom, was the stick:

> A good horse and a bad horse need the spur
> A good woman and a bad woman need the stick
>
> (Meurier, sixteenth century)

From the eighteenth century onwards, however, this method of imposing one's authority appears to have been questioned: 'One must be the companion of one's wife and the master of one's horse', one reads in a work as early as the *Dictionnaire comique* of Le Roux (1786); and the proverbs reflecting the bourgeois mentality, published in a collection in 1861,[23] reiterate the warnings against the older method:

One must be the companion and not the master of one's wife.

Nature has subjected the woman to the man, but Nature knows no slavery.

Beating one's wife does not get rid of her foolish thoughts.

He who strikes his wife is like he who strikes a sack of flour:
the good goes, and the bad remains.

This evolution of the precepts of popular wisdom, which it is difficult to date with greater accuracy, was apparently accompanied by a transformation of behaviour, especially among the élites of society. Observers of the rural areas, from the beginning of the nineteenth century, expressed their indignation at the barbarous way in which women were sometimes treated there: the attitude of men towards women had become one of the principal criteria of civilization. On the other hand, according to the confessors of the nineteenth century, the blows to which the peasant women were accustomed might be less hard to endure than the cruelties of bourgeois husbands. Moreover, proverbs expressing hatred for women became more common during this period: a poor compensation for the man, whom custom had deprived of his traditional means of imposing his will without ceasing to maintain that it was his duty to do so.

The authoritarian behaviour of the man in the household was not merely a manifestation of a desire for power, which is natural in every individual. Traditional society gave him the means to impose his will, but also demanded that he did impose it.

His right to beat his wife was recognized by most of the ancient compilations of customary laws.[24] That of Beauvaisis, in the thirteenth century, declared: 'It is licit for the man to beat his wife, without bringing about death or disablement, when she refuses her husband anything.' That of Bergerac permitted him to beat her until he drew blood, as long as it was with good intent – 'bono zelo' – in order to reform her. The same provision was made in that of Troyes. In 1404, that of the Barrèges valley stipulated: 'Every master and head of a household may chastise his wife and family without anyone placing any impediment in his way.' In this region, where the heiresses held sway over their husbands and their younger brothers, it was apparently necessary to combine the qualities of being a man with those of being head of the household in order to have the right to use the stick. There were also, perhaps, certain variations between one set of customary laws and another with regard to the limits that were not to be overstepped. In Béarn, if the husband beat his pregnant wife and she died as a result, he was considered a murderer. But what was the position when the dead woman had not been pregnant? In Bordeaux, the book of customary laws declared in 1359 that a husband, who in a fit of rage had killed his wife, did not incur any penalty if by a solemn oath he confessed himself to be repentant.

On the other hand, these ancient customary laws treated with severity husbands who failed to impose their authority.[25] According to the customary law of Senlis, compiled in 1375, 'husbands who let themselves be beaten by their wives shall be arrested and condemned to ride on an ass, with their face towards the tail of the said ass'. The customary law of Saintonge, compiled in 1404, included a similar article. In Gascony, it was stipulated that the ass should be led on a leash by the closest neighbour of the husband. If the neighbour refused this honour – or this chore – he was obliged to pay a fine of ten *livres*, which was collected by the riotous crowd. In actual fact, Boerius's *Decisiones Burdigalenses*, published in 1593, describes an incident involving a counsellor of the *Parlement* of Bordeaux who, refusing to lead the ass, readily agreed to pay this fine.

All these instances of legal sanctions applied to chastised husbands date from before the sixteenth century. However, from the fifteenth to the end of the nineteenth century, it appears that in all regions of France, they continued to be persecuted, albeit illegally. Around 1530, Jean Gaufreteau wrote in his *Chronique bordelaise*:

> I see that this custom was not followed only in Bordeaux, but also in several places in France. However, it is certain that it has given rise to the proverb which says that *one must make the ass run every time that a woman rebels against her husband and the husband tolerates it*. But it must be noted that this custom is not kept up today in accordance with its ancient form; for in Bordeaux it is no longer spoken of; but in the country and the little shanties in the neighbourhood, when a woman has beaten her husband, they do not make the husband ride the ass and be led around by his nearest neighbour, but it is the nearest neighbour who must ride the ass, and be led about by the nearest neighbour of the person riding the ass.[26]

A similar transformation was taking place in northern France, as is shown, for example, by the letters of remission of penalties issued by the kings of France.[27] In Senlis, in 1376, it was because a couple wished to evade the donkey-ride, in its penal form, that a scuffle occurred; on the other hand, in 1393 in Calvados, in 1404 in the Eure district, and in 1417 in Marennes, in Saintonge, the letters of remission of penalties mention the mocking donkey-rides by the neighbour of the chastised husband. There is no doubt, however, that the latter suffered as a result of these burlesque demonstrations of his misfortune: the letters of remission of penalties mention this practice only because the donkey-rides had led to the death of a man. In Marennes, for example, we are shown the enraged husband exclaiming: 'By God's blood! If I find him riding the ass, I will stab him with my knife and will tear his guts out.'

After disallowing this practice, the judicial authorities denounced it and prosecuted it, as they did the other *charivaris*. This is shown, for example, in a decree of the *Parlement* of Toulouse dated 27 March 1762.[28] We learn from this that, following a dispute between a husband and his wife, the inhabitants of Saint-Gaudens planned 'a sort of *charivari*'. As soon as he was informed of this plan, the procurator-general of the king in the *Parlement* of Toulouse instructed the mayors and consuls of Saint-Gaudens 'to use all their authority to prevent the occurrence of this manifestation, as being contrary to the provisions of the ordinances, the published regulations, good morals and the public peace'. Despite these prohibitions, the riotous assembly took place during the last two days of the carnival of 1762. In fact, the municipal authorities were probably less inimical to this tradition than were the members of the Toulouse *Parlement*: they were reproved not only for having published the prohibitions in excessively vague terms, but for having suspended for the last two days of the carnival a police patrol based on Saint-Gaudens. In addition, the mayor's lieutenant, who was responsible for policing the locality, was admonished and suspended from his functions for three months.

Despite the efforts of the monarchy, and subsequently of the Republic, and the severity of the law-courts, it is known that in the nineteenth, and even in the twentieth, centuries, *charivaris* and donkey-rides still took place in several regions of France. The long survival of these illegal demonstrations is evidence of the perennial character of the scandal provoked by husbands being incapable of imposing their authority on their wives. On the other hand, their prohibition – from the sixteenth century, apparently – and their progressive disappearance show that the relations between husband and wife increasingly escaped from the surveillance of their neighbours and the pressure of public opinion. Which of the two partners was benefited by this development?

It has often been observed that the revival of Roman Law between the thirteenth and the eighteenth centuries had brought about not only an invigoration of private property – which is an important aspect of the right to a private life – but also a strengthening of paternal and marital authority. In fact, in many spheres, the legal status of women deteriorated, as is shown, for example, by the affirmation of the patrilinearity of descent, from the thirteenth century onwards, and the use of the patronymic surname from the fourteenth century; the exclusion of women from the throne of France, and their inability to transmit rights to the Crown, established in the fourteenth century; their inability to fulfil the obligations of a vassal, from the thirteenth century onwards; finally, and above all, the various legal inabilities affecting married women, particularly after the sixteenth century. All this has been frequently emphasized by jurists, sociologists and certain historians.[29]

Nevertheless, in other spheres the development of French law has been favourable to women. Since the thirteenth century their financial interests have been more effectively protected, which is perhaps a compensation for the patrilinearity of descent. The power of the husband, which was considerable from the thirteenth to the end of the fifteenth centuries, was thenceforth diminished, particularly as regards the right of chastisement so freely granted to the husband by medieval customary laws, which is no longer mentioned in the laws of the sixteenth and seventeenth centuries. Finally, separation *a mensa et thoro*, which was only rarely granted to the woman in the Middle Ages, seems to have been much more frequently granted subsequently.[30]

It is against this general background that one must consider the mandates derived from ecclesiastical morality. It is true that they do not mention the legal inabilities of the woman or her dower. However, they appear to confirm that, in the daily life of the household, the wife became gradually and partially emancipated from the tutelage of her husband. Her subordination to her husband, which was most explicitly emphasized at the end of the sixteenth and the beginning of the seventeenth centuries in the manuals of Benedicti,[31] Toledo[32] and Fernandes de Moure,[33] is no longer stressed at the beginning of the eighteenth century in the manual of Antoine Blanchard.[34]

> The wife who does not wish to obey her husband in matters touching the government of the family and of the house, and those concerning virtues and good morals, sins. For the wife is *obliged* to carry out the *commandments* of her husband. If, on the contrary, she tries to assume the government of the house, pertinaciously and against the will of her husband when he forbids it for some good reason, she sins, for she must do nothing against her husband, to whom she is subject by divine and human law.
>
> (Benedicti, nos. 34 and 35)

Tolet and Fernandes de Moure say, more briefly, the same thing and the latter concludes: 'To wish, despising her husband, to govern, is a mortal sin' (no. 8). Benedicti reminds the wife 'who, swollen with pride, with her wit, her beauty, her possessions, her kin, despises her husband and does

126

not want to obey him', that she 'is resisting the judgment of God, according to which He desires that the wife be subject to the husband, who is more noble and more excellent than the wife, seeing that he is the image of God, and Woman is merely the image of Man' (no. 39). And he denounces, as do all the writers, 'her who being quarrelsome, unruly and impatient, provokes her husband to blaspheme the name of God', for, 'even supposing that she is partly in the right, she should rather keep silent and champ the bit instead of making him blaspheme and swear, knowing well his temperament and knowing full well that he is prone to this vice' (no. 37). Similarly he denounces 'the wife who, being seized with the spirit of jealousy, does not cease from quarrelling with and tormenting her husband, under the pretext of a false opinion which she has of him, which is nothing else but an infirmity of the Evil Spirit' (no. 38). All these articles, in addition to establishing the right of husbands to command, give an impression of the difficulties that they encountered most frequently in their households.

At the beginning of the eighteenth century, Antoine Blanchard said the same thing in principle, but in a noticeably different manner. The wife whom he addresses is no longer a shrew hard to tame, but a pleasant and sensible person whom one expects to be reasonable enough for two people. 'Have you obeyed your husband in just and reasonable matters?' (no. 1), he asks her, thus allowing her a considerable latitude of interpretation. 'Have you not scorned the *counsel* of your husband and the *remonstrances* that he has made to you?' (no. 14), he says to her, as though she were, *vis-à-vis* her husband, in the position of a king in relation to his ministers and his parliaments. It is true that Antoine Blanchard appears to demand from his female penitent even more than Benedicti: 'Have you maintained a close union with your husband, suffering his shortcomings with patience and with charity? Have you not given him reason to be angry and have fits of rage on account of your arrogance and your obstinacy? Have you not been insufficiently obliging towards him?' (nos. 2, 3, 4). The reason for this, however, is that the husband is a bad character, but one can, on the other hand, expect a great deal from his wife, whereas in the time of Benedicti, if the husband swore and blasphemed, his wife was, on her part, 'swollen with pride, quarrelsome, unruly and impatient', and at times 'seized with the spirit of jealousy'.

This transformation of roles is seen still more clearly in the chapter devoted to morality. In the sixteenth century, the husband was responsible for the morals of his wife.

> If the husband gives full rein to his wife, allowing her to misbehave, paint her face to be pleasing to men, and adorn herself beyond the bounds set by the decency of her estate, and indulge in other

excesses without reproving her, he sins, at least venially; for he is obliged to correct her, seeing that according to the Scriptures the husband is the master of his wife. And if she goes so far as to commit some mortal sin because he has not kept her on a close rein, he shares in her sin. (no. 28)

If one rightly understands the situation, 'the husband who does not correct his wife when she perseveres in adultery' is 'as it were, the abettor of her sin' (no. 32). At the beginning of the seventeenth century, one finds the same injunction in the manuals of Tolet and Fernandes de Moure, and also in the *Instruction du chrestien* written by Richelieu, who severely lectures husbands 'who are so indulgent that they thus authorize the liberties that [their wives] take to misbehave'.[35]

On the other hand, there is nothing of this in the examination of conscience published by Antoine Blanchard in 1713. He reproaches the husband only for his own excesses. Moreover, it is the wife alone whom he calls to account for her conduct: 'Have you not given your husband reason to suspect your fidelity by some meetings that were suspect to him and which he had forbidden you?' (no. 12). One has the impression that the husband can still supervise the conduct of his wife, but the moralist no longer makes this his duty. One even has the impression that, instead, the Church counted on the wife to improve her husband and to keep him in the conjugal bed: 'Have you not shown indifference or hatred towards him? Have you not thus given him occasion to transfer his affection elsewhere and to attach himself to some other woman, whereby some debauchery has resulted?' (nos. 5 and 6). The man is no longer qualified to supervise and correct the morals of his wife. It is, on the contrary, the wife who, from the beginning of the eighteenth century, has become the emissary of the Church in relation to her husband, as she was to be in an even more glaring manner in the nineteenth and twentieth centuries.

Finally, and unsurprisingly, Blanchard does not even consider authorizing the husband to beat his wife, whereas the writers of the sixteenth century and the early seventeenth century had had an ambiguous attitude to this question: 'He who severely and atrociously beats or chastises his wife', says Benedicti,

even if it be for some fault, sins. He must chastise her gently and not with cruelty: [cruel chastisement] is not allowed to the master even with regard to his servants. . .For this reason, the law ordains that the husband who beats his wife cruelly should be punished. And it is even true that the wife commits no sin if she separates from her husband on account of his cruelty. . .He may, nevertheless, chastise her for her misconduct, as long as he does not overstep the bounds of modesty and reason: for, even though she is inferior, nevertheless she is not the slave or chambermaid but the companion and flesh and blood of her husband. . .   (no. 30)

In common with Tolet and Fernandes de Moure, Benedicti does not purely and simply forbid the husband to beat his wife. He only forbids him to beat her 'severely', 'atrociously', 'with cruelty' or overstepping 'the bounds of modesty and reason'. Tolet forbids him to 'strike her excessively', and Fernandes de Moure forbids him to 'chastise her beyond what is necessary to correct her'. Clearly, the husband had a duty to correct his wife, and this involved at times a certain measure of violence. One can, however, observe the sort of equivalence that exists in this article between the terms 'beat' and 'correct'.

Benedicti also makes it possible to conjecture as to the manner in which the transformation of customs in his time took place. It happened, on the one hand, through the agency of the law-courts, which, after the end of the Middle Ages, appear to have granted 'divorce' more often to wives beaten 'atrociously', 'cruelly' or 'excessively'. It is these legal proceedings that one must examine to discover the precise significance of these terms. One learns from them that, only too often, blows and other acts of violence endangered the life of the wife; but was divorce granted only in such cases?[36] On the other hand, one may surmise that, among the élites of society, women escaped blows by making the most of their social standing. Benedicti emphasizes, and not without good reason, that even the servants must not be chastised with cruelty and that the wife, even though she is 'inferior', 'is not a slave or chambermaid'. Other writers emphasize that she 'is not a servant'. Benedicti is probably changing his tone when he defines the nature of the wife: the words 'companion and flesh and blood of her husband' strike a sentimental chord. It is, however, the contradiction between the companion and the slave and beast of burden that one discerns in the proverbs of the eighteenth and nineteenth centuries. As for Tolet and Fernandes de Moure, they are still bound by considerations of social status when they say that one must 'take into account the person and standing' of the wife, and even that she is 'equal', that is to say, of the same standing as her husband.

Be that as it may, the development was practically completed by the beginning of the eighteenth century. Antoine Blanchard still alludes discreetly to ill-treatment when he asks the husband: 'Have you not outraged her with words or with blows, either from motives of jealousy, or out of dislike which you felt for her?' (no. 65). However, these acts of violence, of which one could still find some instances today, can no longer be justified in terms of a duty of correction, which has disappeared.

Domestic morality

Parents and children

It seems that the authority of parents and their powers of coercion of their children increased from the sixteenth century onwards. This development is generally attributed to the interest of the absolute monarchy in supporting the authority of fathers of families, as well as to the vogue of the principles of Roman Law and of the ideas of antiquity. One observes, for example, the jurist Pierre Ayrault giving his opinion, in his treatise on the power of the father, that 'domestic discipline, in which the father is like a dictator, has decreed that from his voice shall depend all that is subject to him', and the Guardian of the Seals, Guillaume de Vair, writing that 'we should consider fathers as gods on earth'. Moreover, carrying these principles to their ultimate extreme, Jean Bodin demanded for the fathers of families the restoration of the power of life and death, which had been abolished in late antiquity by the Christian emperors.[37]

Although his recommendation was not adopted, fathers nevertheless preserved or recovered, in the France of that time, most of the rights granted them by the ancient Roman laws. Their 'paternal power' covered the person and the property of their children, grandchildren and other descendants. These 'children of the family' were unable to bind themselves by contracts – chiefly those involving loans and marriage – and, even with the agreement of their father, they could not make wills. This was because all their property belonged to the father. The latter enjoyed full ownership of all property that they held of him, for he could always undo whatever he had done; similarly, he was the full owner of the profits that they derived from such property; he possessed, in addition, the usufruct of their other goods, from whatever source they had come, subject to certain exceptions; finally, he was responsible for the dowries of his daughters-in-law.

This paternal power was more or less widespread and, above all, more or less long-lasting, depending on the region. In the written-law provinces, its weight was felt by 'children' of all ages, as long as the father lived, unless he had emancipated them or they had attained very exalted appointments, e.g. that of a bishop, of President of the Royal Courts, of Procurator-General or of Advocate-General. In the customary-law provinces its duration was extremely variable. In Brittany the son remained subject to the authority of his father until the age of sixty, but marriage contracted with the father's consent emancipated him. In Poitou, the paternal authority lasted indefinitely over unmarried children; from the age of twenty-five, however, they became the owners of property that they acquired, and they could make wills even earlier, the men at twenty and the girls at eighteen. In Berri, marriage could emancipate the person at an early age, and unmarried children were liberated from the paternal authority at the age of twenty-five. According to other customs, such as those of Montargis, the unmarried children were emancipated at the age of twenty.[38]

In the Middle Ages, the Church had diminished the paternal authority by recognizing the validity of marriages contracted by the 'children of the family' without their parents' consent, provided that the boys were thirteen and a half and the girls eleven and a half years old. This was because, from the twelfth century, the Church had held marriage to be a sacrament which the spouses administered to themselves by the exchange of consent. It is true that it considered such disobedience to one's parents to be a grave sin, more especially since marriages contracted in these circumstances were generally clandestine – that is to say, the young people exchanged their consent without witnesses and without having apprised anybody of their intention – and often led to divorces, acts of perjury and the crime of bigamy. Being extremely conscious of the gravity of these disorders, the Council of Trent reaffirmed the condemnation of clandestine marriages, and obliged the couple to exchange their consent in the presence of a priest after the banns had been published, under pain of nullity, but it continued to consider as valid marriages contracted without the parents' authorization. 'The Holy Church of God always execrates clandestine marriages, for the most sound reasons, and has forbidden them; however,' asserted the Council,

> one should not doubt that when they do take place with the free consent of the contracting parties they are true and perfect marriages, as long as the Church has not annulled them; and, consequently, they should with good reason be condemned – as, in fact, the Holy Synod condemns them under pain of anathema – who deny that these [marriages] are true and perfect; and [also condemned] are all those who falsely assert that marriages entered into by the children of a family without their parents' consent are null, and that it depends on the parents whether they are or are not perfect.[39]

However, the Protestants, including the Anglicans, considered the consent of the parents to be as essential to the marriage as the consent of the bride and bridegroom. They based their attitude not only on a traditional practice associated with marriage in western society, but also on a passage in the Epistle to the Corinthians in which Saint Paul, taking cognizance of this tradition, leaves the father free to marry his daughter or to keep her as a virgin (I Cor. 7.36–8). To them, the liberal attitude of the Catholic Church was scandalous, and many people, among the Catholics, shared their view without daring to express it so disrespectfully. The Court of

France, for example, had brought considerable pressure to bear on the Council to revise the Church's doctrine in this sphere, and this is not explained merely by the scandal that had been provoked by the clandestine marriage of the heir of the Montmorency family and a young lady of the lesser nobility. It was the viewpoint of all lay society – or at least that of the fathers of families, who alone were entitled to express their opinion – that the French delegation had defended at Trent. In view of the failure of his efforts, the king refused to allow the decrees of the Council to circulate in France, and took a number of measures designed to strengthen paternal authority without engaging in a direct confrontation with the Church.

Even before the vote on the decree reforming marriage, he had, by the edict of February 1556 'against clandestine marriages', automatically disinherited, and to all intents and purposes made outlaws, all 'children of families' who contracted marriage without their parents' authorization. Going further than this, the ordinance of Blois, in its Article 42, considered as ravishers – and as such punishable by death 'without hope of grace and pardon' – those who married without their parents' consent men or girls under the age of twenty-five: if the Church persisted in not regarding these 'abductions of seduction' as on an equal footing with abductions with violence, declaring the nullity of marriages resulting therefrom, the execution of the guilty party constituted a drastic method of 'liberating' the minor from a marriage objectionable to her parents.

If one envisages marriage as the outcome of the love that two individuals feel for one another and as the means of ensuring their emotional happiness, one cannot fail to find these royal laws odious. However, in a society in which marriage had the effective and avowed function of perpetuating the 'house' and of ensuring honourable matrimonial alliances for it, it was normal that the master of the house should assume the responsibility for marriages. Besides, each marriage implied financial agreements which concerned not only the two spouses but all the members of their families of origin. To marry a son unsuitably might make impossible the marriage of his sisters, either because of the dishonour that this first marriage had brought on the house, or because it had not contributed the resources needed to provide them with dowries. The right of the father of the family to choose marriage partners for his children was not, therefore, an arbitrary privilege; it was a burdensome, but logical, responsibility. Besides, morality as well as the civil law obliged him to assume it in deadly earnest.[40]

In spite of the tension that existed between the Church and the French State concerning this matter, one should not minimize the similarity of their positions. Both Church and State claimed to be supporting, at one and the same time, freedom of marriage and the authority of parents, and they reconciled these two imperatives in a manner that appears to our eyes somewhat paradoxical. Let us observe, for example, how, in the eighteenth century, the jurist Houard justified the royal doctrine on this question.

> The laws have as their chief end to make the undertakings of the parties *fully free and voluntary*: that is to say, that their liberty and their will be exercised, without constraint either from the passions or from persons; in a word, that reflection alone should guide all actions: one cannot say that, when he is agitated by the most imperious of the passions – we are referring to that which impels one sex to unite with the other – a man is exercising his will freely. The law, therefore, foreseeing in how many circumstances a violent passion may extinguish in a man the faculty of reflection, has taken all the precautions necessary to restore it to him when he has had the misfortune to lose it. For this reason the Sovereign, who acts only in the name of the father and mother, and who knows that he cannot be better informed than they as to the imperative motives of the undertaking into which their children desire to enter, has. . . determined to what point the respect of the children for the advice and intentions of their father and mother should be carried.[41]

And, in actual fact, when parents stubbornly insisted on an unreasonable choice of partner, the children could appeal to the royal courts, which, either after consulting a family council if the children were minors, or by the arbitrary decision of the civil lieutenant-governor if they were adults, often found in their favour.[42]

Neither, from the ecclesiastical side, was the necessity of freedom of consent on the part of the spouses presented as contradicting the right of the father to impose on his child the partner of his choice: 'The father can command him to do it', wrote Benedicti, 'not by threats of beating or death, for the marriage should be free'; but the child was, nevertheless, 'obliged to obey under pain of mortal sin',[43] that is, under the threat of eternal damnation. This attitude was not found only among the French clergy. The Spaniard, Fernandes de Moure, after asking himself whether fathers and mothers could 'compel their children to enter into an honourable marriage', replied categorically: 'They can do so. . .and the Council of Trent does not forbid this to fathers and mothers, but only to temporal lords, who were accustomed to ordaining or forbidding marriages at their sole command.'[44] The only point of divergence between the Catholic Church and the supporters of paternal authority was concerned, in principle, with the sacramental character of the exchange of consent, whatever the circumstances: 'Marriage takes place by mutual consent, expressed in words spoken in person, *even if it is love that leads to this*', Peter Lombard had written in the twelfth century;[45] and the Church felt

133

itself unable to reject this traditional doctrine or to separate those whom God had thus joined together. However, it refrained from taking any measures against the prerogatives of fathers, and its condemnation of marriages compulsorily imposed by 'temporal lords or magistrates' protected the freedom of the father and mother to choose the partner of their child as much as the freedom of consent of the latter.[46]

However, the respect which the Church professed for paternal authority was as ambiguous, and even as artificial, as that professed by the French monarchy for freedom of marriage. Ever since its origins, Christianity had staunchly opposed the paternal power when it ran counter to God's will: 'He that loveth father or mother more than me is not worthy of me', one reads in the Gospel (Matthew 10.37): and again, 'Call no man your father upon the earth: for one is your Father, which is in heaven' (Matthew 23.9). This lesson was not forgotten in the sixteenth and seventeenth centuries. 'It must be noted', wrote Benedicti,

> that the command of the father may obligate the child under pain of mortal sin, principally in matters which are not against his conscience and the honour of God. For otherwise the child is not obliged to obey him. For example, if the father commands the child to go to hear the preaching of heretics, to steal, to kill, to traffic at festivals, to lend money with usury, to leave the religious state, to fornicate, to swear, to lie and to bear false witness, etc., he is not to be obeyed. Likewise, if the father or the mother, wishing to sell the honour of their daughter, command her to submit to intercourse in order to earn them something, the daughter must definitely not obey them, but rather suffer death, however poor her parents may be.[47]

One finds similar precepts in the writings of the Anglicans and Puritans:[48] they dispense the child from obedience when the parents forbid him to attend Protestant services, ordering him to go to Mass, to pray in a language which he does not understand – Latin, for example – to swear, to marry an idolatress – this category included the Catholics – to steal, to lie, to use false measures, to bear false witness, etc. To this list the Puritan William Gouge added a prohibition against avenging one's parents, even when the latter on their deathbed have made the child swear to do this, and even if their ghosts come at night-time to haunt forgetful children.

Protestants and Catholics never limited the authority of the parents by the natural rights of the child, but always by what was due to God, because God is our real father, as the majority of writers remind us, quoting in this connection the Gospels of Saint Matthew and Saint Luke. It was also to safeguard what is due to God that the Catholic Church had imposed 'freedom' of marriage: 'Parents who marry their sons or daughters against their will sin most gravely, as do those who force their daughters into the religious state against their will', wrote Tolet;[49] and Fernandes de Moure considered that one rendered oneself guilty of mortal sin in wishing 'to compel one's children to enter into marriage or into the religious state'.[50] All the confessors and compilers of catechisms who, in these early days of the Catholic reforms, referred to this question of the freedom of marriage, referred at the same time to the freedom of religious vocations, and they supported their arguments by the decrees of the Council of Trent regarding this freedom of vocation.[51] The choice of the spouse belonged by right to the father, but it was God's privilege to dedicate young people to marriage or to clerical celibacy. 'Fathers and mothers', declared P.-J. Dorléans, preaching in the second half of the seventeenth century,

> God has given you a share in his parenthood; it is just that he should share its functions with you. The function which He assigns to you is to give them education. . .The function which He reserves to Himself is to assign them an estate; it is an unjust usurpation if, in that sphere, you dare to thwart the commands of Providence. . .[52]

Nevertheless, from the seventeenth century onwards, the rights of the child in this sphere began to develop, in the shadow of the rights of God. 'Miserly father', exclaimed Dorléans,

> you are giving this unfortunate girl to that rich man!. . .you will answer to God for this innocent victim, of whom you make so cruel a sacrifice to your avarice and your ambition. For, after all, it is not thus that one should treat the children of God. Even though He is more master than you, He does not dispose of them as you do, He considers their inclinations, He assesses their vocation in the light of their capabilities, in short, He has regard for them, and, as the Scriptures say, He disposes of them with respect.[53]

As early as the first half of the century, Richelieu denounced not only fathers who impeded the religious or matrimonial vocation of their children, but also those 'who marry them to persons whom they cannot love',[54] thus supposing that in conjugal love there entered a necessary element of inclination. This point of view, which was apparently exceptional among the Catholic writers of the first half of the seventeenth century, seems to have become generally held during the course of the eighteenth century. In 1713 Antoine Blanchard asked fathers: 'Have you not compelled him. . .to enter into marriage with a girl for whom he felt dislike, even though you have foreseen or should have foreseen that they would make a bad household together?'[55] It was to protect religious vocations that the medieval Church had ordained the freedom of marriage; the Council of Trent had been concerned, above all, to put an end to forced vocations, in order to get rid of unworthy monks; the Catholic moralists of the eighteenth century questioned the right of fathers to be the sole choosers of the spouses of their children, in order to avoid unhappy marriages. In this attitude they had been preceded, by more than a century, by the Puritans and the Anglicans, as we shall see below.

Rather than the rights of the child, however, it was the duties of the parents which underwent development. In accordance with the mentality of former times, the father had full powers over his children, as did the master over his slaves; they belonged to him as his own property, because he had made them; he owed them nothing. According to our present-day mentality, however, procreation gives him more duties towards them than rights over them. This is a fundamental inversion of the principles of familial morality, and we must try to understand the reasons for it and to trace accurately its chronological development.

In the domain of the history of ideas, this inversion seems to have taken place from the very earliest days of Christianity: the Epistle to the Ephesians affirms, as we have observed above, the reciprocity of duties in father–child relationships, as in others. Christian fathers are no longer fathers except by delegation of power, and must consider their children 'as trusts which God places in their hands'. 'Christian fathers', Dorléans reminded them, 'if God is the principal father of your children, you are only, strictly speaking, their foster-fathers and guardians.' It is by virtue of this principle that paternity has come to involve more duties than rights. Moreover, even in antiquity, the Christian emperors had emphasized this by depriving fathers of the right to kill and sell their children. This logic, however, was implanted only slowly in the mentality of the faithful.[56] Throughout the early Middle Ages, infanticide appears to have been still frequent, and the theologians themselves admitted so categorically that children were things belonging to their parents, that they thought that God could punish parents in the persons of their children. There still remained, in the modern era, some vestiges of this traditional outlook, encouraged as it was by certain passages of the Old Testament. As an example of this, we may consider this sermon of Claude Joly, Bishop of Agen, which he preached in the middle of the seventeenth century:

> Children are sometimes rewarded for the virtues of their fathers and for the good examples that they have given of a holy and edifying life...Solomon, as you know, gave himself up to all manner of impurities and idolatry; his son Rehoboam was no better than he; nevertheless, on account of the virtues of David their father, God maintained Solomon on his throne, and of twelve tribes, he preserved two for Rehoboam. But these same children are also, sometimes, punished for the sins of their fathers, and it is in this

sense that Saint Gregory explains these words of the Scriptures: *Filius portabit iniquitatem patris*, the son shall bear the iniquity of his father. One often complains of the affliction of families and of the misfortunes that befall them. . .One says that it is the maladies and the evildoing of that family which have reduced the poor children to beggary; but, if one could see more clearly, one would look further back, and one would see that it is the sins of the fathers that these children bear. Your father has made profits by unjust means, he has engaged in business transactions by which he has ruined the people, in order to establish his house. . .Wretched children, you shall pay the penalty for it; the Holy Spirit has said so, and every day we see fresh examples, goods unjustly acquired shall not pass to the fourth generation.[57]

In a society in which privileges, honour, wealth and poverty were founded on birth, there is no doubt that such words were still understood.

In the seventeenth century it was still thought that the child owed everything to his father because he owed him his life. 'If both the one and the other find themselves in the same necessity, the son should give help to his father rather than to his son', Fernandes de Moure considered, 'inasmuch as he has received a greater good from his parents than from his children.'[58] That a father could sacrifice himself for his children was one of the paradoxes of Christianity, and in the seventeenth century the sacrifice of Christ still had this paradoxical character: 'Fathers give life to their children, and this is without any doubt a great favour', exclaimed Father Cheminais in the second half of the century, 'but one has never seen a father who has preserved the life of his children with his own blood, and who has died so that they might live, as did our Heavenly Father.'[59]

In accordance with the ancient principle, the Decalogue ordained that children should honour their parents, but gave parents no instructions as regards their children. For centuries, commentators remained unmoved by this absence of reciprocity: when they did amplify the scope of the Fourth Commandment, it was to find a justification for the duties of inferiors towards their superiors, particularly of laymen towards the clergy. After the Council of Trent, however, their attitude changed abruptly: of the eleven manuals for confessors that we have examined, the four written between the middle of the fourteenth century and the middle of the sixteenth century contain no reference to the duties of parents or of superiors, whereas the seven published between 1574 and 1748 all discuss, at varying degrees of length, these duties. Similarly, of the eighteen post-Tridentine catechisms examined, the ten which were not addressed exclusively to children emphasize, in connection with the Fourth Commandment, that parents also have obligations towards their offspring: 'This commandment imposes obligations not only on children towards their fathers, but also on fathers and mothers towards their children, inasmuch as love should be reciprocal', stated Richelieu, for example, in his *Instruction du Chrestien.*

> This means that God, when He commands children to love and honour their fathers, *tacitly* enjoins fathers to love their children, and there is no need for Him to do so explicitly, seeing that the love of fathers for their children is so natural that, to oblige them to bestow it, the law which they have written in their hearts is quite sufficient, without any other.[60]

However, it is still a fact that no writer had emphasized this before the Council of Trent, and that all felt obliged to do so subsequently.

This change is too abrupt to have had a cause other than an order emanating from above, and it is, therefore, only to a small degree significant of a transformation of attitudes. More interesting in this respect are less sudden and less conscious developments. Among the works which we have been considering, let us examine, for example, the seven manuals for confessors which refer to the duties of parents and the six most voluminous catechisms, which devote six or more pages to commentaries on the Fourth Commandment. In the two works published before 1580, over 80 per cent of the text is devoted to the duties of children and less than 20 per cent to those of parents, while between 22 and 34 per cent of the text is devoted to the duties of parents in the three works published between 1580 and 1638, and between 40 and 60 per cent in the eight works published between 1640 and 1794. Once it was understood that it was necessary to speak of the duties of parents in connection with the Fourth Commandment, writers gradually became more aware of the importance of such duties.

Moreover, the duties became more numerous. In the sixteenth century and at the beginning of the seventeenth century, moralists insisted only on the obligations of maternal assistance and of religious and moral education. In the second half of the seventeenth century and in the eighteenth century, Catholic writers – more than a century after the English Puritans[61] – emphasized the duties of giving professional education and of settling one's children: 'Have you taken care to make them learn the occupation suitable for them according to your station?' asked Antoine Blanchard, for example. Of the seven manuals for confessors considered, only the last two, published in 1713 and 1748, refer to this duty; and, of the six catechisms studied, only the last four allude to the future of the children, in terms which have also changed: those of 1667 and 1765 speak of settling the children, whereas those of 1778 and 1796 refer to learning a trade.

This insistence on the duties of parents was sometimes accompanied by warnings, addressed to those who wished to act justly, as to the difficulties of their task. Let us listen, for example, to the sermon that Dorléans preached to parents seeking ways to settle their children.

> There are no human lives long enough to foresee a thousand un-
> fortunate experiences that will befall them in certain estates and
> will not happen to them in others. You destine this child to the
> legal profession, because he appears to you temperate; but you do
> not perceive, underlying this temperance, a strain of evil com-
> plaisance which will allow him to be governed by all those who
> wish to make themselves masters of his intelligence. . .You consider
> this girl fitted for the cloister, because she appears to you docile;
> but you do not see that this docility stems from an idleness which
> will make the observances of the religious life intolerable to her. . .
> You imagine that that boy is bound to be happy in an estate in
> which you see nothing, you say, that can cause him distress; but
> you do not foresee a thousand events, independent of his tempera-
> ment, his character and even his prudence, which will fill his life
> with affliction. Since you do not and cannot foresee these things,
> leave matters to God who does foresee them.[62]

In the sixteenth century, the only recognized vocation had been the religious one; apart from that, parents were left free to choose the occupation of their children. By the end of the seventeenth century, however, every estate had become a 'profession' and required a 'vocation', which parents were forbidden to thwart.

However, at the same time they were required to help the child to find his vocation.

> Do not, I agree, abandon the destiny of your children to the first
> sallies of a youthful ardour, which should always be suspect. Take
> care not only that an ill-regulated passion does not lead them to
> take one of those wrong decisions which reason always disavows
> when it returns to its senses, and which it often disavows only
> when it ceases to be fashionable; you must even prevent that levity,
> always to be feared among young people, from leading them to
> take the right decisions, for that same levity which has led them to
> take the decisions in haste leads them to forsake them out of
> distaste. However, do not, on the pretext of taking precautions
> against caprice and passions, take the liberty of opposing true
> vocations; and, even though it is your duty to test the vocations
> themselves, do not transform, as many do, a useful test into a
> dangerous temptation.[63]

There was, in such sermons, enough to cause anguish to scrupulous parents. The contradictory and repeatedly belied injunctions of modern psychologists and other educationalists, which cause such an anguish, evident nowadays, are important only in so far as parents consider themselves responsible for the good or evil fortune of their offspring. It seems that it was the Protestant and Catholic reformers of the sixteenth, seventeenth and eighteenth centuries who first convinced parents of this responsibility.

Before the promulgation of the Revolutionary laws it was they, too, who tried to establish among children an equality characteristic of the regions where individualism prevailed. Let us observe, for example, the sermon that Claude Joly, a native of Verdun, where equality between children was traditional, preached in Agenais, where the 'house spirit' held sway.

> The second thing that he requires of you is equality. Do not show more love or tenderness to one child than to another...You love this eldest son too blindly and you desire too ardently to enrich him, you rebuff this younger son too harshly and you are too indifferent as regards settling him. Do you have to strip some in order to dress the others? Must you force this poor younger son into the clerical estate, to which he is not at all suited, in order to make a fortune for that eldest son? Must you so harshly ill-treat this daughter, that you compel her to hasten into a convent, for which she has no vocation whatsoever, so that she surrenders her legitimate portion of the inheritance in favour of those whom you prefer? O unjust fathers, O barbarous mothers: do you realize what you are doing? Saint Ambrose says: you are kindling the fire of discord in your family, you are sowing there the seeds of enmities and litigation...They are all your children, they come from you, do not create so cruel a difference between them; on the contrary, arrange things so that those who share equally one and the same nature also share equally the same favours.[64]

Of the seven manuals for confessors that we have studied, only the last two, published in 1713 and 1748, thus advocate equality among children. However, in the series of catechisms, although the word 'equality' does not appear until 1772, from 1667 onwards parents were exhorted not to provoke jealousy among their children.

Masters and servants

It must be observed once again that it is an anachronism to reduce the family of former times to the father, the mother and the children. The servants were part of the family, and all contemporary texts bear witness to this. The Anglican and Puritan moralists, like the Catholic ones, all refer to the servants when they discuss the government of the family. They were referred to even in the sermons that resounded in the cathedrals: 'A father, head of a family, who has children and servants, cannot labour usefully for his own salvation unless he leads along the same path that he treads those whom Divine Providence has entrusted to his care', observed Claude Joly. 'Moreover, when Scripture praises these fathers and these masters, it nearly always regards them as being accompanied by their children and their servants.'[65]

It is true that this patriarchal image had been, to some extent, lost in the course of the Middle Ages. For a long time the Catholic moralists had referred to the master only in the presence of the king, the pope and other superiors, and to the domestic servants only through the broader concept of 'servitor', which included other inferiors. This medieval tradition is still found in the writings of Benedicti, Tolet, Fernandes de Moure and even Richelieu: in our series of manuals for confessors, domestic servants appear for the first time in 1713, in the manual written by Antoine Blanchard, in which the commentary on the Fourth Commandment is situated entirely within the context of the family. On the other hand, like the sins of parents, those of masters attracted an increasing share of the attention of the moralists: in 1584, Benedicti devoted only two articles to the subject, as against eight dealing with the sins of servants; in 1713, Antoine Blanchard devoted thirteen articles to the sins of masters, as opposed to fourteen to those of servants.

Benedicti was concerned only with the moral and religious surveillance of the servants; he feared the indifference of the master, and counselled severity.[66]

> Masters who do not care about the salvation of their men and women servants, and do not try to correct their faults, allowing them to swear, blaspheme, fornicate, steal, etc., share in their sins. Likewise, he who does not keep himself informed as to the lives of his servants, contenting himself with merely exacting physical service from them: this is common among many masters nowadays. Likewise, he who does not trouble about making them go to Mass, go to Confession and receive Communion, and have Extreme Unction administered to them when necessary. Likewise, he who keeps them busy on holy days with mechanical labour, as has been said above: all these people commit offences.
>
> And if the master has incorrigible servants, he should expel them from his house rather than retain them unless there is a danger of their becoming worse, or of some calamity overtaking them because they have been expelled and punished. Sometimes, too, the master can refuse some necessary things to the servant for a time, so as to give him an opportunity to remedy his faults, since necessity opens

the understanding to the Spirit, according to the Prophet Isaiah. Moreover, the Catholic master should expel from his house his Huguenot servant, unless he desires to retain him with a worthy intention, that is to say, to convert him to the Church and to the way of Salvation.

In acting otherwise, masters would be guilty of mortal sin ('M.S.').

At that time, therefore, the Church required masters to mobilize all their authority to ensure the salvation of their servants, in accordance with the principle *cuius regio eius religio*. However, also approaching the question from the opposite angle, it required servants to disobey unjust orders.

He who, through fear of death or of losing his estate and goods, obeys orders contrary to the commandments of God. . .he commits an offence. . .M.S. He who obeys his masters and lords contrary to the commandments of the Church, commits a mortal sin, unless he was compelled by fear of violence, that is to say, of death, or physical torments, and of losing all his goods. . .V.S. or M.S.

(nos. 45 and 46)

It was again out of anxiety for the salvation of the servants that Benedicti devoted a second article (no. 42) to the duties of masters. 'Those who prevent their men and women servants from marrying when it is opportune for them to do so, and who see that otherwise they will be in danger of fornicating and forming some guilty liaison, commit a sin. M.S.' In this respect, therefore, the masters were, in relation to their servants, in a situation comparable to that of fathers, who were also enjoined to marry as early as possible those of their children who did not have a vocation for celibacy. They prevented the servants from marrying, not by means of a legal veto, like the fathers of families, but by not giving the servant the wherewithal to establish himself independently. At that time, in fact, when the notion of wages was nebulous, it was by ensuring the material independence of a servant that one recompensed his services. However, the master was subject to two temptations: either never to marry off a good servant, in order to keep him in the house, in which case he would be encouraging him to fornicate; or to reward him cheaply by imposing him as a husband on the heiress of a rich villein – a practice which the Council of Trent had denounced.[67]

Antoine Blanchard, writing at the beginning of the eighteenth century, still admonished the master to supervise the morals and religion of his domestic servants. 'Have you supervised the behaviour of your domestic servants? Have you not tolerated their disorderly conduct? Have you taken care to see that your servants frequent the sacraments every so often? Have you not kept depraved servants in your house?' (nos. 50, 55, 62).

However, the struggle against immoral behaviour is considered more important than the struggle against heresy; furthermore, these duties of surveillance have a much more limited role than in the writings of Benedicti.

There is greater insistence, however, on the bad influence that the superior may have on the inferior, exclusively in the moral sphere. He asks: 'Have you not scandalized them by your bad example? Have you not uttered dirty words in their presence? Have you not said anything before the servant-girls with evil intent? Have you not tempted them to crime [that is, to the sins of the flesh] by promises and presents?' (nos. 57, 58, 59, 60).

Above all, there is much more concern than in the time of Benedicti over the wrongs that the master could do to his servants in this world: 'Have you not treated your servants too harshly? Have you taken care of them when they were sick?' (no. 56). 'Have you not ill-treated your servants, either by addressing insulting words to them, or by striking them out of bad temper or in anger?' (no. 51). The sixteenth-century writers might have asked such questions; if they failed to do so, the reason was that they were obsessed with the struggle against heresy and immorality. Besides, by imposing on masters the duty of correcting their servants, they appeared to justify some of their brutal treatment of them. Blanchard's next two articles emphasize not only the new attention paid by the moralists to material wrongs, but the newly acquired importance of the contract and of wages in the relationship between the master and his servants: 'Have you not refused them their needs? Have you not infringed the agreements that you have made with them, with regard to either food or clothing? Have you not retained their wages on the false pretext that they have lost, taken or broken something? Have you not excessively delayed payment of their wages after dismissing them?' (nos. 52 and 53). Finally, there is this article, which would have been unthinkable in the sixteenth century: 'When someone has come to you to seek information as to their conduct, have you not wronged them purely from motives of vengeance, discrediting them by making false accusations against them, in order to prevent their being engaged in some house?' (no. 54). One seems to have already passed from the brutal paternalism prevailing in the sixteenth century to the pettiness of bourgeois society.

One can also discern, in the questions that Antoine Blanchard asks the masters, a new distrust of the traditional domestic promiscuity: 'Have you not dressed or undressed in their presence with immodesty and indecency?' (no. 61), a question which one can compare with that asked of parents regarding their attitude towards their children: 'Have you not put them to sleep in a bed that is too close to your own? Have you not put to sleep in your own bed any of your children who have reached the age of reason?' (nos. 36, 37). Even more emphatically than promiscuity between parents and children and between masters and servants, the moralists of that age denounced familiarity between the servant and the child. 'Have you not suffered him to be too often in the company of some servant, with whom he might be debauched by the immoral conversations that he had with him?' (no. 29). It is worth noting that none of the manuals published at the end of the sixteenth and the beginning of the seventeenth centuries denounced such familiarity.

Leaving aside general considerations regarding what inferiors owed to their superiors, Antoine Blanchard draws a very detailed picture of the bad servant, as he was represented at the beginning of the eighteenth century. Like the bad servant of the sixteenth century, he despises his masters and disobeys them (nos. 36, 37, 45, 47); or, by a misplaced obedience to them, he infringes the commandments of God (no. 49). Furthermore, he does not have their interests at heart:

> have you taken care to fulfil the duties of your estate and your standing, watching over their interests and preventing, as much as you ought, anyone doing them any injury? Have you not caused some detriment to them through your lack of care or your lack of thrift? Have you taken care to warn them when some one of the house or of another house has been doing them some injury, above all when you were entrusted with the responsibility for looking after this matter? (nos. 38, 39, 41)

He is lazy or inept: 'Have you not fruitlessly wasted the time that you should have employed in your master's service?' (no. 48). He is a thief, or an accomplice in theft:

> Have you not retained anything when buying or selling on their behalf, on the pretext that your wages were not sufficient? Have you not taken wine, salt, candles, bread or other things to distribute as gifts, or with the object of obtaining help from someone in your work, when you can and should do it yourself? Have you not lent your services to the son of your master or mistress, to help him in thefts he has committed? (nos. 40, 42, 43)

Finally, he is indiscreet: 'Have you not reported things that have happened in the house? The moods of your master or mistress, their quarrels, and other things which demanded your silence and discretion?' (no. 46).

The moralists of the early period of the Catholic Reformation evince a certain optimism with regard to the servants: they thought that, provided they were supervised and corrected, one could make good fellows out of them. In the course of the seventeenth century, this optimism appears to diminish: rather than emphasizing surveillance and correction, Claude Joly, in the middle of the century, speaks of the need to choose them carefully:

> The obligation of masters is to choose good servants...You are

144

obliged to make this choice: 1. for the tranquillity of your conscience; for if you love virtue then you should love virtuous servants...2. You are obliged to make this choice for the spiritual good of your family. A depraved manservant and an evil maidservant can ruin an entire family...This daughter is most often with this maidservant, this son is almost always with this manservant; if he is unchaste, he will teach him unchastity; if he is a drunkard, he will accustom him to drink too much wine; if he is a blasphemer, he will induce him to blaspheme.

He still refers to the need for correction, but he wishes it to be gentle, and does not seem to expect great results from it: 'I admit that they often deserve that you should chastise them, but it should be rather...with the charity of a father than with the harshness of a tyrant.'[68] Finally, in the eighteenth century it was no longer demanded that masters should have virtuous servants, nor that they should chastise them or dismiss the depraved ones. The essential consideration appears to have been to prevent the children being corrupted by contact with them.

3. MORALITY AND THE FEELINGS

In drawing attention to the respect and obedience which the wife, the children and the servants owed to the head of the family, and to the duties of protection, supervision and chastisement of the latter, it is not certain that we have characterized domestic relationships with sufficient precision, since most of the other social relationships were similarly based on the principle of authority, and on the duties of protection, supervision and chastisement which were incumbent on the superiors. Did one not also expect the members of a family to feel for one another those specific sentiments of family relationships which we term conjugal love, maternal love, paternal love and brotherly affection, and which, rightly or wrongly, we distinguish from what Christianity understands by 'love of one's neighbour'? To what extent did the morality of family relationships refer to these specific sentiments and to others, and how did it characterize them?

An examination of conscience in 1713

For the purposes of such a study, let us examine closely the terminology employed by a particular moralist, Antoine Blanchard; we have already seen to what extent he was an innovator, in comparison with the confessors of the late sixteenth and early seventeenth centuries. In the total of 153 articles which he devotes to domestic relationships, he refers eighty times to sentiments, passions and moods, and uses thirty-seven different concepts. Table 11 shows an inventory of these, with an indication of the

Table 11. Inventory of the sentiments and moods mentioned by Antoine Blanchard in his chapter on the Fourth Commandment

Terms relating to sentiments, moods, attitudes, etc.	Sins of servants	Sins of masters	Sins of children	Sins of parents	Sins of husbands	Sins of wives
Respect	—	—	1 (C)	—	—	—
Deference	37 (S)	—	—	—	—	—
Arrogance	45 (S)	—	5 (C)	—	—	3 (W)
Contempt	—	—	3, 9, 35 (C)	—	64, 66, 77 (H)	14 (W)
Scandal	—	57 (S)	—	—	72 (C, S, W)	—
Harshness (in deed or word), harshly	—	56 (M)	2, 20 (C)	—	76 (H)	—
Brusqueness	—	—	—	22 (P)	—	—
Rage	—	51 (M)	15 (P)	42 (P)	64 (H)	3, 8 (H)
Anger	44 (M)	—	—	8 (P)	—	3 (H)
Bad temper	—	—	—	—	73 (H)	—
Ill-humour	46 (M, S)	51 (M)	—	22 (P)	—	—
Obstinacy	—	—	—	—	—	3 (W)
Obligingness	—	—	—	—	—	4 (W)
Patience	—	—	—	—	—	2 (W)
Charity	—	—	—	—	—	2 (W)
Maintaining union	—	—	—	—	—	2 (W)
Shame	—	—	5 (P)	—	76 (W)	—
Contrariety	—	—	—	—	—	—
Resentment	—	—	13 (C)	—	74, 76 (W)	—
Repugnance	—	—	—	—	—	—
Vexation	—	—	—	18 (P)	73, 75, 78, 88 (W)	15 (H)
Sadness	—	—	—	17 (P)	—	—
Sorrow	—	—	—	17 (P)	—	—
Envy	—	—	6 (C)	—	—	—
Jealousy	—	—	6, 7 (C)	—	65 (H)	—
Suspecting fidelity	—	—	—	—	—	12 (H)

147

moods, attitudes, etc.	Sins of servants	Sins of masters	Sins of children	Sins of parents	Sins of husbands	Sins of wives
Dislike	–	–	–	6, 16 (C)	65 (H)	–
Hatred	–	–	12, 13 (C)	5 (P), 7 (C)	63, 87 (H)	5 (W)
Desiring death	–	–	12 (C)	10 (P)	68 (H)	–
Intention of causing death	–	–	–	8 (P)	79 (H)	–
(Not) loving	–	–	–	–	–	–
Affection (transferring it elsewhere)	–	–	–	–	69, 70, 73 (H)	6 (H)
Attachment (excessive)	–	–	–	5 (P)	–	6 (H)
Indifference	–	–	–	5 (P)	–	5 (W)
Coldness	–	–	5 (C)	–	–	–
Number of terms	4	4	12	13	14	15
Number of times terms used	4	4	16	16	24	16
Number of articles	14	13	35	49	26	16
Number of times used in relation to number of articles	8/27 = 30%		32/84 = 38%		40/42 = 95%	

(S) = Servants	:	3 sentiments; 3 mentions
(M) = Master or Mistress	:	5 sentiments; 5 mentions
Total	:	8 sentiments; 8 mentions
(C) = Children	:	12 sentiments; 18 mentions
(P) = Parents	:	14 sentiments; 14 mentions
Total	:	26 sentiments; 32 mentions
(H) = Husband	:	16 sentiments; 23 mentions
(W) = Wife	:	13 sentiments; 17 mentions
Total	:	29 sentiments; 40 mentions

The head of the family (H + P + M) experiences 21 different sentiments, mentioned 42 times.

Source: A. Blanchard, *Examen général sur tous les commandements et sur les péchés de plusieurs états* (2 vols, Paris, 1713), vol. 2, pp. 189–202.

articles in which they are mentioned and, in parentheses, that of the person who is subject to these sentiments or moods.

In the first category we have grouped the sentiments connected with the hierarchical character of domestic relationships. *Respect* and *deference* are what the writer expects from inferiors, that is, in this context, the children and servants. He asks the children (no. 1): 'Have you not been lacking in respect towards your father and your mother?' and the servants (no. 37): 'Have you shown to [your masters] all the deference due to them?' *Contempt* was another, and negative, way of referring to the respect due to one's superiors. It could happen that children felt contempt for their parents 'on account of their poverty or of some natural defect' (no. 3); as for the servants suspected of having 'had contempt' for their masters, they are asked in the same article: 'Have you not spoken ill of them?' The wife also, as an inferior, is capable of having 'contempt for the counsels of her husband' and for his 'remonstrances' to her. On the other hand, parents are not asked if they have felt contempt for their children, nor masters if they have felt it for their servants, because they did not owe them any respect. This being the case, it is worth observing that, when examining the sins of the husband towards his wife, Blanchard asks: 'Have you not treated her too harshly and with contempt?...Have you not rendered her contemptible to your children and your servants by the contempt that you have shown for her...Have you not allowed that creature [meaning the husband's mistress] to insult her and speak to her with contempt?' (nos. 64, 66, 77). The reason for this is that the wife, in spite of being subordinate to her husband, is his equal, as Fernandes de Moure had emphasized a century earlier; and she was, within the house, superior to the children and the servants, and most certainly to that despicable creature, her husband's mistress.

One would also place *scandal* among the sentiments characteristic of hierarchical relationships, for it was never an inferior who scandalized his superior but always the latter who scandalized the former. It is when examining the sins of the master towards his servants that the question is asked: 'Have you not scandalized them by your bad example? Have you not uttered dirty words in their presence?' (nos. 57 and 58). Or it might be the guilty attachment of the husband for some woman that risked 'causing a scandal in his family' (no. 72). In fact, when the inferior committed a sin, his superior knew that he should chastise him for it, under pain of himself sharing in that sin. The inferior, however, had no power to correct his superiors. In the face of the sin that the latter committed in his presence, the inferior did not know what attitude to adopt to avoid sharing in it. He knew full well that all sin merits vengeance, and he would have liked to escape that which would assuredly come crashing down on his superior, but he could do nothing: he was apprehensive, dumbfounded, scandalized. Furthermore, the superior who scandalized his inferiors would eventually provoke their contempt.

Servants, as such, do not appear to have been capable of feeling sentiments other than deference, contempt and scandal. They were neither supposed nor required to have other sentiments. The confessor watched over their acts – laziness, theft, indiscretion, etc. – rather than their feelings. Let us, however, examine those of the master towards them.

'Have you not ill-treated your servants, either by addressing insulting words to them, or by striking them out of bad temper or in a fit of rage?' (no. 51); *ill-humour, rage* and *anger* are the only sentiments to which Blanchard refers when he examines the behaviour of the master towards his servants. Speaking in more general terms, these moods are the exclusive prerogative of the head of the family in his capacity as father or husband as well as master. Parents are asked if they have not beaten one of their children 'excessively and without cause, out of bad temper' (no. 8). And again: 'In chastising him, have you not overstepped the limits, abandoning yourself to your ill-humour and your fit of rage?' (no. 22). 'Have you not cursed them out of anger?' (no. 42). And, to the husband: 'Have you not shown bad temper in your house, swearing, raging and finding fault with everything that your wife has done. . .?' (no. 73). The master of the house should not give way to bad temper and fits of rage: he should chastise his servants, his children and possibly his wife coldly and reasonably.

On their side, however, those subject to his governance are guilty when they arouse the master's anger. 'Have you not given them reason to become angry with you and to use abusive words to you?' Blanchard enquires, when examining the sins of servants against their master. Examining those of children against their parents, he asks: 'Have you not given them reason to be angry with you on account of your disobedience and your bad behaviour?' (no. 15). He asks the wife: 'Have you not given him reason to be angry and have fits of rage on account of your arrogance and your obstinacy?. . .Have you not refused him his conjugal rights without legitimate cause? Has your refusal not been the motive for some fit of rage or some other disturbance?' (nos. 3, 7 and 8). And she is urged to show *patience, obligingness* and *charity*: 'Have you maintained a close union with your husband, suffering his shortcomings with patience and charity?. . .Have you not been insufficiently obliging towards him?' (nos. 2 and 4). The reason for this is that fits of rage and anger are the normal reactions of the head of the family to the clumsiness or impertinence of his servants, the disobedience of his children, the obstinacy of his wife or, worse still, the refusal of her body. In this, he is doing no more than follow the example of Yahweh, whose anger was so often aroused by the insubordination of the Jews. Anger formed part of the manifestations of authority. One could reproach the master of the house only for indulging in it to excess.

The wife, when she is thwarted, reacts differently: she gives way to *resentment* and *vexation*. It is, above all, the husband who provokes this, by his infidelity and his cruelty: 'Have you not enticed that creature to your house just to spite your wife? Have you not bestowed on that creature indiscreet favours, which have given your wife reason to feel resentment? Have you not treated your wife badly in her presence, crossing her in every way just to spite her and continually addressing harsh words to her?' (nos. 74, 75, 76). Vexation, as opposed to mere resentment, might have serious consequences. 'By the ill-treatment and the vexation that you have given your wife, have you not made her sick? Have you not been the cause, by reason of your ill-treatment, of her being injured during the time of her pregnancy', 'or that vexation has caused her to have a confinement all the more troublesome because it has been premature?' (nos. 78 and 88).

However, the wife did not have a monopoly of vexation. She could also cause her husband to feel it: 'Have you not caused him vexation by your bad behaviour and your lack of diligence in the education of your children?' (no. 15). Likewise, children could vex their parents, and cause them *sorrow, sadness* or even *shame*:

> Have you not reproved them with arrogance, filling them with shame, not only in private but even in public?...Have you not plunged them into sorrow and sadness, even to the extent of making them sick, by your debauchery and your keeping company with certain persons of dissolute behaviour, having taken no account of their prohibitions? Have you not contributed to their death by the extreme vexations that you have caused them?
>
> (nos. 5, 17, 18)

No one other than the husband and his wife – either individually, or collectively as parents – appears to be liable to entertain these unhappy emotions. Contrary to what we would expect, it was not among the more humble members of the family that these sentiments were supposed to exist, but among the most highly honoured – those who, in principle, wielded domestic power. The confessor of that age was not interested in the vexations and resentments of the humble. It must, however, be observed that, even though the children and the servants were equally uninteresting as the subjects of these doleful sentiments, they were in an entirely different position as regards their ability to provoke such sentiments in others. Servants could arouse, in their masters, only bad temper and fits of rage; children, on the other hand, were capable of provoking in their parents, in addition to anger, shame, sorrow, sadness and a vexation that was at times mortal: this is an evident sign of the dominion that they held over their hearts.

It was to evil sentiments, even more than to sorrowful sentiments, that Antoine Blanchard alluded with great frequency: *envy, jealousy, dislike, hatred, desire for someone's death.* These evil sentiments are the most numerous (seven different notions), the most frequently mentioned (nineteen times), and the most evenly shared, since they could be felt by the husband towards his wife and by the wife towards her husband, by the children towards their parents, by the parents towards their children, and by the children towards one another. Only the servants, apparently, were incapable of feeling or provoking such sentiments.

Envy is found only among children: it is logically derived from the iniquity of the parents, and is accompanied by a host of other evil sentiments. Moreover, it was parents who were asked:

> Have you not had too much attachment for one of your children at the expense of the others; conceding everything to this one, and refusing almost everything to the others; forgiving everything to the first and nothing to the others. . .? Have you not provoked, by this behaviour, dislike, envy and jealousy among them? Have they not abused and insulted one another owing to this implanting of hatred and jealousy? (nos. 5, 6 and 7)

Jealousy is somewhat more common because, when the husband abuses or beats his wife, it may be 'from motives of jealousy' (no. 65). It must be observed that the word does not appear when the wife is asked: 'Have you not given your husband reason to suspect your fidelity by some meetings that were suspect to him and which he had forbidden you?' (no. 12). Is this the result of chance, or is it because the husband's jealousy is a less justifiable sentiment than his anger? As for the woman, we have observed that the liaisons of her husband might provoke in her resentment and vexation, but never jealousy.

Dislike is not only a gratuitous and irrational sentiment, but it, too, is generally felt by a man, with his wife as the object. Parents, for example, are asked whether they have not forced any of their children 'to enter into marriage with a girl for whom he felt dislike' (no. 16); and when the husband outrages his wife 'with words or with blows' this could be, just as much as out of jealousy, 'out of dislike which you felt for her' (no. 65). If more concern was shown for dislike on the part of the husband than on that of the wife, this was perhaps because it was more dangerous, both on account of the authority that was acknowledged as being his in the government of the house, and because of the active role that was supposed to be his in the conjugal bed.

151

It is true that the confessor was concerned about the *hatred* that the wife might harbour towards her husband (no. 5). However, he was worried less by the gravity of this sentiment or the acts to which it might induce the woman than by his fear that this hatred might give the husband 'reason to attach himself to some strange woman', and that 'some debauchery' might ensue as a result. It is only on the part of the other members of the family that hatred appears dangerous.

The husband is first asked some innocuous questions: 'Have you not had hatred for your wife?' or 'Have you not uttered abusive reproaches to your wife out of the hatred that you had for her?' (nos. 63 and 87). Then he goes on to enquire about desire for her death and attempts to murder her:

> Have you not desired her death, in order to be able to marry another?. . .By the ill-treatment and the vexation that you have given your wife, have you not made her sick? Have you not refused her needs and the necessary assistance in that condition? During the course of her illness, have you not tried to make it even worse, with the object of procuring her death, heaping imprecations and curses on her? (nos. 68, 78, 79)

It is true that in none of these three articles is hatred specifically referred to: it may simply be that the husband loves another woman, as no. 68 supposes. The Frenchmen of pre-Revolutionary times, too, were suspected of practising 'divorce Italian style'.

Children were suspected of somewhat heinous intentions towards their parents: 'Have you not desired their death? Was it out of hatred or with the object of acquiring the inheritance earlier? Have you not continued to harbour hatred towards them? For how long did it last? Have you given them external signs of it which they were able to perceive?' (nos. 12 and 13). If one is to believe Freud, of course, this desire for one's parents' death is present in all ages and in all countries. However, the confessors of past times were not dealing with the unconscious, and all of them, from Gerson to Blanchard, asked the same question. The reason is that, in a society in which one lived, to a far greater extent than nowadays, on an ancestral patrimony, the child was really – and not just unconsciously – dependent until his father's death. The ownership of the patrimony, as much as laws and morality, gave the father the power to impose on his children an occupation or a spouse, and to correct his 'depraved' tendencies – that is, to oppose what the child wanted to be. This dependence, in relation to the parents and the patrimony, lent further strength to the hatred of unloved children for an unjustly favoured child.

More surprising, at first sight, is the hatred that parents might harbour for certain of their children. This sentiment was envisaged as being entertained by fathers who favoured one of their children at the expense of the others 'out of the indifference or hatred' which they felt for them (no. 5).

Should one assume that, in this context, the term 'hatred' is incorrect, or that it had at that time a less strong connotation than today, which its association with the term 'indifference' in this article and in others in fact suggests? The following articles provide evidence of the possible force of this hatred: 'Have you not beaten any of your children, excessively and without cause, out of bad-temper and because you did not love him? Have you not refused him his needs? Have you not desired his death?' (nos. 8, 9, 10). There is no doubt about the fact that this hatred could be carried to great lengths. Why? How were children, so defenceless legally and economically in relation to their parents, capable of inspiring their hatred – and not merely their dislike?

Among the social élites at that time, a number of heads of families were bent on achieving the ascent of their house, and an excessively numerous family threatened to wreck that ambition. This seems to have been especially true of commoners trying to gain entry into the nobility in regions where the customary laws did not allow for the right of primogeniture among commoners. In these families, the child who embodied the hopes of social ascent of the father was cherished. On the other hand, when a dozen other children arrived who would prevent the father rounding off his fortune and would filch from the heir a part of the patrimony, thus imperilling the rise of the family, it is understandable that he should have taken a dislike to them. Speaking in more general terms, the inability to control births multiplied the unwanted children. And the hope of getting rid of them by death might suggest itself all the more easily to some minds because infant mortality was, as is known, considerable, especially among the children from the towns put out to nurse in the country. It may well have been not without malign intent that, in many bourgeois families, the mother nursed the heir, and the younger children were put out to nurse.[69]

It might also happen that a father had not found, in the heir whom customary law had imposed on him, the qualities he expected of him; that he had tried in vain to change his character, and this futile tyranny had provoked a ferocious hatred between father and son. This would be all the more strong on the part of the father, who knew that one day he would have to leave his heir to act as he pleased. One can observe, among reigning families, the relations between Charles VII and the future Louis XI, between Francis I and the future Henri II, between Frederick William of Prussia and the future Frederick II, and, to take an extreme example, the history of Peter the Great, the judge and executioner of his own son. However, the same thing could also happen in families of less exalted rank: history has preserved traces of the disputes between Mirabeau 'the friend of men' and Mirabeau the orator; it has forgotten many others equally characteristic of a society in which, more frequently than nowa-days, the heir embodied the hopes of his father.

In that society, absolutely any of the children could, in addition, dis-honour his family by his wrongdoings and his personality. Since the father was responsible for both, one can understand what vexation, what sadness, what grief and, finally, what hatred he might feel. Many fathers requested from the king a letter under his private seal for use against their unworthy sons.[70]

In short, the spouses and their children were already distinguished, within the household, by the wrongs that they could do or wish to do to one another. If these evil sentiments were characteristic of the family as we conceive it today, this was because its members were indissolubly linked to one another by Christian marriage, the solidarity of honour, the legal authority of the father, and the economic dependence of all on the common patrimony. However, even if these traditional structures encour-aged evil sentiments, they did not necessarily arouse them. It remains to be investigated whether our confessor did not expect the members of the family to harbour towards one another the good sentiments supposedly characteristic of family ties.

The notions of *love*, *affection* and sentimental *attachment* in fact appear either directly or by reference to their opposites, *indifference* and *coldness*. They concern only family relationships in the sense in which the term is understood nowadays, not the relations between masters and servants. Nevertheless, the requirements of Antoine Blanchard in this sphere are still very different from those of the moralists of the twentieth century.

The noun 'love' does not appear, and the verb 'to love' appears only once. It is still expressed in negative terms, and in connection with the relations between parents and children: 'Have you not beaten any of your children, excessively and without cause, out of bad-temper and because you did not love him?' (no. 8). If modesty impelled Corneille's heroine to say 'I do not hate you' instead of 'I love you', in this context it appears to have led the writer to say 'you did not love him' instead of 'you hated him'.

The notions of *affection* and *attachment* appear not, as one might imagine, because the confessor is complaining of the absence or weakness of these sentiments; on the contrary, he is denouncing their excessive force or the illegitimate object towards which they are directed. He is afraid, as we have observed, that the wife's indifference to or hatred of her husband may have given the latter 'occasion to transfer his affection elsewhere and to attach himself to some other woman' (no. 6). In addition, he asks the husband: 'Have you not formed an attachment for some woman other than your wife? Has this attachment not given rise to some licentiousness in your family and in your household? When you have been keeping company with that creature for whom you had that attachment, have you not shown bad temper in your house. . .?' (nos. 69, 70, 73). And the parents are asked: 'Have you not had too much attachment for one of your children at the expense of the others. . .?' (no. 5). It would seem, therefore, that, far from uniting the family, affection and sentimental attachments were suspected of provoking all kinds of disorders.

One could, quite evidently, read between the lines and conclude that, if the husband were in danger of 'transferring his affection elsewhere', this was because he should feel it for his wife; that if he had 'not formed an attachment for some woman other than his wife', he was expected to have an attachment for the latter; that, as regards the children, if 'too much attachment' for one of them was dangerous, a moderate and equitably shared attachment was desirable. However, the text says nothing about this, and what it does say does not necessarily imply this. One could, in fact, just as easily suppose that the confessor favoured cold and rational behaviour and distrusted all affective impulses.

The only proof that Blanchard demands of affection between spouses on the one hand, and between parents and children on the other, is that he condemns the *indifference* of the woman towards her husband or of parents towards their children, and the *coldness* of children towards their parents. Furthermore, it must be noted that when the wife is asked if she has not had 'indifference or hatred' for her husband, the juxtaposition of these two notions does not suggest a very emphatic demand for affection; and that, besides, this indifference or even this hatred were feared less for themselves than because they could 'give reason' to the husband 'to transfer his affection elsewhere'. As for the husband, affection is not demanded of him in either positive or negative terms, doubtless because his indifference was not considered liable to impel the wife to adultery.

Similarly, the indifference that parents were reproached for showing to certain of their children was associated with hatred; and they were reproached for these sentiments in so far as they aroused envy and jealousy between the children. The only question in which a lack of affection is in itself denounced is this one, addressed to children: 'Have you not shown coldness or callousness towards [your parents] because they were a burden to you?' (no. 20). Even so, the terms 'coldness' and 'callousness' appear to refer to external conduct rather than to the absence of good sentiments which it manifests.

Like the moralists of the nineteenth and twentieth centuries, Antoine Blanchard asked the members of the household to examine the sentiments that they felt for each other. Like them, he was chiefly concerned with the relations between husband and wife. In connection with these relations, he refers to twenty-five different sentiments, mentioned forty times, in 64 per cent of the questions that he asks them. He refers to only twenty-two, mentioned thirty-two times, in only 23 per cent of the questions put to parents and children, and seven, mentioned only eight times, in 26 per cent of the questions put to masters and servants. However, in contrast to the moralists of today, he was hardly concerned at all about the absence or lukewarmness of good sentiments: it was the bad ones which attracted his exclusive attention. It is true that this provides evidence, above all, about the morality of former times – and particularly that of confessors – which was a morality of sin rather than a morality of love. It also suggests, however, that the strength and the indissolubility of the ties of marriage and of consanguinity in the direct line, the burdensome authority of the head of the family, the close legal and economic dependence of those who were subject to him, and his own dependence on them as far as his honour and his ambitions were concerned were more pronounced in former society than in our own, and encouraged the crystallization of evil sentiments. The servants, however, because they were freely chosen and freely dismissed, and because they had no part – or very little – in either the honour or the patrimony of the house, were not suspected of feeling or provoking such hatreds. It is true that, besides this, the confessor worried very little about their troubles, or about those of the children. Fundamentally, he was interested in the sentiments of the members of the household only in so far as they might disturb the life of the house. It remains for us to examine to what extent the evidence of the other moralists agrees with that of Antoine Blanchard.

The attitude of the Catholic moralists: long-term changes

For comparison, let us examine Benedicti's *Somme des Péchez*, of which the first edition was published in 1584. The attention paid to the sentiments connected with domestic morality is already considerable, whether one measures this by the wealth of the vocabulary referring to the sentiments or by the frequency of allusions to them in relation to the length of the text. Measured by these standards, however, less attention was paid than in the work of Antoine Blanchard (Table 12). Above all, the vocabulary employed was manifestly different, and was apportioned very differently among the various chapters devoted to domestic relations.

From the sixteenth to the eighteenth century, the confessor seems to have paid less attention to the sentimental content of the relations of the master with his servants, and more to that of the relations of the husband with his wife, if one is to judge by the number of sentiments referred to in

Table 12. *Consideration of the sentiments in the context of domestic morality:
its evolution from Benedicti to Blanchard*

	Benedicti (1584)	Blanchard (1713)
Number of sentiments referred to	37	37
Number of allusions to sentiments	82	80
Length of text (in words)	43,610	17,840
Frequency of allusions to sentiments	19/10,000	45/10,000

the various chapters (Table 13A), or by the frequency of references to
these sentiments (Table 13B).

Table 13. *Evolution of consideration of the sentiments in different categories
of domestic relationships*

	Benedicti (1584)	Blanchard (1713)
(A) According to the number of sentiments referred to		
Masters–servants	13	8
Parents–children	23	22
Husband–wife	10	25
(B) According to the frequency of allusions to sentiments		
Masters–servants	37/12,320 = 30/10,000	8/3,240 = 25/10,000
Parents–children	34/24,500 = 14/10,000	32/9,280 = 34/10,000
Husband–wife	11/6,790 = 16/10,000	40/5,320 = 75/10,000

In the chapter on the relations between masters and servants, the
vocabulary expressing degrees of respect and contempt was much more
extensive in the work of Benedicti. Moreover, in common with all the confessors of his age, Benedicti demanded that the master should have
concern for the salvation of his servants, which Blanchard no longer
demanded. Conversely, Benedicti did not worry about the *anger* of the
master. Was it for this reason that, among the sentiments of the servant,
he notes on several occasions *fear*, which Blanchard no longer mentions?
After all, Benedicti is no more interested than Blanchard in the *sorrow*,
jealousy, *hatred* or *love* of masters and servants, but he is interested in
these sentiments in the relations between husband and wife or parents and
children. In short, although the sentimental observations are more extensive in the chapter on master–servant relations and less extensive in the
chapter on conjugal relations, this is because Benedicti devotes much
fuller consideration to respect, fear and other sentiments of the kind, and

much less to the sorrowful and aggressive sentiments about which Blanchard was so concerned.

Nevertheless, it should not be too hastily concluded that Catholic morality was uninterested in the sentiments of affection between masters and servants. Richelieu exhorts superiors and inferiors to 'live together with *love* and honour towards one another'; and among them he counts 'masters and servants' as well as fathers and children, 'the secular magistrates and those who are subject to them', 'wives and husbands' and 'guardians and wards'. In the second half of the eighteenth century, one catechism prescribed love, when addressing the servants, in a much more specific manner. 'What are the duties of servants towards their masters?' asked the *Catéchisme de Mâcon* in 1765. And the reply was: 'There are four: love, respect, fidelity and obedience', and it was further explained that 'love' in this case meant 'a sincere affection which attaches them to the interests of those whom they serve'. Similarly, the *Catéchisme de Blois* (1778), to the even more specific question 'What are the duties of domestic servants towards their Masters and Mistresses?' replied: 'They should *fear* to displease them and anger them. *Love* and *respect* them. Serve them with *affection*. Obey them promptly. Look after their property carefully, not giving it even to the poor without permission. Say nothing of what happens in the house of their masters and mistresses, complaining of their *ill-temper* and their other faults.'[71] On the other hand, although the *Catéchisme de Mâcon* mentions love when it examines, in general terms, the duties of superiors, it no longer mentions it when it records in greater detail the duties of the master towards his servants: his only duties are 'the maintenance, instruction, charitable correction, assistance, good example and wages'. There is the same absence of any mention of love among the duties which the *Catéchisme de Blois* prescribes for the master. One possible interpretation of this asymmetry is that the Christianity of that period was more concerned with attaching servants to their masters than masters to their servants. This is the least hazardous interpretation, given the present state of research, but it is not the only possible one.

With regard to the requirement of love between parents and children or husband and wife, not all the moralists were as discreet as Benedicti and Blanchard: of nine manuals for confessors written in the period between 1388 and 1713, four explicitly mention love, and sometimes also friendship and affection; and, of eighteen catechisms published between 1563 and 1815, fifteen use the noun or verb 'love' and one prescribes friendship, finding too violent the concept of love, which it nevertheless mentions once, though pejoratively.

Can one discern a development in this sphere? Of the five works written between 1388 and 1574, none refers to love, friendship or affection in connection with the Fourth Commandment. Between 1578 and 1814, how-ever, one finds only one manual for confessors – that of Blanchard – and one catechism which does not prescribe love or friendship. The develop-ment in the years following the Council of Trent is too abrupt to indicate an evolution of mental attitudes. However, one can discern other changes, which occurred later and were less abrupt, which are probably more significant.

Between 1578 and 1687, of nine catechisms enjoining children to love their parents, four make this the first of their duties, while five mention love only in second or third place; between 1688 and 1815, seven cate-chisms out of eight ordain love as the first of the child's duties. However, between 1578 and 1687, only one catechism out of nine reciprocally enjoined parents to love their children, whereas between 1688 and 1815 one finds four out of eight that do so. Finally, of the twelve catechisms of the sixteenth and seventeenth centuries only one took the trouble to explain to the child what was to be understood by the expression 'love one's parents', while all five catechisms published between 1765 and 1815 provide an explanation.

To an equal or greater extent than the increasing use of the word 'love', what appears significant is the evolution of the concept of love in this context of domestic morality. In 1688, the *Catéchisme de Bourges* clarified this by asking the question: 'Who are those who do not love their parents?' The answer is worth noting: 'Those, firstly, who hate them; secondly, who insult them; thirdly, who strike them; fourthly, who desire their death; fifthly, who do not take compassion on their ailments and do not console them; sixthly, who do not pray and have prayers said for them after their death.' At that time, love was confined to the absence of hatred and the fulfilment of one's duties towards one's parents. However, the five cate-chisms published between 1765 and 1815 explain the nature of filial love in terms that we might use today. Children must 'love their father and mother', 'having for them a heartfelt affection, giving them proof of it on the appropriate occasions', declared the *Catéchisme de Mâcon* in 1765; 'to love one's father and mother', explained the *Catéchisme de Lausanne* in 1794, 'one must have tenderness of heart towards them, and desire them and do them all the spiritual and temporal good that one can'. All the catechisms represent love as an inwardly felt tenderness or as an impulse of the heart which impels one to do all that one can – and not just what one ought – for the person one loves.

One should not, however, too hastily concede that love between children and parents is therefore an invention of the eighteenth century. Benedicti explained what this love should be, giving a description entirely external, but less derisive than that of the *Catéchisme de Bourges*.

Children who never show any sign of affection towards their fathers and mothers, never saying a kind word to them, but instead looking askance at them and speaking to them harshly, even though they do not otherwise hate them in their heart, commit a sin. And why do they sin, since they do not hate them? Because they grieve them, and also because they are obliged to show them externally, that is to say, by words and deeds, the love which they should bear them. (no.2)

Tolet makes a similar observation. Such attitudes are, however, almost exceptional at that time. Besides, Tolet himself added: 'children are obliged to have an inwardly felt love; therefore, anyone who has hatred for his father and mother, and deliberately desires for them some considerable injury, whether of the body or the soul, commits a mortal sin'. One could quote many more analogous texts. The people – or, at least, the theologians – of that time appear not to understand what we call love. They seem emotionally desiccated. They know only duty: for them to love is, essentially, not to hate.

Furthermore, it may be said – and this opens up quite different perspectives – that they distrust love. An anonymous work entitled *Exercices spirituels qui se font en l'église Saint-Etienne-du-Mont* (1667) enjoined friendship between parents and children, not love. Moreover, when the word 'love' is used by the writer, it appears in the inventory of sins that children can commit, to warn them against any excess of this sentiment: 'If owing to an immoderate love towards one's father or mother one has not worried about offending God.' Conversely, it was a commonplace of the age to compare fathers who were insufficiently strict with their children 'to monkeys that kill their little ones through hugging and cherishing them too much' (Benedicti, no. 23). Also one should perhaps not ignore the observation of Richelieu 'that the love of fathers for their children is so natural that, to oblige them to bestow it, the law which they have written in their hearts is quite sufficient, without any other'. Rather than teaching parents and children to love one another, the moralists of the end of the eighteenth century perhaps only left them free to do so, whereas those of the sixteenth and seventeenth centuries sought ways to restrain that affection, which was suspect because it was natural and profane. It is probably not fortuitous that the only important works not to ordain that parents and children should love one another are the Jansenist *Exercices* from Saint-Etienne-du-Mont and the work of Antoine Blanchard, published during the austere epoch at the end of Louis XIV's reign.

To an even greater extent than excessive love between parents and children, there was a distrust of 'natural' love between spouses. Of our eighteen catechisms, sixteen enjoined love between parents and children.

two enjoined it between masters and servants, and only one between husband and wife: this was the *Catéchisme de Blois*, published in 1778. It is true that in the seventeenth century the author of the *Exercices* of Saint-Etienne-du-Mont asks the wife 'if she has loved her husband for God's sake'. This, however, was less to enjoin her to love him than to warn her against a 'natural' and excessive love: in fact, the very next question is 'if she has consented to criminal acts with him'.

Married love according to the teaching of the Church

The theologians of that time distinguished several kinds of love, of which some were good, others bad, and still others morally neutral. The Christian should love his neighbour out of his love for God, and because God commanded him to do so. This 'Christian' love was considered to be greatly superior to 'natural' or 'human' love. Even within the latter, one distinguished 'love stemming from concupiscence', which was bad, and 'love based on affection', which was better. 'We call "love stemming from concupiscence"', explained a great theologian of the sixteenth century, 'that with which we love our neighbour principally for our own good, not for his; on the other hand, love based on affection is that with which we love him principally for his good or his pleasure.'[72] This 'love based on affection', although it was not in itself culpable, could nevertheless be dangerous. It was this that often impelled fathers to damn themselves by practising usury or other crimes in order to round off the inheritance of their children, and it was this, too, which might impel certain wives to give their husbands 'consent to criminal acts'.

Love stemming from concupiscence was supposed to impel young people to contract marriages disapproved of by their parents, and against which the royal laws claimed to defend the prerogatives of reason; it was this, too, that married couples almost inevitably encountered in the marriage bed. Since ancient times, theologians had emphatically condemned it. Saint Jerome wrote:

> He who is too ardently amorous of his wife is also an adulterer. With regard to the wife of another, in truth, all love is disgraceful; and with regard to one's own wife, excessive love is. The wise man must love his wife with judgment, not with passion. Let him curb his transports of voluptuousness and not let himself be urged precipitately to indulge in coition. Nothing is more vile than to love a wife like a mistress. . .[73]

This attitude, inspired by Stoicism and, more generally, by the wisdom of antiquity, has been constantly supported by medieval and modern theologians who, for the most part, have emphasized the first and last sentences

161

of this text. 'The man, who behaves towards his wife more as a licentious lover than as a husband, is an adulterer', asserted Benedicti, for example; and he likewise condemned 'the wife who behaves towards her husband like a mistress' and 'the husband who, carried away by excessive love, had intercourse so violently with his wife, to satisfy his voluptuous urges, that even if she were not his wife he would want to have an affair with her'.[74]

The theologians of the twentieth century continue to condemn, even within marriage, indeed especially within marriage, the pursuit of a selfish pleasure incompatible with true married love. They forbid one, during the sexual act, to consider the other partner as simply an object of pleasure, for the other partner is a person whom one must love for himself or herself. Some of them have thought themselves able to identify this selfish attitude in certain modes of coition, traditionally deemed to be 'against nature'. However, although all these moralists of former times devoted a chapter to these modes of copulation 'against nature by reason of the position adopted', and although they, too, associated these with the pursuit of a pleasure which they termed excessive, it was never in the name of love that they condemned them.[75] The *retro* position – not to be confused with sodomy – was 'against nature' because, being characteristic of the coupling of animals, it degraded man to the level of the beasts. The *mulier super virum* position was condemned, because it was contrary to the nature of woman – which is passive, as Aristotle had demonstrated – and to the nature of man, which is active. 'Who can fail to see', they asked, 'that in this position the woman acts and the man submits?' Many of them even thought that Sodom and Gomorrah had been destroyed because their inhabitants had thus reversed the 'natural' order of the relationship between the man and the woman. Other positions 'against nature' were so described for less understandable reasons; but all were suspected of being adopted in order to obtain an 'excessive pleasure' and of being unfavourable to procreation. Coition was only truly 'natural' and 'conjugal' when the woman lay on her back, with the man on top of her, because, they asserted, this position was the most favourable to procreation, and, probably above all, because it symbolized masculine domination and the fertilizing gesture of the tiller of the soil.

Although they denounce the pursuit of selfish pleasure, the twentieth-century theologians, rejecting the ideas passed down from the moralists of antiquity, no longer concern themselves with the notions of excess and moderation in this sphere. Moreover, although married love, as they define it, must necessarily embrace 'love based on affection', it appears that there also enters into it legitimately 'love stemming from concupiscence'. Anyway, they recognize in it an entirely legitimate dimension of sexual desire. They make the sexual union of the married couple the character-

162

istic manifestation of married love and condemn, more or less as if they were sacrilegious, acts of coition which are not inspired by love.[76] In contrast to this, the theologians of former times not only did not demand that the sexual union of the married couple should be a manifestation of love, but they considered it legitimate only when it took place from motives other than love, and held it to be culpable when it was the expression of what we term love, in which, being still hidebound by concepts inherited from antiquity, they insisted on seeing only the pursuit of pleasure. Moreover, the most liberal-minded among them undertook to legitimize this pursuit of pleasure: this was true of Thomas Sanchez who, at the beginning of the seventeenth century, considered as sinful only those acts of coition in which married couples indulged 'for pleasure alone', that is to say, excluding not only in intention but physically the possibility of procreation.

Taking literally, and in a judicial sense, the words of Saint Paul to the Corinthians 'The wife hath not power of her own body, but the husband: and likewise also the husband hath not the power of his own body, but the wife' (I Cor. 7.4), the theologians envisaged conjugal intercourse not as an act of love but as the fulfilment of a duty ordained by God and by men. In this matter they admitted the perfect equality of the man and the woman, and either of them could 'demand the conjugal debt' (*debitum conjugale*) and oblige the other to 'pay' it. From the thirteenth century onwards, they even tended to grant a privileged status to the woman, whom the 'natural' timidity of her sex prevented from demanding payment of the debt with as much effrontery and determination as her husband, and imposed on him a duty to understand her hints, her gestures or mere attitudes of her body or her face as indicative of her desire. Whatever the manner in which the payment of the debt was demanded, there were always, in their view, a debtor and a creditor, and it was this pedestrian image of the couple and of coition that was taught to the faithful, essentially in the confessional.

Each of the spouses owed his or her body to the other on condition that it was for a 'conjugal' use, and not 'against nature'; hence the importance of the debates concerning what was or was not against nature; the debtor could not claim exemption on such trivial grounds as his or her psychological or physical indisposition, and had no right to know why the spouse demanded it. The latter, however, had accounts to render to God. The moralists of antiquity and of the Middle Ages considered his demand fully legitimate only if he made it with the intention of procreation. Any other motive was culpable. In the last centuries of the Middle Ages, however, it was admitted that he might sin only venially or even not sin at all if he demanded it to escape from an impure temptation, for example the temptation to possess another woman – on condition that when possessing his wife from this motive he did not imagine himself to be possessing the other woman, which would constitute adultery – for marriage had been given to man, in Saint Paul's words, 'as a remedy for fornication'. Although they never explicitly formulated this paradox, theologians less liberal-minded than Sanchez seem, therefore, to have been suggesting that it was more sinful to make love to one's wife on account of the desire that one had for her than on account of the love that one had for another woman.

The traditional attitude of the laity in France

This image of marital relationships was not, perhaps, that of the common run of the faithful, but it certainly permeated the mental attitudes of the pious and also circulated in other, entirely different, sectors. One may read once again, for example, what Montaigne wrote about conjugal relationships.

> These shameless caresses which our first excitement suggests to us in this game [of love] are not only indecent but also injurious when indulged in with our wives. *Let them learn shamelessness, at least, from another hand.* They are always aroused enough for our needs. I have used only natural and simple instruction. Marriage is a religious and devout tie: that is why the pleasure that one derives from it should be a pleasure circumspect, serious and mingled with a certain severity; it should be a voluptuousness in some ways prudent and conscientious. And, since its principal end is procreation, there are some who cast doubts as to whether, when we are without the hope of that fruit – as when the women are beyond child-bearing age, or pregnant – it is permissible to seek their embraces.[77]

Going further, he uttered a warning against an excess of conjugal affection.

> The affection which we have for our wives is quite legitimate: nevertheless, theology does not neglect to curb and restrain it. I think I have read in the past in the works of Saint Thomas, in a passage in which he condemns marriages between kinsfolk within the prohibited degrees, this reason among others: that there is a danger that the affection that one has for such a woman may be immoderate; for if marital affection exists there entire and perfect, as it should do, and one overburdens this further with the affection that one owes to one's kinsfolk, there is no doubt that this addition will transport such a husband beyond the bounds of reason.[78]

This passage supports the idea recently expressed by an ethnologist, that all societies – with the exception of our own, in which the intermediary structures have disappeared, leaving the State and the conjugal nucleus face to face – have distrusted the excessive love of married couples for

one another because it risks making them forget their other social obligations.[79]

It is true that the evidence of Montaigne is vitiated by the fact that he
was an adherent of those Stoics from whom the Church had adopted its
doctrine of marriage. Let us examine, therefore, the observations of
Brantôme, who was not a follower of the Stoics; nor can he be suspected
of being excessively pious.

> We find in our Holy Scriptures that there is no need for the
> husband and wife to love each other so fervently: this is understood
> to refer to lascivious and dissolute loves; more especially as, com-
> mitting and entirely occupying their hearts with these lewd
> pleasures, [they] think of them so much and give themselves up to
> them so excessively that they forsake the love that they owe to God;
> thus, I myself have seen many women who love their husbands so
> very much, and their husbands love them, and they burn with such
> ardour, that wives and husbands entirely forget the service of God;
> for the time that they should have devoted to it [they] employed
> and consumed in their debaucheries.[80]

The reference to those married couples who burned with love for one
another reminds us that morality and practice do not always coincide, but
it is vague, debatable and, in any case, less interesting than the evidence
provided by this passage of the mentality of the author. This 'good companion', with a taste for risqué stories, had an attitude towards conjugal
relations analogous to that of Montaigne and the theologians. In his view,
to love one's husband too much meant to 'be dissolute', and a woman who
found too much pleasure with her husband would seek it with other men.

Certain bridal customs – if one is to believe those who described them in
the early nineteenth century – suggest that similar mental attitudes existed
among the common people. One example was that which, around 1830,
still prevailed among the peasants of the Côtes-du-Nord:

> Before letting the bride depart, the girls surround her, to snatch
> from her the bridal wreath, and thereupon the bride redoubles her
> tears; she escapes with her companions, and the bridegroom runs
> after her with his groomsmen. There ensues a struggle which gives
> the impression of being in earnest. The efforts to take the bride
> forcibly to the conjugal home often result in her clothes being torn,
> which for her is a mark of honour, for the more resistance a girl
> offers on this occasion the more virtuous she is considered in the
> canton, and the more her husband thinks himself entitled to count
> on her fidelity.[81]

Denounced by the moralists as a motive for the sexual union of the spouses, love was even more openly condemned – at least during the period with which we are concerned in this study – as a motive for marriage. Peter Lombard, who established for a long time the Catholic doctrine of marriage, conceded that the spouses gave themselves the sacrament of marriage by the exchange of 'words spoken in person, even if it is love that has led to this'. However, drawing up an inventory of the reasons which might impel people to marry, he classed as among the least honourable – *minus honnestis* – 'the good looks of the man or of the woman, which often urge hearts afire with love to pursue the possibility of satisfying their desire'. Love of this kind was madness, and most of the ecclesiastical writers of the sixteenth and seventeenth centuries agreed on this with the defenders of the royal edicts. The married love which the Church commanded spouses to have for one another was a Christian love, quite different from this: it was founded not on the vain appearance of the body, nor even on mysterious affinities between souls – such as that which linked, for example, Saint François de Sales and Saint Jane Frances de Chantal, these being modes of affection that he permitted his women penitents to have for men other than their husbands – but on the love of God and the grace which He had bestowed on the couple by the sacrament of marriage. It was, perhaps, because it believed in the strength of the sacrament of matrimony to assist the couple in their life together, that the Catholic Church was able to be so categorically opposed to marriages of love.

The ethics and practice of married love in England

It was different in the case of the English Puritans: 'unlesse there be a ioyning of harts, and knitting of affections together, it is not Mariage indeed, but in shew & name', wrote Henrie Smith, as early as the second half of the sixteenth century.[82] The love of which these Puritans spoke resembled, in many respects, that which Catholic couples should have for one another: it consisted of desiring the true good of the other person, which implied for the husband not only providently ensuring the material well-being of his wife, honouring her in every way, not humiliating her or exasperating her by his idleness, his prodigality, his keeping bad company or feeling an unjustified jealousy, but also reproving her with patience and gentleness when she committed a fault, instilling good manners into her and educating her as a co-heiress of the Kingdom of God.

Nevertheless, the Puritans were already more insistent than the Catholics on married love as a duty. 'For the first', wrote William Whately, 'a man must love his wife above all the creatures in the world besides. . .no neighbour, no kinsman, no friend, no parent, no child should be so near and dear.'[83] Also, more than being a duty, love is a grace that permits, and alone permits, the fulfilment of conjugal obligations. In the view of Robert

Pricke, this 'is not only the fountain and cause, but also the director and life of all duties. For where it is wanting, either no duties will be performed, or untowardly and from the teeth outward, or not continually.' And Robert Bolton added: 'Without this mutual complacency, that I may so speak, and loving contentment in each other, I doubt whether I should encourage any to proceed.' This 'lovingness which is drawing into action' is also 'a sweet, loving and tender-hearted pouring out of their hearts, with much affectionate dearness, into each other bosom; in all passages, carriages and behaviour, one towards another'.[84]

There is also, however, an honourable sexual dimension in this love. One does not have to repudiate it and purge oneself of it, as Catholic morality of former times proposed; on the contrary, the sexual instinct exists, according to a recent analyst of Puritan thought, to bring the man and the woman together and to permit them, in marriage, to express, sustain and fortify their love. This already foreshadowed present-day Catholic teaching.

This love of the married couple for one another comes from God and cannot be made to exist by human fiat. 'As Faith', wrote Thomas Gataker, 'so love cannot be constrained.' And he went on to explain: 'The Woman that thou wouldest be suitor to is God's Daughter...It is God who disposes of her heart...Parents who have the power to grant her in marriage cannot command affections, but God is able to incline them.' He inclines them, the Catholics might have said, by the grace of the sacrament of marriage. The Puritans, however, did not believe that marriage was a sacrament, but they did believe in predestination: it was, therefore, from all eternity that God inclined the future spouses to that love, in order to lead them to marriage. Love is mysterious, observes Daniel Rogers; the pagans attribute it to the stars, but it is God who has made it particularly strong between certain men and certain women for the purpose of marriage.[85] It was in this respect that the Puritan teaching differed most markedly from the earlier Catholic doctrine of marriage, and it is in this respect, above all, that it seems to constitute the origin of our present-day 'marriage of love'.

More insistent than the Catholics on the consent of the parents, and scandalized that the Council of Trent had not considered this necessary for the validity of marriage, the Puritan moralists were, at the same time, more respectful of the feelings of young people. This was true of the Anglicans as well as of the Puritans. One can observe, for example, the Bishop of Norwich, Joseph Hall, in the first half of the seventeenth century, berating with a vehemence that one never finds in contemporary Catholic writings parents who did not take account of the inclinations of their children:

which also seems to be intimated by the Apostle in that he supposes and gives a power to the parent either to give or keep his virgin; and how apt parents are to make use of this awful authority in matching their children for their own worldly advantage, contrary to their affections and disposition, we have too lamentable experience every day...but especially if the affections of the young couple have been before (as it oft falls out) placed elsewhere; what secret heart burnings; what loathing of conjugal society; what adulterous plottings do straight follow; what unkind defiances pass between them? How do they wear out their days in a melancholic pining, and wish each other and themselves dead too soon? Yea, herein an imperious or covetous parent may be most injurious to himself...[86]

This text does not conceal the tendency of English parents to marry their children out of considerations of material interest, which were, perhaps, more sordid than in France, because, in the England of that time, money seems to have had more importance and birth less. This was especially true in the eighteenth century, when social gatherings became veritable markets for dowries and husbands, and marriages were arranged through small advertisements which indicated the girl's dowry.[87] Until the end of the nineteenth century a host of English writers, both moralists and novelists, denounced these mercenary marriages. However, their indignation, which made itself heard from the late sixteenth century onwards, is probably a historical phenomenon more worthy of attention than the sad stories that they recount. One realizes this when one observes that French writers of the same period were, instead, indignant at the folly of sons of good family marrying for love girls of inferior standing.

When a French aristocrat stayed in England in the late eighteenth century, what impressed him was the good understanding that existed between English couples, and the freedom that fathers allowed their daughters to express their inclinations, even in high society. 'Husband and wife are always together, they belong to the same society', wrote François de la Rochefoucauld in 1784.

It is extremely rare to see one of them without the other. The richest people have only four or six carriage-horses; they have no need for more, because they do all their visiting together. It would be more ridiculous in England to do otherwise than it would be in Paris to go around always with one's wife. They give the impression of the most perfect harmony...

I do not know if the custom of marrying late is a consequence of the obligation to live always with one's wife; I would be inclined to think so. To have a wife who displeases you must, in England, make your life most unhappy. One therefore seeks, rather, to know her before marrying her; she feels the same, and I think it is for this reason that it is unusual to marry before the age of twenty-five or twenty-eight. This also, perhaps, results from the fact that it is the custom to set up house as soon as one is married. One never remains in the house of one's parents, and one must be judicious enough not to indulge in follies, as regards either expenditure or conduct. I consider this custom of marrying late to be much better; it is more in accord with nature.

Also, it is much easier for people to know each other before marriage, for young people are in the world of society from their infancy; they always accompany their parents. Young unmarried girls form part of the company, and talk and amuse themselves with as much freedom as if they were married. Three-quarters of marriages are based on mutual attachment, and one sees by experience that most of them are entirely successful.[88]

It is true that among the popular sectors one found examples of a barbarity that scandalized other nations. The Viscount of Vaudreuil, at the beginning of the nineteenth century, made a fleeting allusion – as though referring to something quite familiar to the French – to those English husbands who led their wives to the fair 'to sell them there with a halter round their necks' like cattle. This is apparently not an anglophobe myth, since one can read in a note to Blackstone's celebrated commentary on the laws of England:

It is surprising that there are no prosecutions initiated against those who sell their wives publicly and against those who buy them. Such a practice is in itself a disgrace, a scandal, and it encourages other criminal and perverse acts. It is sufficiently common today for it to be a salutary example to punish by exposure in the pillory those convicted of this offence.[89]

The philosophy of the Enlightenment and the right to love

Leaving girls free to meet young men seemed to the French less barbarous, but to them it had rustic connotations: 'In Lower Brittany, as in England, girls enjoy great freedom', wrote one observer around 1830. 'They run around day and night with young men, without there having resulted for a long time any noticeable licentiousness.'[90] The notion that anglo-mania had made fashionable among the French élites in the eighteenth century was married love. One finds, it is true, only six mentions of it, among the 31,716 titles registered by the Booksellers' Administration between 1723 and 1789. It is, however, significant that of these six titles, five were published after 1770, and that the first of these five, published in 1772, was *Sophie ou l'amour conjugal, drame en cinq actes imités de l'anglois.*[91]

In order to make as close as possible a comparison with the ecclesiastical documents which we have analysed earlier, let us examine, as an example of the 'Enlightened' attitude towards love, the evidence of the 'philosophical' and anonymous *Catéchisme de la morale. . .à l'usage de la jeunesse*, published in Brussels in 1785. The whole of the first chapter is devoted to love. 'The term Love signifies, in general, all affection that has its source in nature; and which leads, despite itself, so to speak, towards the loved object.' This is a far cry from the cold definition given in the *Catéchisme de Bourges* in 1688. However, the distrust inculcated for centuries persisted:

> We will say nothing here about the attraction which nature gives one sex for the other; a sweet and terrible sentiment, and one may wonder whether the Supreme Being imparted it to man in His goodness or in His wrath; it makes for the happiness of all beings and the misfortunes of man. . .and, if it sometimes softens fierce souls, it even more certainly degrades weak ones; it is the most seductive pleasure of all, but nature herself which presents it to us seems to have wanted to keep us away from it, by the perils with which it has surrounded it, and the wise man renounces it in order to avoid the innumerable ills that it brings in its train.

When speaking of married love, the author no longer portrays it as a terrible passion, but as a duty,

> that which possesses from the first, and which ought to maintain, the most absolute dominion over the heart. The sacred knot of marriage imposes on both the spouses a solemn duty to love one another. What a Hell is the life of a disunited couple! To live happily under the yoke of Hymen, do not commit yourself to it unless you are loved. Make firm that love by founding it on virtue. If it has had no other object than beauty, graces and youth. . .it would soon pass away with them, but if it is attached to qualities of the heart and the mind, it will stand the test of time.

Couched in 'eighteenth-century' language, this is a morality still influenced by Christianity, but by a Christianity more Puritan than Catholic.

The continuation breaks more deliberately with the principles of traditional morality.

> Ignoble interest has proscribed love within marriage, and has relegated it to novels, to such an extent that if one really feels love, one must at least, for fear of scandal, treat one's wife in public only with frigid politeness, under pain of incurring the disapproval and the gibes of polite society. Those sacred terms 'husband' and 'wife'

are banished by etiquette and relegated, along with tenderness and duties, to the lower orders. Nevertheless, a marriage contracted without tenderness is a sort of abduction; the person only belongs, following a natural instinct, to him or her who possesses the heart. One should receive the gifts of Hymen only from the hands of Love: to acquire them in other ways is, strictly speaking, to usurp them. Sacred knot, you are the prey of brute force and of interest; just like gold and sceptres!

There is, in the sentimentalism of the late eighteenth century, a shameless-ness that sometimes shocks our modern sensibilities. Bernardin de Saint-Pierre, Greuze and even Rousseau provoke among many of us a certain repugnance. However, to give way to this feeling, to class their shameless-ness as nothing more than a superficiality of sentiment, would be to refuse to perceive, and to comprehend, a great historical transformation. Their shamelessness is a form of aggressiveness. It was battling against a traditional order of things that was no longer acceptable and with which we have not renewed our connections, however much admiration we may profess for the civilization of seventeenth-century Europe. Love had existed for centuries. Among the social élites, and particularly, perhaps, for the women, it constituted an essential value, one of the principal motives for living. However, one could only speak about it in profane literature – since the twelfth century, this had been almost exclusively devoted to the topic – and one could only live it outside marriage or at the risk of upsetting the social order. Yet illicit love-affairs had been severely harassed both by the public authorities and by the Church. After the twelfth century the latter slightly liberalized its doctrine of marriage – and the same could be said of the Protestants – but only to put an end to adultery, concubinage and prostitution. More or less convinced of the immorality of this type of love, the élites of society, in the second half of the eighteenth century, refused to repress any longer their feelings and their desires. They claimed the right to satisfy them openly, legiti-mately, within marriage. This was a first revolt against the traditional morality, before that of the twentieth century, which is beginning to cast doubts on the virtues of the marriage of love and to wonder whether it is not a new form – the Puritan form – of repression.

Behind the overt gestures of defiance, the underlying developments were slow and unobserved. The series of catechisms and of manuals for con-fessors have indicated some of these. Others can be revealed by an ex-amination of the legal proceedings involved in the breaking-off of engage-ments. In 1527 a certain Gabriel Songis complained to the officiality of Troyes that his fiancée refused to celebrate their wedding. The girl, an orphan, retorted that she had been forced into this 'so-called marriage' by her guardians, and that she was unable to contract a valid marriage, being only 'ten or twelve years old'. The plaintiffs contested this defence by alleging that she was thirteen or fourteen. In a judgment delivered on 18 January 1528, the accused girl was 'adjudged to Gabriel Songis as his future wife' and condemned to pay costs.[92]

To break a promise of marriage, at that time, one had to have more serious grounds. In the second half of the seventeenth century, this was no longer the case. In 1665 Jeanne Pluot declared that she had never intended to fulfil the promises made to a certain Lasnier 'against her will and out of the respect that she bore to her father and mother who had browbeaten her'; that she 'has never loved and still does not love the said Lasnier, and would choose death rather than marry him'. The court released her from her promises.

Others obtained the same liberation without adopting this tragic tone: in 1666, Elizabeth Bernard said simply that she 'has never had, any more than at present, any affection for the said Grosos', her fiancé. Odart Courtois, a painter and glazier who had become engaged to a comparatively rich widow at the instigation of his parents, said that he had not been given 'time to know her' and that, now that he did know her, he did not have 'any affection' for her; in 1673 Nicole Mussot wished to break off the engagement because her fiancé 'has not fulfilled the duties that a fiancé owes to his fiancée, which has chilled the affection that she had for him'. In short, all those who refused to get married despite their promises won their cases.[93] It is true that between the beginning of the sixteenth century and the middle of the seventeenth, there was an essential change of attitude of the Church, not towards love but towards the sacredness of 'promises for the future'. Whatever the reason, however, the effect is evident: young men and girls could now be freed from their promises of marriage, giving as the sole reason the fact that they do not love or no longer love their proposed future spouse.

Both a progressive development, and a failure to complete the process, can be observed. In 1785, the author of the *Catéchisme de Bruxelles* still does not carry his discussion of the marriage of love to its logical conclusion. 'It is, nevertheless, just', he writes,

> that a child who is not capable of discernment should not be free to bind himself, without the authority of his parents, by an indissoluble knot. This would be, on the part of the latter, an act of outrageous inhumanity, to abandon him to thoughtlessness and temerity, which are only too common at his age; when it is a question of deciding, by a marriage, the happiness or misfortune of his life. His natural guardians may, without his being able to complain about it, prevent his committing himself, or defer his commit-

ment, if they consider it unworthy of him or precipitate. Of course, they should consent to it when the match appears *eligible*.

Whereas in the preceding passage the author based marriage on love and love on virtue, it is no longer to the absence of virtue that the word 'eligible' refers: it is to disparity of social standing. Fundamentally, the author has contented himself with clothing in a fresh argument – based on the notion of the immaturity of young people, and the pursuit of their personal happiness – the traditional position defended by Houard, which visualized love as an act of folly that vitiates consent. In the view of this 'Enlightened' author, as in that of the Catholic or Puritan moralists, marriages should unite individuals of the same social standing, with the agreement of their parents. The Enlightened élites of the eighteenth century dreamed of instituting the love-match, but they were incapable of doing this as long as their social power remained based on a material patrimony. The love-match was to cease to be a fantasy, in that social milieu, only when the essence of inherited capital became cultural – that is, in the twentieth century. The new aspirations were expressed for a long time before economic changes made possible their realization. However, the revolution of the conjugal system did not take place until after that of the economic system, for only then could the marriage founded on love be instituted without challenging the hierarchical structures of society.

4. *Reproduction and sexual life*

1. THE FAMILY AND REPRODUCTION IN CHRISTIAN THOUGHT

It is surprising that the constitutive cell of our societies should be the conjugal family. There are a great many other possibilities, as anthropologists testify, and there have been, in fact, in France itself, all sorts of other types of household, as we have observed. However, when the French or English moralists referred to the family, they recognized only one type: the conjugal family with domestic servants. All the other elements were regarded as accessory and contingent. It was the result of chance that, in a given family, there might not be servants or children; there might no longer be a father or mother; or the man or wife might not be the father or mother of all the children. However, like the historians of the Cambridge group, the theologians visualized, in such households, a conjugal family with certain elements added or subtracted. Similarly, they seem to have considered that to extend the family to various kinsfolk or even other couples did not alter its fundamental essence. It was the conjugal family that God had instituted, and the theologians succeeded in identifying it in all societies. They saw it as a 'natural' institution. Nevertheless, 'it is not a thing that men could stumble on by chance', observed the Puritans Dod and Cleaver, 'but the wisdom that we speak of is not natural, but fetched from the fountain of all wisdom, God himself, who by his Word giveth unto us pure light to walk by. . .even within the secret of our own walls.'[1]

If the ties of marriage and of consanguinity in direct line are the basis of the institution of the family, the reason is that its essential function is reproduction. In the case of a man, the Catholics envisaged in this world only two states in which he could normally attain salvation: the married state and the clerical state. Access to the former was by the sacrament of Holy Matrimony, and to the latter by that of Holy Orders. The first had as its function the reproduction of the species, its biological multiplication, while the second had as its function the multiplication of Christians by preaching and religious instruction.

This apportionment of roles, on which the Fathers of the Church had

174

insisted, does not explain, however, why in addition to procreation the couple was entrusted with the maintenance and education of their children – these two things were so closely connected that, in former times, to 'nourish' also meant to 'educate'. Saint Augustine distinguished three properties in marriage – *proles*, *fides* and *sacramentum* – that is to say, progeny, fidelity and indissolubility. However, he emphasized, even at this early date, that *proles* implied not only procreation but also the material responsibility for the children and their education. Saint Thomas observed that, among certain species of animals, the female was incapable of bringing up the young by herself. 'Especially, however, in the human species, the male is required for the offspring's education, which is expected not only as to nourishment of the body but more as to nourishment of the soul.'[2] This task of 'nourishing' the children appeared so essential to the married state, that he referred to it to explain the prohibition of all sexual activity outside marriage. If one accepts the premise that sexuality has been given by God only for the purpose of procreation, and that it is always a grave sin to use it for pleasure alone, why cannot any man procreate with any woman? The answer to this is that only the married couple is capable of bringing up and suitably educating the children whom they bring into the world. In saying this, Saint Thomas was doubtless thinking not only of the supernatural graces that marriage bestows, but also of the stability of the conjugal tie, the social prestige of the legitimate family and its economic potential. Only marriage creates the ties of kinship that will permit the child to become integrated into society, whereas children born of fornication, adultery or concubinage are mere bastards, without kinsfolk, spurned by all. Moreover, the legitimate family is an association possessing the economic means of feeding and educating the children, and capable of apportioning the individual roles involved in this task. Finally, and above all, this association is stable by virtue of 'fidelity' and the 'sacrament'.

Should one attribute to Christianity the association of the procreative and the educative function, or did Christianity find it in the societies in which it originated? In Jewish, Greek and Roman society, it appears that the association derived from the ownership by the father of those whom he procreated. It was this ownership that made it possible for the God of the Old Testament to avenge on the son the wrongs committed by the father. In Greece, the city undertook the maintenance and education of children only in so far as it claimed a right of ownership over them. For example, if the Spartan State took charge of the children from the age of seven, this was because it claimed absolute power over them: it manifested this from the moment of their birth, by exercising its sovereign judgment as to whether they were to live or to be hurled into the ravine of Taygetus.

The other cities allowed the father more power over his offspring, but nevertheless supervised the education of young people in their capacity as future citizens.

Christianity seems to have brought about the disappearance of the powers of the State over the child, and thereby increased the responsibilities of the parents as regards their maintenance and their education. These responsibilities were, at the same time, shared between the father and the mother. In the eleventh century, for example, Burchard of Worms asked the mother: 'Hast thou put thy child near a fire, and another person has come and upset over the fire a cauldron of boiling water, so that thy child has been scalded to death? *Thou who shouldst watch carefully over thy child for seven years*, thou shalt fast for three years. . .'³ And at the end of the sixteenth century, Benedicti wrote: 'Mothers who do not take good care to nourish their children, or at least provide them with good nurses, until the age of three – after which the fathers are obliged by natural law to further their interests and give them what is necessary – commit a sin.'⁴ One can detect here an increase in the legal responsibilities of the woman.

However, for the man as for the woman, this responsibility had become a servitude rather than a right. According to Christian doctrine, in fact, the true father of children was God: 'Call no man your father upon the earth: for one is your Father, which is in heaven.'⁵ It is no longer because they are the owners of their children that the parents are responsible for their feeding and education; it is because God has ordained it. And the more the writers insist on the fatherhood of God, the more they also insist on the duty of parents to care for their children and to educate them.

'Christian fathers, if God is the foremost father of your children, you are only, strictly speaking, foster-parents and guardians; this office concerns their education, and this is what God demands of your care', Dorléans reminded them.

> The diligence that they are obliged to apply to the education of their children should not be a half-hearted concern, because it should be not only that which nature compels them to have, not only what is demanded by the good qualities of their children, but what is demanded by the respect which they are obliged to have for God Himself, Who has entrusted these children to their charge. . .If parents considered their children as trusts which God has placed in their hands. . .not only would they not abandon them, not only would they not have for some of them a predilection so detrimental to the others, but they would not even entrust the responsibility for their education so completely to other people that they did not retain for themselves the principal control of it.⁶

In order to convince people of the necessary association of the functions of biological reproduction and of education, the Fathers of the Church had conceived images which were still being used by the preachers of the seventeenth and eighteenth centuries.

> Saint Ambrose says that men are born more or less like bears, brutish, unformed and imperfect; and that, just as the bears succeed in giving their young the shape that they should have by polishing them with their tongues, so fathers and mothers should, so to speak, perfect the formation of their children, whom nature has only rough-hewed in the maternal womb, by their words and their precepts. For, just as it is in the tongue of the she-bear, or rather in her heart and her affections, that nature has placed that quality appropriate to perfecting the formation of the young, and another animal would not succeed in doing so; so it is in the tongue, or rather in the heart of a father and a mother that nature has deposited the virtue capable of perfecting their children. If they do not pay due attention to this, then the diligence of the most capable stranger is unsuccesful. . ., but even if others could be successful, would it be a fitting response to the honour that God has bestowed on them, confiding these children to their care, to rely upon some-body else?[7]

Even though there is a great deal of rhetoric in a sermon of this kind, it may be supposed that, even if only out of a rhetorical preoccupation, its arguments would make an impact on those who heard them: parents might love their children and take care of them out of a 'natural inclina-tion', or for the honour of their house; but then they would be good parents only to certain of their children. For them to be good parents to all of them, it was necessary to remind them that these children were sent by God.

> If parents considered their children as trusts which God places in their hands. . .one would not see. . .those excessive inequalities which are usually, within families, such disastrous seeds of discord, and which often cause fathers vexations which are all the more bitter because it usually happens that those of their children in favour of whom they have neglected all the others are those who, by a redoubtable but just judgment of God, give them least satis-faction. Thus, the father and mother should not devote all their care to the education of the eldest son, because he has a better appearance than the others or because he is better fitted for the world, to the neglect of the others. . .[8]

Their duties towards their children were derived not from their paternity but from their duty to God.

177

Other preachers, it is true, did in fact employ arguments more consistent with our attitudes towards these matters.

> It is a principle generally admitted by philosophers and theologians that what gives being gives at the same time the consequences of being; this principle is so firmly established that Saint Thomas, who acknowledges that God owes nothing to His creature, nevertheless asserts that, having once created it, it is up to Him to preserve it. . . likewise, since fathers and mothers have brought their children into the world, they are obliged, by a parallel principle of justice, to give them a good upbringing.[9]

However, this line of argument was exceptional, and never displaced the preceding one; it was presented in philosophical terms – that is to say, beyond the reach of ordinary minds – and was, therefore, probably not attuned to the mentality of the mass of the faithful in the mid seventeenth century.

Furthermore, to insist on the responsibility that parents assumed in procreating their children might have diverted their attention from their conjugal duties, which were essential from the point of view which interested the Church, that is, chastity. The Church, therefore, tried to allay the anxieties of those of the faithful who might be afraid of being unable to feed and suitably educate the children that they brought into the world. 'The upright man should never be afraid of having too many children', wrote Benedicti,

> on the contrary, he should think of them as a blessing from God and believe what David says: 'I have', he says, 'been young, and now am old; yet have I not seen the righteous forsaken, nor his seed begging bread', *for since God has given them, He will give him in consequence the means of feeding them,* for it is He Who feeds the birds of the Heavens; otherwise He would not have given them to him.[10]

Exhortations of this nature continued to be made until the end of the eighteenth century, and again in 1930 in the encyclical *Casti connubii*.

In Benedicti's formulation, it is worth noting the expressions 'the upright man' and 'the righteous man'. On the one hand, these imply the conviction, inherited from the Old Testament and the mentality of the early Middle Ages, that God makes children live or die in accordance with the merits of their parents; on the other hand, they might also be derived from the Augustinian doctrine of the elect and the damned. Whether or not this is the case, the apparent optimism of Benedicti was not valid for all men, which saved him from being too brutally belied by the experience that his readers might have had of the infant mortality of the age, and of the need for many poor people to abandon their children because they lacked the means to feed them. It was valid only for the righteous man, the upright man; not everybody does possess these attributes, but everybody *can* possess them, according to the Catholic doctrine of free will.

This exclusive interest of the Church of former times in individual problems, and its deep-seated indifference to social problems, becomes evident when one reflects, from a sociological point of view, on the coherence of its doctrine concerning reproduction. The Church has never obliged Christian societies to redistribute land periodically, in order to adapt resources to the needs of each family, as was done, for example, by the ancient Scandinavians or the Incas. It was fully conscious of the inequality of resources – inadequately palliated by individual charity – but, despite this, it never accepted the measures enabling people to adapt their needs to this inequality: neither the sterile fornications of the poor, nor the polygamy of the rich, after the manner of the Hebrews or the Muslims; nor prohibiting the marriage of the poor, a measure by which the Bavarian State, in the nineteenth century, tried to limit the increase of the abandonment of children; nor the right of married couples to limit their offspring by infanticide at birth, abortion or contraception, a right which the Greeks and Romans generally granted to fathers of families. In the Christian system, the adaptation of demography to inegalitarian social structures could logically only take place through the death at an early age of poor children and the swift enslavement of the survivors to the possessors of the land.

Being a gift of God, the child was taken back by God when it pleased Him, and parents should accept both events with the same piety. 'The Lord gave, and the Lord hath taken away'; such was the usual comment of devout parents when faced with the deaths of their children. Moreover, the state of biological knowledge left them as defenceless in the face of the mysteries of fertility as in the face of those of death. It is true that western society had known for millennia that procreation is a result of sexual union. However, because people did not know the details, nor even the fundamental organs of the process of generation, and because it had been observed that sexual relations were not always fertile, one could believe that conception depended immediately on the will of God. By their sexual union, the parents provided the raw material for the future child, but it was God himself who decided whether or not to make a child from this seminal material, and who, in any case, introduced the soul at a particular moment in the process of gestation. This could not be doubted by married couples who waited for years for a conception that never occurred; nor by those who, living a normal sexual life, were, to a greater extent than others, overburdened with children. God sent children to whomsoever He wished, and in such numbers as He wished, and the spouses generally did not imagine that it depended on them to increase or diminish their fertility. Most writers were even agreed in recognizing that fertility was in inverse ratio to the frequency of sexual intercourse. 'And that is why prostitutes very rarely conceive', wrote Guillaume Bouchet.[11] This transference of responsibility doubtless explains both the importance of fertility and that of infant mortality in Christian society in former times.

However, after analysing Christian ideology concerning the reproductive system, one must observe what the latter actually was between the end of the Middle Ages and the end of the eighteenth century.

2. THE SYSTEM OF BIOLOGICAL REPRODUCTION IN REAL LIFE

In practice, the Christian system was never fully enforced. Its lack of realism and its harshness were offset by the concubinage of the rich, the prolonged or definitive celibacy of the poor and its corollary, the 'dissolute' sexual life of the unmarried. It is true that although, to quote the demographer Moreau, 'debauchery does not populate', certain forms of it nevertheless led to the birth of an excessively large number of children destined to abandonment and a swift death. In addition, the system was still further aggravated by the habit of townspeople of putting their children out to nurse in the country.

From concubinage to the abandonment of children

Concubinage was, like marriage, a comparatively long-lasting union, which made it possible to bring up the children thus procreated. It is true that they were born bastards, and as such had more difficulty in integrating themselves into society than the children born of a legitimate marriage: the clerical state was barred to them; heraldry symbolically stamped their arms with a 'bar of bastardy'; sometimes they were even subject to a special tax, as for example, in Normandy. It is this practice which permits historians to ascertain their number. In the Middle Ages their numbers were high, and the resources that they obtained were fairly considerable. Moreover, medieval history is filled with their deeds, which proves that they often succeeded in playing important roles. William the Bastard, who became King of England under the name of William the Conqueror, is well-known, as is the valiant Dunois, the Bastard of Orleans and companion of Joan of Arc. This prominence of bastards in medieval history, compared with their almost total absence from ancient history, suggests that they owed their survival to Christian morality. And, in fact, the moralists of the Middle Ages declared that men had a duty to bring up and educate their bastards as much as, if not on the same level as, their legitimate children.

In contrast to marriage, which was a social institution by which families of the same standing entered into an alliance to perpetuate themselves, concubinage was a personal union, an affair of love, at least on the part of the man. It could become established at all social levels. In the Middle Ages, as in the eighteenth century, one finds examples of the very poor living in concubinage because they could not afford to get married. In the case of such people, the archives rarely show traces of their children. Other unions could not be transformed into marriages because one of the partners was already married. In the Middle Ages, concubinage was widespread among the parish clergy and other holders of ecclesiastical benefices, whose solemn vows prevented them from taking a wife legitimately, but who nevertheless had the means to support a woman and to bring up her children. Another classic case was that of the rich man, married or unmarried, living with a girl of lower social standing, whom it would have been more scandalous to marry than to keep as a concubine. Saint Augustine, even at that early date, although he repented of having thus lived in sin with an honourable girl of inferior status, never considered marrying her, even though he had a son by her.

Among the rich, in general, concubinage was a form of polygamy: this was true not only of the kings and other great lords, but also of respectable married bourgeois who, having seduced a girl of lower social standing, had by her several children, whom they often brought up in their homes along with their legitimate children. We have observed how the Sire de Gouberville lived in company with a half-brother and two half-sisters, bastard children of his father, and he felt great affection for them. He himself had only bastard daughters, whom, however, he succeeded in marrying to gentlemen of the neighbourhood. It is not known why he remained a bachelor all his life, nor if he had several concubines. Jean Bottigny, lord of Morembert, explained on his part 'that since his youth he has always followed the men acting on the king's orders and also the wars, and that having seen in those wars many gentlemen lamenting the fate of their wives and children, he has never had any desire to marry'. However, being incapable of continence,

> he has always led, since his youth, an improper and dissolute life, and has committed sins of the flesh with several women and girls, both in Vendeuvre and in Morembert, namely: in Vendeuvre a certain Jeanne Brethaigne, by whom he has had several children; then a certain Colonne, and at present another widow, named Jeanne, by whom also he has had children

181

and who 'is still living with him', as he attests.[12] The important fact, for the purposes of our analysis, is that he maintained these women and their children: concubinage was adapted to the inegalitarian structures of society, and allowed the bastards to survive.

From the sixteenth century onwards, the Church took upon itself the abolition of the practice. At the beginning of the century, the era of un-molested concubinage was already over for the parish priests: of the fifty summoned before the officiality of Troyes between 1515 and 1531 for offences against chastity, only five were living in concubinage. The rest, who were equally incapable of sublimating their sexual impulses, were all the more dangerous to the virtue of their female parishioners and the lives of the children who they had by them. At best, they gave the girls whom they had deflowered a dowry which permitted them to set up a household.[13] The concubinage of laymen, too, was already threatened: in 1529 the lord of Morembert was required, under pain of excommunication, to expel from his house the widow whom he was keeping. The court does not appear to have worried about what this measure implied for the children whom he had had by her.

Almost everywhere, those living in concubinage were denounced from the pulpit and excommunicated. In the seventeenth century, they had virtu-ally disappeared from sight: only the kings and the most powerful lords still reared their bastards in public. Louis XIV himself, before the end of the century, decided to marry secretly the last of his mistresses, Madame de Maintenon, whereas the gallant Henri IV had never dared to marry the women he loved, who were, however, of much higher social standing. As for the bourgeois and the worthy peasants who made a servant-girl pregnant, instead of bringing up her children as in former times, they drove her from the house, out of fear of scandal as much as out of avarice.

Demographic statistics confirm this change in customs. In Nantes and the neighbouring villages, in the sixteenth century, 50 per cent of illegiti-mate births were still the result of concubinage.[14] In the town of Nantes itself, this rate fell to 5.5 per cent between 1735 and 1750, and to 2.5 per cent between 1751 and 1787.[15] Moreover, in all the villages of France, it had become extremely rare for a girl to have more than one illegitimate child in the same parish: at Isbergues, in Artois, the proportion of illegiti-mate births was 2.5 per cent before 1650, but between 1598 and 1803 one finds only two unmarried mothers who had had more than one illegitimate child.[16]

This banning of concubinage partly explains why the number of illegiti-mate births decreased considerably between the sixteenth century and the middle of the seventeenth century (see Figure 4). However, for the

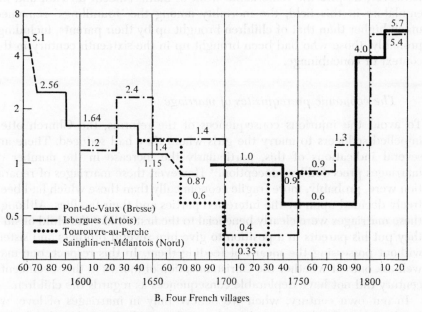

A. A sample of twenty-four English parishes

B. Four French villages

4. Trends in the rate of illegitimacy of births in the rural areas. (A) from Peter Laslett and Karla Oosterveen, 'Long term trends in bastardy', *Population Studies* (July 1973), p. 267; (B) from J.-L. Flandrin, *Les Amours paysannes* (Paris, 1975), p. 238.

children who, despite everything, were born out of wedlock, the chances of survival were much smaller than in the past. Unmarried mothers, repudiated by their seducers and often chased out of their villages, were without the means to bring up the child of sin. When they did not stifle the child in secret to preserve their honour, they generally abandoned it to public charity. We know, for example, the fate of thirty-nine unmarried mothers recorded between 1681 and 1790 in five parishes of the Vallage (Haute-Marne): twelve succeeded in getting married, only one remained in her village unmarried, and the remaining twenty-six had to leave their villages – fourteen of these abandoned their children.[17] Often, the seduced girl was driven away as soon as the pregnancy became evident, and it was in isolation, in the country or in a big town, that she gave birth to and then abandoned her child. This explains, at least partly, why in the seventeenth century and the first half of the eighteenth, the rate of illegitimate births decreased markedly in the rural areas, while it increased quite perceptibly in the towns. One can judge this by the example of Bayeux (Figure 5). This doubtless also explains the increase in the number of foundlings, occurring in an age of reformation of morals, principally in the towns where, as in Paris, their reception had been reorganized (Figure 6). However, despite the remarkable work of Saint Vincent de Paul and his emulators in this field, the mortality among the 'foundlings' remained much higher than that of children brought up by their parents, including, probably, those who had been brought up in the sixteenth century in the context of concubinage.

The economic prerequisites of marriage

To avoid the injurious consequences of the reforms, the Church often impelled seducers to marry the girls whom they had seduced. There are several indications of this, particularly the increase in the number of marriages preceded by conception.[18] However, these marriages of reparation were, probably, more fragile economically than those which had been freely decided upon by the interested parties and their families. Although these marriages were clearly beneficial to the first child – the child of sin – they put his parents in a position to give him several brothers and sisters without possessing the means of feeding them. In this respect, one may well ask oneself whether the Christianization of morals in the seventeenth century did not have deplorable consequences as regards the children.

In our own century, when we believe only in marriages of love, we laugh at, or are indignant at, 'marriages of reason' arranged by families, in which there is a tendency to see only 'marriages of money'. However, in a society in which the vast majority of families owed their subsistence to a small or large capital, which they made, or failed to make, to bear fruit by their own efforts or those of others, it was criminally thoughtless to marry without having the capital needed to maintain the future children. This

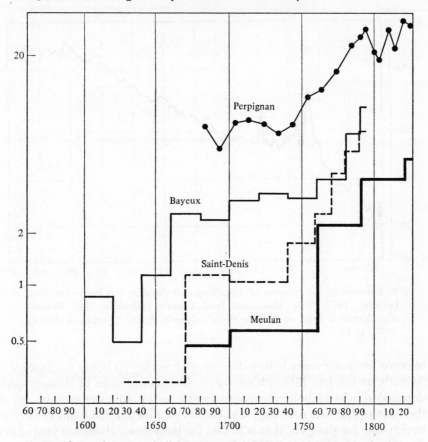

5. Trends in the rate of illegitimacy of births in some French towns. From J. Guibeaud, 'Les Naissances hors mariage à Perpignan de 1684 à 1894', *Société Agric. Sciences et Litt. des Pyrénées Orientales*, vol. XXXVI (1895), pp. 431–46; M. El Kordi, *Bayeaux aux XVII et XVIIIe siècles* (Mouton, 1969); J. Beaud and G. Bouchart, 'La Population de Saint-Denis en France', AUDIR microfiche no. 73.944.73; M. Lachiver, *La Population de Meulan du XVIIe au XIXe siècle* (Paris, 1969), p. 67.

was, apparently, realized: in regions where 'marriage in the house of the parents' was not the practice, the young men waited until they were in a position to establish the agricultural, craft or commercial business that would provide a living for their wife and children before getting married. This might oblige them to remain single, either for life – as was often the case with the younger sons in the south of France – or until an advanced age. As for the girls, they found a husband only on condition that they provided him, as their dowry, with part of this necessary initial capital: those whom their parents could not provide with a dowry were obliged

185

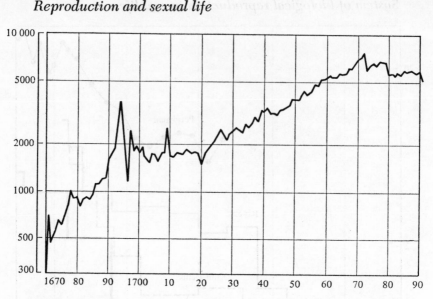

6. Increase in the number of foundlings admitted to the Paris foundling hospital, 1670–1790. Abstracted from Claude Delasselle, 'Les Enfants abandonnés à Paris au XVIIIe siècle', *Annales E.S.C.* (January–February 1975), p. 189.

to serve for many years before dreaming of setting up house on their own. As early as the late fifteenth century – in circumstances of demographic depression, when labour was consequently well paid – the average age at the time of the first marriage was twenty-five for the men and twenty or twenty-one for the girls, that is to say, for both sexes, about ten years later than the legal minimum.[19] Subsequently, this average age at first marriage appears to have increased continuously throughout France (Figure 7), no doubt partly on account of the increase in population which produced a fall in wages, but also because of the gradual conquest of the peasant 'inheritances' by the nobles and bourgeois. For the same reason, the proportion of the permanently unmarried increased in some villages where the young people did not have the habit of emigrating and which were not affected by industrialization. However, despite this, it seems that people married with more lack of foresight in the eighteenth century than in the sixteenth, judging from the increase in the number of foundlings in the course of the century (Figure 8), in proportion to the fall in the level of real wages.[20] It is, in fact, certain that a number of these children were legitimate children who had been abandoned by parents who considered themselves to be incapable of feeding them.[21]

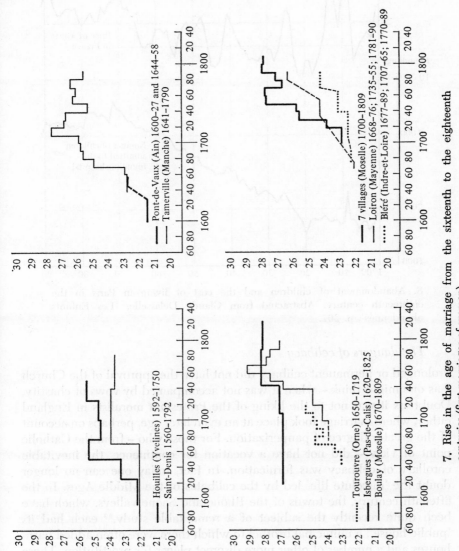

7. Rise in the age of marriage from the sixteenth to the eighteenth centuries (first marriages of women).

Pont-de-Vaux (Ain) 1600–27 and 1644–58
Tamerville (Manche) 1641–1790

7 villages (Moselle) 1700–1809
Loiron (Mayenne) 1668–76; 1735–55; 1781–90
Bléré (Indre-et-Loire) 1677–89; 1707–65; 1770–89

Houilles (Yvelines) 1592–1750
Saint-Denis 1560–1792

Tourouvre (Orne) 1650–1719
Isbergues (Pas-de-Calais) 1620–1825
Boulay (Moselle) 1670–1809

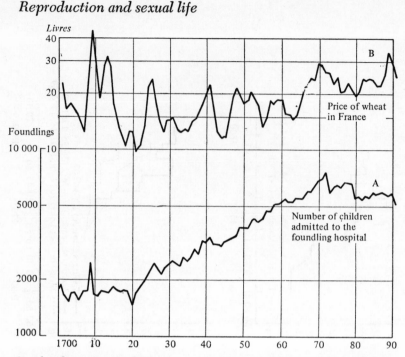

8. Abandonment of children and the cost of living in Paris in the eighteenth century. Abstracted from Claude Delasselle, 'Les Enfants abandonnés', p. 207.

The dangers of celibacy

Prolonged or permanent celibacy did not have the approval of the Church – as one might think – when it was not accompanied by vows of chastity. Doubtless it was not to the liking of the Protestant moralists in England either, where marriage took place at an even later age, perhaps on account of the greater degree of pauperization. For those who – from the Catholic point of view – did not have a vocation for continence, the inevitable corollary of celibacy was fornication. In fact, today one can no longer doubt the 'dissolute life' led by the celibates of the Middle Ages. In the fifteenth century, the towns of the Rhône and Saône valleys, which have been quite recently the subject of a remarkable study,[22] each had its 'public house', a municipal brothel to which there were often added bathhouses and a number of other more discreet places for prostitution. These establishments were frequented not only by the ill-behaved young men and the travellers, but by all the bachelors of the town, without their incurring any obloquy. Only their married clients in the towns occasionally attracted reprimands. It appears that during the same period there was also a number of prostitutes in the rural areas, as is shown, for

188

example, in the archives of the officiality of Troyes.[23] Also, in both the country and the towns, groups of bachelors often perpetrated collective rapes, under the pretext that their victims were suspected of debauchery, and probably to put them into the category of girls 'public and common to all', that is to say, girls for bachelors. It must be observed, in fact, that in all these incidents, they beat the girl, called her a 'whore' as publicly as possible and, after raping her, forced her to accept money as a symbolic gesture. There is no doubt that, to these young men leading a life of pleasure, celibacy was no great burden, and they could wait until they had the means to establish themselves before getting married. For that, they also needed to possess the means of entertaining their companions of bachelor days, under pain of undergoing the *charivari*.

From the first half of the sixteenth century, however, even before the Council of Trent, the public authorities had reacted. Still tolerating, as a lesser evil, the burlesque entertainments occurring in the haunts of youth, they began to deal severely with rape, close down brothels, round up prostitutes, flog them publicly on the charge of pimping, and drive them out of town under the threat of the direst penalties. It is true that prostitution did not disappear, and neither did rape. However, the former, like the latter, became clandestine and punishable. Since, at the same time, illegitimate births became much less frequent, the civil authorities – and, in our own day, the devotees of statistics – were able to feel satisfied with this semblance of chastity.

The Church of the time, however, was not so easily deceived. For example, the *Instructions pour les confesseurs du diocèse de Chalon-sur-Saône* asked the question: 'What are at present the most widespread habits of mortal sin?' and replied: 'In the case of young people, they are improper thoughts, and the sins of impurity',[24] that is, in the language of today, erotic reveries and solitary masturbation. Having been apprehensive about these practices since the end of the fourteenth century – although then they had been so infrequent that they could be made a 'case reserved' for submission to the bishop – confessors and educators appear to have been, in the seventeenth century, more worried about them than before. They used every possible means to stamp them out: the children of princes were watched closely even in the most private places,[25] and those of the common people were advised to confess their sin three times a week.[26] In the second half of the eighteenth century and later, it was laymen – doctors, guardians and parents – who took the matter in hand, panic-stricken by the medical lucubrations of the celebrated Doctor Tissot, whom nobody thought of doubting. This already amounted to a veritable delirium of repression, in the face of the irrepressible. Furthermore, the ecclesiastics did not scorn this support from the physicians, to

189

judge from the case of the Abbé Barruel, then tutor to the children of the Prince of Saxony, who inspired in his pupils a holy dread of the solitary act by reading to them the works of Doctor Tissot.[27]

What is important, for the purpose of our analysis, is that in these solitary pleasures the customs of the seventeenth and eighteenth centuries conflicted with the precepts of Christian morality more fundamentally than did those of the fifteenth century. Long regarded by laymen as a lesser evil – and probably also by the pastors, so long as it did not cause scandal – masturbation was, in theological terms, a 'sin against nature', that is, it was classed, along with coitus interruptus, sodomy and bestiality, among the most grave of the sexual sins. From a pastoral point of view, it was too widespread for it to be treated with as much rigour as these last two sins. However, it caused apprehension, more especially, as a sin that was liable to become a habit; when, until an advanced age, people did not know other sexual pleasures, there was a risk of their developing a fixation on this one and not wanting to get married. 'There will be found some so enslaved to the filth of this sin, as is, most often, the youth of both sexes', wrote Benedicti, 'that the men will not want to marry, nor the women to take husbands, when by this method they assuage their lewd appetites, spending their years in it even, alas, until the grave. . .'[28] Or, if they did marry, they risked remaining addicted to their sin after marriage. It is this fear that explains the intransigence of the moralists in the matter of the conjugal duty: in all circumstances, even when it entailed a serious risk to her health or that of the child, the wife was obliged to 'pay the due' to the husband who demanded it, for fear that the latter might 'pollute himself' voluntarily, or, as they say even more explicitly, might be led 'to satisfy his passion himself'.

To avoid these impurities into which a man was liable to fall on account of his sinful nature, God had given him a remedy – marriage. It was because he did not make use of it that he committed all kinds of fornications. At the beginning of the fifteenth century, when exhorting confessors to question young men and girls regarding the sins of the flesh, Gerson emphasized that 'there is hardly anyone, after they come of age, who does not commit vile and abominable sins *if they do not get married early*'; Benedicti, at the end of the sixteenth century, forbade masters to prevent their servants from marrying 'when it is time for it, and when they see that otherwise they will be in danger of indulging in debauchery'; Antoine Blanchard, in 1713, asked fathers: 'Have you not neglected to establish your children, when in a position to do so? Have you not been the cause, by this failure to establish them, of your children abandoning themselves to debauchery?' It is probable that the logic of economic development would have made marriages even later and celibacy even more widespread than they actually were, if the Church had not opposed this tendency, either directly through its exhortations to fathers and masters, and its pressure in favour of marriages of reparation, or indirectly by the abolition of medieval liberties. This would explain why an increasing number of legitimate couples were incapable of maintaining all the children that they procreated.

These exhortations are, however, less numerous than one might have expected; they are discreet, and remarkably imprecise as to the age at which young people should marry, compared with the precepts of the Councils of the early Middle Ages: 'The sons, when they reach the age of puberty, should be compelled to take a wife or to embrace ecclesiastical continence [as they please]; as for the daughters of the same age, it depends on the will of their father whether they should be dedicated to chastity or to marriage.'[29] From the sixteenth to the eighteenth centuries, no moralist any longer recommends marriage at puberty, which followed logically from Saint Paul's teaching, even though all of them were conscious of the sins against purity committed by adolescents, and it does not appear that it was favoured any longer by the English moralists, who were nonetheless even more convinced of the necessity of marriage. One may, therefore, ask oneself whether both groups were not sensitive, more than they were prepared to admit, to the need to have the means to establish oneself before getting married. Their silence regarding marriage at the age of puberty, their struggle to impose continence on young people who had no vocation for it – are those not the earliest shadows of a genuine Malthusianism before Malthus?

The fertility of households

One must also enquire as to whether the increase in the number of foundlings in the seventeenth and eighteenth centuries was not due to an increase in conjugal fertility. This idea appears inconceivable to the French demographers, who are convinced that fertility was 'natural' until the middle of the eighteenth century – with the exception of specific social groups without numerical importance – and that it was, on the contrary, in the second half of the century, when the graph of abandonments literally soars, that people began to practise contraception. They are, probably, essentially right. It is clear that one of the two important facts of French demography is the transition from the very high and apparently uncontrolled fertility which characterized the seventeenth century and the first half of the eighteenth century to a fertility increasingly lower and increasingly controlled by the couples themselves, which was characteristic of the nineteenth and twentieth centuries. It has recently been conclusively shown that this progressive fall in fertility began in the

191

second half of the eighteenth century, not only among the urban population, but also among the peasants, at least in a considerable number of villages of the Paris Basin.[30] However, since in this matter one has only ever bothered to confirm, by superabundant and often unconvincing statistics, *a priori* ideas inherited from the demographers and moralists of the eighteenth century, just as one has never enquired *whether* fertility in former times was entirely 'natural', but merely *when* it became artificial, let us try to carry this paradoxical hypothesis to its conclusion, if only to assure ourselves that it has in fact been irrefutably proved.

Recent research has brought to light an increase in the fertility of young women, after 1750, in most western countries, even in those French villages where the fertility of the older women decreased as a result of contraceptive measures. This increase might be due to a greater frequency of pre-marital relations, or to a more rapid sexual maturation, due to economic, sanitary or climatic reasons.[31] In Colyton, the only village in England where it has been possible to study the fertility of couples,[32] it increased in all age-groups in the eighteenth century, after having declined in the seventeenth (Table 14).

Table 14. *Evolution of legitimate fertility in Colyton (Devon)*

Period	15–19 years	20–24 years	25–29 years	30–34 years	35–39 years	40–44 years	45–49 years
1560–1629	0.412	0.467	0.403	0.369	0.302	0.174	0.018
1630–1646	0.500	0.378	0.382	0.298	0.234	0.128	0.000
1647–1719	0.500	0.346	0.395	0.272	0.182	0.104	0.020
1720–1769	0.462	0.362	0.342	0.292	0.227	0.160	0.000
1770–1837	0.500	0.441	0.361	0.347	0.270	0.152	0.022

Source: E. A. Wrigley, 'Family limitation in pre-industrial England', *Economic History Review*, no. 1 (1966), p. 89.

In this village, the age at marriage was already very advanced between 1560 and 1646. Between 1647 and 1719, it increased still further, by three years for the women and by one year for the men. The British demographers see in this raising of the age at marriage a response to a difficult combination of circumstances revealed by the clearly perceptible reduction in the expectation of life. However, as if this response were not sufficient to solve the difficulties of the households, they may have used another – the limitation of their fertility. In fact, fertility fell quite sharply, then rose again in the eighteenth century, at the same time as the age of marriage fell and the expectation of life increased: no doubt because the 'Industrial Revolution' had provided them with extra resources. This apparently coherent thesis is supported by a series of statistical tests which

in principle demonstrate controlled fertility: the fertility of women between the ages of thirty and forty-five, for example, diminished much more
among those who had married young than among the others; those who
had married before the age of thirty had had their last child two years
earlier, on average, between 1647 and 1719 than in the course of the period
1560–1646. Finally, only 18 per cent of those who had lived with their
husbands until the normal age of menopause had had six or more children,
whereas the proportion had been 55 per cent in the preceding period.

It may, however, be doubted whether the peasants of Colyton voluntarily limited their fertility, and it is still more improbable – in the absence
of any explicit evidence – that they did so by means of coitus interruptus.
Indeed, other classic tests of contraceptive practices have shown negative
results. Moreover, most of the data assembled by the British demographers
could be explained in 'natural' terms by the bad conditions of sanitation
that characterized that era: an increase in the deaths of infants before
christening (the latter usually took place, in England, between ten and
fifteen days after birth); temporary sterility provoked by malnutrition;
permanent sterility resulting from an inefficiently conducted delivery,
with all the greater probability, at age 'X', that the woman, who had
married younger, had already had other children; and miscarriages, which
the British demographers are not the only scholars to neglect, probably
unjustifiably.[33] Finally, it is the reversibility of the process which causes
most surprise among French historians, accustomed to regard the control
of fertility as an irreversible acquisition of our modern societies. For all
that, the 'Colyton case' remains disconcerting, and obliges the French
demographers to consider with an equally critical eye their own methods
and their own conclusions.

The statistical tests patiently elaborated by Louis Henry to demonstrate
the natural or Malthusian characters of a given fertility,[34] are based, on
the whole, only on common sense and the psychology of the Malthusian
couples of the present day. Compared with patterns of behaviour in
former times, of which the logical basis is insufficiently known, they have
not always given convincing results. We have just observed, in the case of
Colyton, how they might be ambiguous. Moreover, it was demonstrated
some years ago that some of them could give positive indications in a
population in which contraception was definitely non-existent or exceptional, and negative ones in a population where contraception was
certainly practised.[35]

In more general terms, the very notion of 'natural fertility', inherited
from Christian theology, is ambiguous. This is true, in the first place,
because contraception and abortion are not the only methods of voluntarily limiting fertility: there are others, such as sexual abstinence, the

prolonged or definitive refusal of one of the partners to fulfil his or her 'conjugal duty', with or without 'illegitimate' compensations. In the sixteenth century, Benedicti denounced married couples who, for fear of having too many children, 'content themselves only with satisfying themselves in their marriage by means of contacts and illicit indecencies'. Later, even in the absence of voluntary limitations, fertility has always, to a great extent, depended on the culture of each human group – for example, sexual taboos or nursing habits. It is, therefore, impossible to give an accurately calculated definition of 'natural fertility' and to prove in purely statistical terms that a given type of fertility is natural or otherwise. Although it is well known that in France the peasants of the south-west have traditionally had a lower fertility than those of the north, the Paris Basin or Brittany (Table 15), was this less 'natural'? One cannot, at present, be certain about this.

Was contraception unknown?

It was thought, about twenty years ago, that contraception had been unknown in western medieval society.[36] Although this view remains tenable for the mass of the faithful – we have developed this theory above – it is now certain that Christian moralists have denounced it in all periods of history, because, most probably, there were methods of contraception which were used by, at least, certain hardened sinners. It is, of course, possible that these denunciations were inconsistent with the customs of the period and simply constituted an inheritance from antiquity – an inheritance preserved by the clergy and not by the faithful.[37] This hypothesis is, however, difficult to reconcile with the changes, in the course of the centuries, in the methods denounced and with the details given regarding the users of such methods.[38] Finally, one might question the effectiveness of these methods. In fact, many of the practices denounced appear to us to be symbolic, magical and without real efficacy. Others, however – like the 'sterility poisons' denounced in the penitential books of the early Middle Ages – may have had abortive, if not contraceptive, properties. Besides, some contraceptive methods were of necessity effective, for example those used by prostitutes – vaginal tampons, perhaps – and coitus interruptus, which historians agree in designating as the contraceptive weapon of the 'Malthusian revolution' in France.

A detailed study of works of moral theology and of manuals for confessors also demonstrates that, from the fourteenth century onwards, moralists were especially preoccupied with this 'sin of Onan', and that between the sixteenth and the eighteenth centuries they became increasingly obsessed with it. This is probably an indication of a spread of this practice, at least among the élites of society. Indeed, Brantôme asserted that in the sixteenth century high-born ladies who indulged in adultery

Table 15. *Comparative fertility in various regions of France*

Region and locality	15–19 years	20–24 years	25–29 years	30–34 years	35–39 years	40–44 years	45–49 years	'Complete progeny' 20–44 years
South-west								
Sérignen (Hérault) 1650–1792	0.339	0.423	0.392	0.363	0.284	0.143	0.010	8.02
Thézels and S. Sernin (Lot) (Bas-Quercy) 1700–1792	0.208	0.385	0.355	0.290	0.242	0.067	0.000	6.59
Lévignac-sur-Save 1750–1790	NDA	0.396	0.424	0.308	0.253	0.096	0.000	7.38
Thirteen parishes of the south-western quarter of France (married women aged 20–24) 1720–1769	NDA	0.449	0.356	0.288	0.215	0.129	0.014	7.18
North								
Sainghin-en-Mélantois								
1690–1739	NDA	0.512	0.521	0.419	0.402	0.220	0.031	10.37
1740–1769	NDA	0.592	0.519	0.472	0.412	0.213	0.015	11.04
Paris Basin								
Three villages (Oise) 1740–1779	NDA	0.527	0.515	0.448	0.368	0.144	0.021	9.86
Coulommiers (Seine-et-Marne) 1670–1715	0.330	0.522	0.482	0.439	0.305	0.128	0.059	9.38
Rumont (Seine-et-Marne) 1720–1790	NDA	0.496	0.504	0.444	0.370	0.186	NDA	9.95
Meulan (Yvelines)								
1660–1709	0.541	0.486	0.465	0.498	0.410	0.159	0.014	10.09
1710–1739	0.643	0.555	0.547	0.508	0.357	0.155	0.013	10.61
Brittany								
Saint-Méen (Ille-et-Vilaine) 1720–1792	0.484	0.582	0.548	0.476	0.385	0.202	0.032	10.96
Saint-Aubin (Ille-et-Vilaine) 1749–1789	NDA	0.582	0.520	0.489	0.358	NDA	NDA	NDA
La Guerche (Ille-et-Vilaine) 1740–1789	0.382	0.507	0.487	0.458	0.270	0.145	NDA	9.33

imposed it on their lovers, and he was indignant at people behaving the same way within marriage.[39] Some people, from that period onwards, probably regarded it in a different light, because at the beginning of the seventeenth century Saint François de Sales denounced 'certain heretics of our days' who defended Onan's act, claiming that God had punished not the act itself but 'the perverse intention of that wicked man'.[40] Furthermore, the demographers see a proof of the spread of this practice among the élites in the fact that, from the beginning of the eighteenth century, the legitimate fertility of the dukes and peers of France and that of the bourgeoisie of Geneva diminished quite perceptibly.[41] We will examine, at a later stage in our study, the beginnings of the 'Malthusian revolution'. Is it certain, however, that the struggle of the post-Tridentine clergy against infertile practices within marriage was ineffective? Might it not have had the effect, not only of retarding the spread of 'Malthusian' practices, but of making conjugal life more fertile?

In an identical region – for example, the Paris Basin – the rates of fertility that we have been able to ascertain are perceptibly lower in the seventeenth century than in the first half of the eighteenth, the era in which the Catholic reforms made their full impact on the rural areas (Table 16).

Table 16. *Fertility rates in the Paris Basin in the seventeenth and eighteenth centuries*

	15–19 years	20–24 years	25–29 years	30–34 years	35–39 years	40–44 years	45–49 years	'Complete progeny' 20–44 years
	Late sixteenth and seventeenth centuries							
Argenteuil 1625–1669	0.258	0.410	0.396	0.413	0.325	0.267	0.065	8.91
Villepreux 1590–1680	0.250	0.386	0.425	0.287	0.228	0.198	0.075	7.62
Marly-le-Roi 1596–1695	0.411	0.483	0.431	0.380	0.354	0.191	0.030	9.20
Aubervilliers 1634–1699	0.250	0.404	0.460	0.436	0.399	0.173	0.011	9.36
	Late seventeenth and early eighteenth centuries							
Saint-Denis 1670–1709	0.545	0.566	0.502	0.463	0.369	0.223	0.016	10.62
Coulommiers (Type I cards) 1670–1715	0.364	0.573	0.500	0.429	0.302	0.127	0.000	9.66
	Eighteenth century							
Rumont 1720–1790	NDA	0.496	0.504	0.444	0.370	0.186	NDA	10.00
Argenteuil 1740–1770	0.460	0.554	0.521	0.478	0.360	0.147	NDA	10.30
Three villages 1740–1779	NDA	0.527	0.515	0.448	0.368	0.144	0.021	10.01

Source: Partially unpublished research by Marcel Lachiver and his students.

System of biological reproduction in real life

Moreover, when, in the same locality, it is possible to ascertain the evolution of fertility, one can verify that a period of increase generally precedes the period of decrease – which begins around 1750 in the Paris Basin but after the Revolution in other regions, or even after the middle of the nineteenth century in still others, such as Brittany (Table 17). It is true that this rise is partly explained by a more efficient registration of newborn babies dying before baptism. It is true, also, that the famines occurring at the end of the reign of Louis XIV may have diminished the physiological fertility of women, and the improved conditions of the reign

Table 17. *Periods of increase and decline in fertility in northern France*

	15–19 years	20–24 years	25–29 years	30–34 years	35–39 years	40–44 years	45–49 years	'Complete progeny' 20–44 years
Paris Basin								
Meulan								
1660–1709	0.541	0.486	0.465	0.498	0.410	0.159	0.014	10.09
1710–1739	0.643	0.555	0.547	0.508	0.357	0.155	0.013	10.61
1740–1764	0.533	0.467	0.490	0.420	0.306	0.107	0.017	8.95
1765–1789	0.480	0.515	0.465	0.385	0.283	0.115	0.013	8.81
1790–1814	0.476	0.433	0.331	0.253	0.159	0.053	0.006	6.09
1815–1839	0.359	0.363	0.273	0.203	0.127	0.063	0.005	5.14
Pays d'Arthies								
1668–1719	0.432	0.419	0.425	0.362	0.283	0.129	0.010	8.09
1720–1744	0.222	0.422	0.452	0.411	0.314	0.135	0.019	8.67
1745–1769	0.555	0.497	0.426	0.373	0.258	0.145	0.023	8.49
1770–1789	0.364	0.431	0.354	0.284	0.212	0.088	0.009	6.84
1790–1804	0.500	0.430	0.333	0.227	0.172	0.058	0.000	6.10
1805–1819	0.235	0.318	0.246	0.175	0.115	0.039	0.001	4.46
Cormeilles-en-Parisis								
1610–1667	NDA	0.464	0.442	0.395	0.394	0.177	0.022	9.36
1668–1699	0.338	0.515	0.512	0.435	0.423	0.226	0.017	10.55
Brittany								
Saint-Méen								
1720–1755	0.487	0.560	0.527	0.464	0.379	0.185	0.036	10.57
1756–1792	0.473	0.632	0.591	0.502	0.400	0.262	0.016	11.93
North								
Sainghin								
1690–1739	NDA	0.512	0.521	0.419	0.402	0.220	0.031	10.37
1740–1769	NDA	0.592	0.519	0.472	0.412	0.213	0.015	11.04
1770–1789	NDA	0.417	0.466	0.428	0.289	0.158	0.008	8.79
Isbergues								
1620–1745	0.489	0.428	0.442	0.404	0.390	0.328	NDA	9.96
1746–1789	0.400	0.559	0.463	0.457	0.411	0.200	NDA	10.45
1790–1825	–	0.514	0.446	0.406	0.381	0.200	NDA	9.73

of Louis XV may have increased it.[42] However, this does not seem sufficient to prove that this rise was in no way due to the reform of morals.

When the demographers attempt to explain the rise in the rates of illegitimacy at the end of the eighteenth century, they refer only to the process of dechristianization, and never to the boom in population, the 'proletarianization' of the peasants, their uprooting, the rise in the age of marriage and the increase in the numbers of the unmarried. Similarly, they refer only to morality and religion to account for the great increase in the number of foundlings or the drop in fertility. However, when they attempt to explain a perceptible, though slight, rise in fertility, they consider only registrations of births and the economic situation, and do not formulate the hypothesis – even if only to demonstrate its futility – that it might have resulted from a 'Christianization' of conjugal life. Nevertheless, the moral reform is a major phenomenon in the history of the seventeenth and eighteenth centuries. It became statistically evident, as we have observed, in the slump in the rates of illegitimacy of births in the rural areas of France and the virtual disappearance of concubinage. The failure of the demographers to consider it as an explanation for the rise in fertility is surprising.

It has been necessary to formulate this hypothesis, because at the moment we are discussing traditional behaviour and not the 'Malthusian revolution'. However, whatever its degree of relevance, it remains true that overall, even at the beginning of the seventeenth century and even in the south-west of France, the fertility of households was fundamentally different from what it became in the nineteenth and twentieth centuries. Let us examine, therefore, what the effects of this were.

Fertility and infant mortality

In Canada and in the English colonies in America, a level of fertility analogous to that of couples in France and England produced a boom in population which has never been equalled in western Europe. The 'full countries' of western Europe could not maintain the same rates of demographic growth as these 'new' countries, which were still empty in comparison with the densities of population which European agricultural techniques allowed. It does not appear, however, that immigration played, at that time, an important part in the growth of the population of North America: this is probably true in the case of the English colonies, and proven in the case of Canada. The most probable explanation of this boom in population is, therefore, that advanced by Malthus: the age at marriage was markedly lower than in Europe, at least in the case of the girls. Also, the parish registers in some English colonies show that infant mortality was much lower in America than in Europe[43] – except where winters were tremendously cold, as they were in Canada – although this may be a result of defective registration of babies dying before baptism.[44]

In France, a moderately careful examination reveals geographical and chronological correlations between the level of the rates of fertility and that of the rates of infant or juvenile mortality. Where the fertility of women between the ages of twenty-five and twenty-nine was over 500 per thousand – for example, in the north of France, Beauvaisis, Brittany and the small towns – the rates of infant mortality were generally between 200 and 300 per thousand, and sometimes even exceeded 300 per thousand; on the other hand, in the south-west, where women between the ages of twenty-five and twenty-nine had a fertility of under 400 per thousand, the rates of infant mortality were generally below 200 per thousand (Table 18). When, after 1750, legitimate fertility decreased, probably owing to measures voluntarily taken by married couples, in the north and in the

Table 18. *Infant mortality and fertility: geographical correlation*

Region and locality		Evaluation of fertility		
	Rate at 25–29 years	'Progeny' 20–44 years	Average number of children per complete family	Infant mortality per 1,000 births
(A) High-fertility regions of northern France				
Brittany–Anjou				
21 parishes	1740–1789	–	NDA	–	249
Saint-Méen	1720–1792	0.548	10.96	–	c. 235
Saint-Aubin	1740–1789	0.520	–	–	243
North and Paris Basin				
Sainghin	1740–1789	0.519	10.04	–	c. 267
Auneuil	1656–1735	–	–	7 to 8	288
3 villages	1720–1792	0.515	10.01	–	c. 212
41 parishes	1750–1789	–	–	–	230
Small towns				
Coulommiers	1670–1715	0.500	9.66	7.2	269
Meulan	1660–1739	0.507	10.33	–	244
Argenteuil	1640–1770	0.554	10.30	–	256
Thoissey	1740–1789	0.546	10.38	–	c. 259
(B) Low-fertility regions of south-western France				
Soudeilles	1740–1779	0.397	8.00	–	154
Thézels	1747–1792	0.335	6.52	–	191
Duraval	1770–1800	–	–	–	199
Pontourville	1756–1798	–	–	–	c. 194
Azereix	1732–1772	–	–	4.7	188
Bilhères d'Ossau	1740–1779	0.400	8.26	–	182

Paris Basin, infant and juvenile mortality also diminished (Table 19); on the other hand, in exceptional regions such as Brittany, where the rates of fertility were increasing, there was also an increase in infant or juvenile mortality. Was this purely fortuitous?

Table 19. *Infant mortality and fertility: chronological correlation*

Locality	Period	'Progeny' 20–44 years	Infant mortality
Meulan	1660–1739	10.33	244/1,000
	1740–1789	8.89	226/1,000
	1790–1839	5.69	155/1,000
Soudeilles	1740–1779	8.00	154/1,000
	1780–1819	7.01	124/1,000
	1820–1859	6.59	116/1,000
Bilhères d'Ossau	1740–1779	8.26	182/1,000
	1780–1819	6.07	151/1,000
	1820–1859	5.58	117/1,000
Sainghin	1740–1769	11.04	267/1,000
	1770–1789	8.79	145/1,000
	1790–1809	9.16	175/1,000

The decline in infant mortality has often been attributed to advances in medicine and hygiene. In this sphere, however, detailed knowledge exists at present only of the efforts undertaken at the prompting of Mme du Coudray to improve the obstetric techniques of the rural midwives.[45] This improvement in the conditions of childbirth could only – by definition – diminish endogenous mortality, that which was due to heredity and the conditions of pregnancy and confinement. However, if one can judge by the figures which demographers calculate according to a simple and approximate graphical procedure,[46] it was, above all, exogenous mortality which diminished, in the north and in the Paris Basin (Table 20B). It was this that was responsible for the excessively high rates of infant mortality in the regions of high fertility, and for the low rates in the south-west, whereas endogenous mortality, with certain exceptions, varied little from one region to another (Table 20A).

It remains to ascertain in what sense there was established a relation of cause and effect between the level of the rates of fertility and that of the rates of infant mortality. Is it true that mortality was so high, in northern France, because fertility was excessively high? In support of this hypothesis, there is the fact that the limitation of births, from the mid eighteenth century onwards, seems to have led to a decrease in infant mortality – a decrease which, at the present stage of historical research, cannot be explained by any other cause – whereas in the Breton villages where fertility increased, infant or juvenile mortality also increased.

Table 20. *Infant mortality: endogenous and exogenous causes*

		Infant mortality	Endogenous	Exogenous
(A) Exogenous origin of excessive infant mortality in northern France				
Northern France				
21 parishes in Brittany and Anjou	1740–1829	228/1,000	85	143
41 parishes around Paris	1750–1789	230/1,000	96	134
Sotteville-lès-Rouen	1760–1789	245/1,000	85	160
Meulan	1668–1739	244/1,000	61	183
Argenteuil	1740–1790	256/1,000	64	192
Sainghin	1740–1749	259/1,000	120	139
South-western France				
Thézels and St-Sernin	1747–1790	191/1,000	102	89
Bilhères d'Ossau	1740–1779	182/1,000	98	84
Present-day France	1953–1955	36/1,000	13	23
(B) Exogenous causes of the decline in infant mortality in northern France				
Meulan	1668–1739	244/1,000	61	183
	1740–1789	226/1,000	85	141
	1790–1839	155/1,000	74	81
Sainghin	1740–1749	259/1,000	120	139
	1780–1789	148/1,000	107	41
	1820–1829	132/1,000	90	42
(C) Endogenous causes of the decline in infant mortality in south-western France				
Soudeilles	1610–1699	210/1,000	142	68
	1700–1779	154/1,000	94	60
	1780–1819	124/1,000	68	56
	1820–1859	116/1,000	57	59
Bilhères d'Ossau	1740–1779	182/1,000	98	84
	1780–1819	151/1,000	65	86
	1820–1859	117/1,000	34	83

However, it is known that the death of a child at an early age shortens the 'dead time' of its mother, that is, the sterile period which always follows a confinement. In fact, in the absence of contraception, the woman who is not nursing her child conceives again much more quickly than the woman who is nursing. The 'nursing effect', it is true, does not occur in all women, and it generally does not last as long as the nursing, especially when the latter was prolonged for two years or more, as was *in principle* the rule in medieval and pre-industrial societies. Many doctors today have a tendency to doubt the physiological influence of nursing on fertility, with all the more reason because, in our society in which few women breast-feed their children, and in which few do not practise some form of contraception, it is difficult to apprehend the problem in statistical terms. However, the writers of former times were quite familiar with it, and historical demography has confirmed their assertions: this influence is statistically evident. It can be shown by comparing the fertility of women who nursed their children with that of women who entrusted them to a wet-nurse (Table 21), or, to eliminate the extraneous effect of any con-

Table 21. *Variations in the fertility of women, depending on whether or not they put their children out to nurse*

			Age-groups			
15–19 years	20–24 years	25–29 years	30–34 years	35–39 years	40–44 years	45–49 years
		Women not putting children out to nurse				
0.429	0.530	0.490	0.421	0.300	0.132	0.016
		Women putting children out to nurse				
0.545	0.589	0.603	0.501	0.417	0.116	0.023

Source: M. Lachiver and J. Dupaquier in *Annales E.S.C.,*
no. 6 (1969), p. 1399.

traception that may have been practised by the latter group, by demonstrating that the death of a child after birth perceptibly shortened the interval before the next birth (Table 22). Even this method also minimizes the real effects, because often, in former times, the mother of a child dying in infancy would accept a strange baby to nurse.

Table 22. *Intervals between births after deaths in infancy at Bléré*

Intervals in months	1st–2nd	2nd–3rd	3rd–4th	4th–5th	5th–6th	6th–7th
Normal	18.3	22.7	23.3	24.9	23.4	24.2
After death	15.7	17.6	19.1	17.7	19.3	22.5

Source: M. Lachiver, in *Annales de démographie historique* (1969), p. 224.

It might, therefore, be supposed that the more precipitate rate of births in northern France can be explained by the more frequent deaths of children in infancy. The high level of mortality would be, therefore, the biological cause of excessive fertility. But how can one explain the difference in the rates of mortality? Physical factors such as climate may have been influential, but it would probably be better, in order to take account of the comparisons between fertility and infant mortality in south-western and northern France, to insist on a composite hypothesis. The lower infant mortality in the south-west, according to this hypothesis, would not be attributable to the particular mildness of the climate, but to the fact that the babies were better cared for. Perhaps this was because the extended family offered them better protection than the conjugal family, in which – as we shall observe later – the economic functions of the mother prevented her from fulfilling normally her maternal obligations. Or perhaps it was because she could, as a result of this, nurse the child for longer, and this simultaneously diminished the risks of conception for the mother and those of death for the child.

Wet-nursing

It is, in any case, certain that it is nursing customs that explain the excessive fertility of urban couples and the excessive mortality of their children. Putting their children out to nurse in the country, mothers in the towns often conceived at the rate of one child every year, both among the poor silk-weavers, for example, and among the wealthy bourgeoisie.[47] The women in the country, on the other hand, who took in a child to nurse when they had lost their own or had finished nursing it, bore children at much longer intervals. In the country, women who had a child every year were exceptional, because only the wives of well-to-do farmers put their children out to nurse.

Neither is there any doubt as to the effects of wet-nursing on infant mortality. In Lyons – probably more than in Paris, where a 'nursing board' exercised a certain degree of supervision – the babies were the victims of the avidity of the nurses as much as of the ignorance and negligence of their parents. One observes, for example, in a village where in 1759 there were only sixteen births, twenty-one families taking charge of twenty-six nurselings. Furthermore, the number of nurselings increased still further in times of crisis – it was as high as thirty-nine in 1767 – although the nurses, being less well fed in those years, probably had less milk than usual.[48] It is true that some nurses might develop affection for the strange babies whom they nursed: there are touching proofs of this, at least in the nineteenth century.[49] However, it seems that in general, at least in the eighteenth century, nurses witnessed the babies' deaths without great commotion and regarded the nurselings essentially as a source of revenue: an example is known of a nurse who, in the course of twenty years of exercising this trade, had had twelve nurselings and had not kept a single one of them alive. She did not let them die intentionally, since their death probably led to her losing money; but the pursuit of her activity for twenty years testifies to her lack of scruples, to the ignorance and negligence of the parents who entrusted their children to her, and to the indifference of the authorities and of society.

We are beginning to acquire some figures which make it possible to evaluate statistically the harmful effects of mercenary wet-nursing. It is known, for example, that the mortality of babies put out to nurse by the Hôtel-Dieu increased continuously in the course of the eighteenth century, in proportion as their number increased: around 1771–3, at the end of this process, the death-rate was between 62.5 per cent and 75 per cent, depending on the provinces that received the babies.[50] It is true that children brought up in a family had greater chances of survival than these foundlings: in Rouen, where 90 per cent of the latter died during nursing before the age of a year, the poor children 'assisted' by the town without having been abandoned by their parents died in the nursing-stage at a rate of 'only' 38.1 per cent. However, of the children in Rouen nursed by their mothers still fewer died – 18.7 per cent.[51] It can, therefore, be acknowledged, in the present state of research, that the practice of putting babies out to nurse doubled infant mortality among urban families. It is this that explains both the excessive mortality of children in the towns and the excessive fertility of urban couples not practising contraception.

These common results of mercenary wet-nursing did not pass unnoticed: '[In Lyons] 6,000 children are born every year. Over 4,000 die in the nursing-stage', wrote Prost de Royer, not without some exaggeration. As early as the sixteenth century, doctors were advising the nursing of babies by their mothers, and in the eighteenth century Enlightened opinion conducted a vigorous campaign in favour of it. However, putting babies out to nurse was customary, and people accustomed themselves to its drawbacks philosophically, if not insensitively. In the sixteenth century, Montaigne no longer remembered even the exact number of children that he had lost in the nursing-stage; and in the century of the Enlightenment, the craftsmen, shopkeepers and workers of Lyons, who in the course of their married lives procreated twelve or twenty children, most of whom they lost during their lifetime, were probably no more sensitive. The mortality of their children, like the fertility of their wives, was apparently, for them, part of the order of nature. These things depended on God, since they had, for their part, fulfilled *normally* their duties as spouses and as parents in making the financial effort – a considerable one, in the case of the workers – of paying the wet-nurse. 'They regard themselves as justified on the grounds of example and custom', wrote Moheau, referring to mothers who took the risk of putting their children out to nurse. He added:

> They deceive themselves, they fail at the same time in their duties as citizens, as wives and as mothers. To surrender a child to a strange woman is a cruel and unnatural act, which, if it were an

isolated occurrence, would be regarded as an atrocity; and the multitude of transgressions does not detract from their perversity! Nature, which has been deceived, avenges herself and inflicts punishment; and the milk which ought to be the food of the children becomes, for the mothers who deprive them of it, a cause of sickness and death.[52]

This line of argument suggests that these mothers were acting under the influence of a customary morality – which Christian morality probably acknowledged, as it was necessary to threaten them with the vengeance of nature – rather than under the influence of 'natural sentiments'. It may, moreover, be supposed that the separation which took place from the moment of the child's birth prevented the crystallization of maternal love. Be that as it may, it is evident that, to those parents who took the risk of putting their children out to nurse, there were more important considerations than the lives of their offspring.

'The wives of the working-men are just as sensitive as we are', wrote one author at the end of the century, 'but, in tears, they take their children to be fed by others, because they really must begin to feed themselves.' In the case of the butchers, pork-butchers, bakers and all the other food trades, the woman was needed to keep the shop; as for the wives of the silk-workers, they had to help their husbands with the task of weaving. Generally speaking, the women of the popular sectors all had, in former times, an important role to play in the economy of the household; if they were unable to fulfil it, the entire family business ran the risk of collapsing. There is no need to enquire any further why, in the parish of Saint-Georges in Lyons, for example, 80 per cent of widowers remarried within six months. Nor could the economic function of households, which impeded the development of the affective function, as we have observed in connection with love between spouses, be put aside, even temporarily, as a result of the needs of the reproductive function. The only exception, perhaps, was in the multinuclear families of southern France: in Bilhères d'Ossau, only 6.6 per cent of widowers remarried within six months.

Among the élites of society women could, perhaps, devote themselves more fully to making themselves loved by their husbands, having children and looking after them. However, they too usually shifted onto mercenary nurses the feeding of the younger children, after they themselves had nursed their eldest son,[53] because they had better things to do: even if the latter were only to manage the household and bring up the children who had passed the nursing stage. Besides, the very number of the children – when fertility was not limited – prevented mothers from looking after them as attentively as in the 'Malthusian' families of the nineteenth and twentieth centuries. Moreover, as soon as one rose in the social scale, women

205

acquired imperative social obligations which competed with or sup-
planted their family obligations. It was to these women especially, one
might suppose, that the Catholic moralists and later the *philosophes*
addressed their exhortations in favour of family life and maternal breast-
feeding; but it is difficult to ascertain what proportion of them were
influenced by the sermons to the point of nursing all their children. At the
time when maternal nursing and family life became fashionable, after
1750, it certainly appears that, in these circles, couples had already become overtly 'Malthusian'.

Maternal nursing and the conjugal duty

If the advocates of maternal nursing attacked only the 'frivolity' of social
life, this may have been from policy or from a sense of decency; for conjugal obligations, also, impelled parents to separate from their new-born
children. As in many other societies, it was thought in the past that sexual
relations could 'corrupt' the milk of the nursing mother, reduce the supply
of it, and even make it disappear completely when she had the misfortune
to conceive again. This risk of premature conception was by no means
imaginary, since the infertility of the nursing mothers generally did not
last as long as did the nursing: research in progress demonstrates that
conception, in the nursing mother, could take place from the sixth month
onwards, whereas nursing, according to the customs of the time, should
last about two years, and a baby weaned before the age of one year rarely
survived. Each society has had its own particular solution to this incompatibility between the functions of wife and those of nurse: some have
obliged the man to practise coitus interruptus or other methods of contraception during the entire period of nursing;[54] many have forbidden the
man all relations with his wife until weaning, but have authorized – or
even organized – his carnal relations with other women. The Church, for
doctrinal reasons, was unable to accept either of these solutions. Being
convinced that a married man was incapable of exercising continence for
more than a few days, it found a convenient solution in the practice of
putting out the child to nurse. One may observe how, as late as the
eighteenth century, Fromageau posed this problem in his *Dictionnaire des
cas de conscience*:[55] 'Jeanne, having had *a first child* by her husband,
wishes to feed it herself; but, since her husband wishes to demand of her
his conjugal rights, she asks whether she is obliged to satisfy him during
all the time that she is nursing her child, or whether she can refuse him
without sinning?' After setting out the arguments, he concludes: 'The wife
should, if she can, put her child out to nurse, in order to provide for the
frailty of her husband by paying the conjugal due, for fear that he may
lapse into some sin against conjugal purity.'

The theologians, for centuries, had advocated the same solution to this problem. This does not mean that they were unconscious of the risks that being put out to nurse entailed for the child, nor that they came to their decision lightly: in other chapters, they take to task mothers who do not nurse their children. Benedicti asked,

> why is it that nature has given them two breasts like two little bottles if it is not for this purpose, but, being the cruel stepmothers that they are, it is enough for them to have pulled their children out of their entrails and put them on the earth, and then they send them off to wretched villages, to have them nursed by strange women, unhealthy and with a poor constitution: a thing so detrimental to the poor little children, that it would be better for them to be nourished by some brute beast, like Cyrus or Romulus, than to be entrusted to the mercies of such nurses. For not only are their bodies affected and damaged...but also, what is much worse, there remains some impression and stamp of the vice of the nurses on the minds of the children...In short, from whence comes that infinite number of maladies, such as the pox, leprosy, tinea and other corruptions, both of the body and the mind, if not from the bad constitution and the corrupted milk of the nurses, to the great detriment of the children and the eternal infamy of the mothers? It would, therefore, be much better and more becoming for these young ladies, who are so rosy-cheeked, to be holding a child in their arms, the fruit of their marriage, rather than a little pug-nosed dog...Christian ladies will take this short digression in good part, both for the benefit of their children, and to avoid sin, if not mortal, then at least venial.[56]

The inconsistency of their prescriptions demonstrates the insolubility of the contradictions between conjugal duty and maternal duty. It is, moreover, evident that not all parents could put their children out to nurse. In the case of those who could not, the medieval theologians had commanded them to give the conjugal due priority over maternal scruples, and, from the sixteenth to the eighteenth century, many still held this opinion. Sanchez, for example, wrote: 'I shall not condemn the man who demands [the conjugal due], because it is justified to imperil one's child so as not to be forced to practise continence for such a long time, which is so very difficult, or rather morally impossible.'[57] Others, such as Fromageau, considered the duties towards the child to be more imperative. We shall return later to the subject of the evolution of these prescriptions between the end of the Middle Ages and the end of the eighteenth century. What is important, at this stage, is to emphasize their uncertainties. To set their own minds, and those of their penitents, at rest, they minimized the risk which a premature conception might entail for the child: 'When the parents are poor, experience shows that they do not observe any period of delay during which they abstain from intercourse, and neither do they put the child out to nurse. Despite this, we see no serious damage to the child.'[58]

This is also the opinion of the demographers of the present day, who nevertheless know to what an incredible level infant mortality rose in the rural areas of France in former times. They consider that, on the one hand, nursing renders the risk of conception extremely slight, at least during the first year, and that, on the other hand, after the first year nursing is more detrimental than favourable to the health of the child. Is this not settling the question rather too hastily, when one knows that a great number of societies have considered sexual relations during nursing to be dangerous?

Normally – that is, when one had the means – children were nursed until they were two years old or more.[59] Whatever the hygienists and pediatricians of today may think about this, it was probably reasonable in a society in which so many children died of diarrhoea because 'artificial' feeding was not really understood and the water was polluted. On the other hand – even though it is difficult to know which women nursed their children themselves – preliminary researches appear to confirm the risk of conception during nursing and the influence that this might have had on infant mortality.[60] Let us examine, for example, the distribution by age of children dying in Cuise-la-Motte (Oise) between the middle of the seventeenth century and 1819 (Figure 9). The frequency of deaths decreases very rapidly from birth to six or seven months, then increases up to twelve or thirteen months and remains at a high level up to twenty months. This resurgence of mortality is familiar to demographers, and they attribute it to difficulties involved in weaning. But why were there so many weanings between eight and fourteen months, when the usual custom was to wean the babies at about two years of age, or eighteen months as a minimum? Partly, no doubt, because the mothers were in a hurry to finish nursing in order to be free for other functions; but also probably because they had lost their milk after a fresh conception. The graph shows, in fact, that the number of children dying after their mothers had conceived again increased regularly between the ages of eight and fourteen months – at the same rate as the total increase in deaths – and remained at a high level until the age of twenty months. However, this phenomenon is not found in all regions. At Germont, in Deux-Sèvres, the distribution by age of child deaths is analogous to that of Cuise-la-Motte, but there is no longer any correlation with the pregnancy of the mother (Figure 10). Until 1740 one finds only one child dying before the age of eighteen months during the pregnancy of his mother; yet this child was,

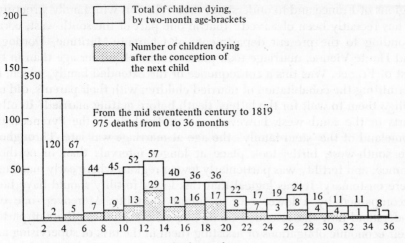

9. Infant mortality and premature pregnancies in Cuise-la-Motte (Oise). Results of research based on the family record cards compiled by the I.N.E.D.

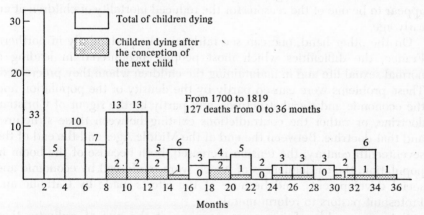

10. Infant mortality and premature pregnancies in Germont (Deux-Sèvres). Results of research based on the family record cards compiled by the I.N.E.D.

almost certainly, nursed by a mercenary wet-nurse. It would seem that – at least before the mid eighteenth century – the women of the south-west contrived to avoid conception while they were nursing their children.

Consistencies and contradictions

Despite the expansion of demographic studies during the last twenty years, much remains to be done to ascertain the customs of the various

209

regions of France and to understand their relations with family structures. It has recently been observed[61] that in one part of the south-west, corresponding to the present departments of Charente-Maritime, Dordogne and Haute-Vienne, marriage took place at a much earlier age than in the rest of France. Was this a consequence of the extended family, which, by permitting the cohabitation of married children with their parents, did not oblige them to wait for the latters' death before getting married? In other parts of the south-west, however, and particularly in the Pyrenees, the homeland of the 'stem family', the age at marriage was late. Throughout the south-west, births took place at longer intervals than in northern France; and fertility was particularly low in regions where early marriages were customary. It was logical that this lower fertility should have been accompanied by a lower rate of infant mortality. Moreover, one can understand how the extended family, by relieving the mothers of part of their economic obligations or assisting them in the task of supervising and bringing up the children, may have preserved the life of the child more effectively than did the conjugal family of northern France. However, it is still not clear in what way the extended family could have prevented mothers from conceiving during the nursing stage, although this does appear to be one of the reasons for the reduced mortality of children at an early age.

On the other hand, one can see fairly clearly, particularly in northern France, the difficulties which most people encountered in leading a normal sexual life and in maintaining the children whom they procreated. These problems were caused partly by the density of the population and the economic and social structures, and partly by the rigour of Christian doctrine, or rather the contradictions existing between those structures and that doctrine. Between the end of the Middle Ages and the end of the seventeenth century, the tension increased, both because of the boom in population, the consequences of which were reinforced by economic and social developments, and because of the efforts made by Catholic and Protestant pastors to reform morals.

Being incapable of imposing marriage at the age of puberty, they resigned themselves, despite some protests on the grounds of principle, to the prolonged celibacy of the majority of the laity, and even to the permanent celibacy of a considerable proportion of them. Engaged in a desperate struggle against extra-marital sexual activities, they seem to have come increasingly to regard continence as normal for young laymen. The Protestant moralists, in this respect, were no different from the Catholics, even though they were in principle even more convinced of the inability of a man to refrain from concupiscence without the remedy of marriage. Even public opinion, which in the fifteenth century quite freely allowed bachelors to frequent prostitutes, found this behaviour scandalous before the end of the seventeenth century. After the middle of the eighteenth century, public opinion also took part in the struggle against solitary practices, which appear to have increased in proportion to the repression of other forms of sexual behaviour. It was universally acknowledged, in the eighteenth century, that continence was necessary not only for ecclesiastics but also for 'infants', in the legal sense of the term, that is, all those who were not 'fathers of families'. Furthermore, the institution of the family was developed to the detriment of the traditional societies of young people, with the overt support of Church and State, in order to reduce the unmarried to the status of 'infants'. This process of sexual repression, which was dominant until the middle of the eighteenth century, then reached its zenith, perhaps on account of the increase in the number of celibates in society.

With regard to married couples, on the other hand, the Church had attenuated its doctrine, between the twelfth century and the end of the sixteenth century; this must be understood as another method of combatting extra-marital dissipation. This liberalization, however, had given rise to contradictions between conjugal rights and duties towards the child – contradictions which had not existed in early times, when conjugal union was justified only for the good of the offspring.[62] Differences of opinion among theologians, and the inconsistency of the precepts formulated by the same writer in different chapters of the same work – for example, on the subject of putting babies out to nurse – are evident signs of this. In real life, poverty might not only prevent parents from feeding all the children that they procreated, but it very often distracted the mothers from their maternal functions. The frequency of conception, in the case of some of the women who nursed their own children, could lead to the death of the children at an early age on account of premature weaning, and, when they did survive, their very number prevented the parents from attending to each one of them as much as would have been desirable: they got rid of them as early as possible by putting them into domestic service when they reached adolescence. In short, the ideal of family life which the Catholic Church, as well as the Protestants, endeavoured to develop was hampered by this excessive fertility.

After the great theologians of the late sixteenth century – Pierre Ledesma and Thomas Sanchez – no one was bold enough to emphasize these contradictions too strongly or to search for theologically novel solutions. Obscure confessors, occasionally, were more daring: Pierre Milhard, for example, generously asserted, at the beginning of the seventeenth century, that 'the wife is quit' of the conjugal duty when she and her husband 'are overburdened with children and lacking the means to feed them'.[63] His work, however, was condemned.

The growth of public charity, which was considerable, was shown to be more and more inadequate with every day that passed in the second half of the eighteenth century. We have already noted the appalling mortality among the foundlings and its aggravation during this period. Was the situation any better in England? The babies of the foundling hospital in London, where the rate of infant mortality was 70 per cent in the middle of the century, apparently survived for more than a year at a rate of 85 per cent at the end of the century. The other foundling hospitals, however, appear to have been slaughter-houses like those in France.

It was in this combination of circumstances that critiques of the demographic system were formulated, by Condorcet in France and by Malthus in England. Contrary to what is often thought by those who have not read him, it was not in the future that Malthus situated the moment when the level of the population would exceed that of the means of subsistence, but in the past. 'It will appear', he wrote, 'that the period when the number of men surpasses their means of easy subsistence has long since arrived; and that this necessary oscillation, this constantly subsisting cause of periodic misery, has existed in most countries ever since we have had any histories of mankind, and continues to exist at the present moment.'[64] And he contrasted, quite justifiably, the remarkable demographic expansion of the new countries, still 'empty' of men, with the demography of Europe, obstructed for centuries by various regulating mechanisms. Carrying to extremes the ideal of continence, he proposed as the most acceptable regulating mechanism a systematic prolongation of celibacy.

In France, however, from the second half of the eighteenth century onwards, an increasing number of couples had discovered another method of escaping from the infernal cycle of excessive fertility and excessive infant mortality – contraception. Let us try to ascertain how and why this occurred.

3. THE ADVENT OF BIRTH CONTROL AND ITS SIGNIFICANCE

Two views of the 'Malthusian revolution'

You may consult those men whom Religion has appointed as depositaries of the secrets of the hearts and frailties of humanity, or those whom a taste for researches in natural philosophy important to the good of the State has made accurate observers of the customs of the country people and the poor; they will tell you that rich women, for whom pleasure is the greatest objective and the sole preoccupation, are not the only ones who regard the propagation of the species as a trickery of past times: already these deadly secrets, unknown to any animal other than man, these secrets have

212

penetrated into the countryside: nature is cheated even in the villages.

If these licentious customs, if these murderous tastes become more widespread, they will be no less fatal to the State than the plagues which ravaged it in past times; it is time to halt this secret and terrible cause of depopulation, which imperceptibly undermines the nation and with which, in a short time, it may be perhaps too late to deal. To prevent these misfortunes, the sole, the one and only means is the re-establishment of morality.[65]

This celebrated passage of Moheau is, on this subject, the *alpha* and the *omega* of the French demographers. After searching for 'Malthusian' peasants in the south-west and in Normandy, it seems that they finally found them in the Paris Basin (see Table 17 above, and Figure 11). Around 1740 in small towns such as Meulan, and around 1760 in the surrounding countryside, the fertility of households began to decline significantly, and this decline continued until the twentieth century.[66] Here one really is dealing with the beginnings of the 'Malthusian revolution' among the mass of the people.

There is still insufficient information, however, as to how far the upper classes of society were more advanced in this respect. Ten years ago, it was acknowledged that they had practised contraception since the end of the seventeenth century, as both the bourgeoisie of Geneva and the dukes and peers of France evinced a decline in fertility from that time onwards. Nowadays it is asserted that in Geneva the fertility of couples in the popular sectors was as low and as sharply declining as that of the bourgeoisie; and one wonders whether the infertility of the dukes and peers might not be explained by their neglect of their wives, or even by a more frequently physiological sterility, rather than by contraception. It has recently been demonstrated[67] that in Meulan the rich – in this case the bourgeois, the merchants and the well-to-do master-craftsmen – limited their fertility before the poor did so (Table 23). There is, however, at present no information about how long the court nobility and the Parisian bourgeoisie had been controlling their fertility, and this renders the explanations of the phenomenon even more uncertain.

Being admirers of Moheau and, like him, 'populationists', the French demographers have in general accepted his thesis: birth control is held to have been caused by a deterioration of morals, by selfishness and – they add – by irreligion, these three tendencies developing *pari passu*. Historians have, indeed, traditionally believed that the French Revolution was prepared by a process of dechristianization, which was especially perceptible among the élites but which could also be gauged among the people through such symptoms of immorality as the increase in illegitimate births and the abandonment of children.

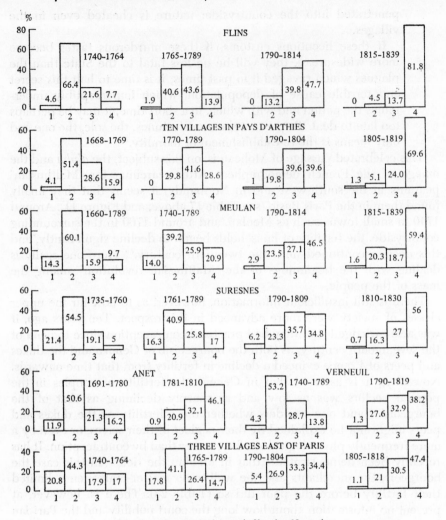

1. Couples with average birth interval of less than 19 months
2. Couples with average birth interval of 19 to 30 months
3. Couples with average birth interval of 31 to 48 months
4. Couples with average birth interval of more than 48 months

11. Contraception and average intervals between births in the Paris Basin. From Marcel Lachiver, 'Fecondité légitime et contraception dans la région parisienne', in *Hommage à Marcel Reinhardt* (Paris, 1973), p. 396.

Nevertheless, we have seen that these two phenomena might have had causes other than irreligion and immorality: for example, the boom in population, and the proletarianization and pauperization of the wage-

Table 23. *Trends in fertility among the poor and among the rich in Meulan* (%)

		Average birth interval					
		Under 18 months	19–30 months	31–48 months	49 months and over	Under 30 months	31 months and over
1660–1739	Poor	9.1	54.6	22.7	13.6	63.7	36.3
	Rich	21.6	55.8	10.0	12.6	77.4	22.6
1740–1764	Poor	17.4	43.5	34.8	4.3	60.9	39.1
	Rich	16.7	44.4	18.5	20.4	61.1	38.9
1765–1789	Poor	4.2	58.3	20.8	16.7	62.5	37.5
	Rich	15.0	35.0	20.0	30.0	50.0	50.0
1790–1814	Poor	0	28.6	25.7	45.7	28.6	71.4
	Rich	0	13.5	37.8	48.7	13.5	86.5
1815–1839	Poor	0	33.3	23.8	42.9	33.3	66.7
	Rich	3.5	17.2	17.2	62.1	20.7	79.3

Source: Unpublished research by Marcel Lachiver.

earners. In addition, one must consider the chronology of these events, which is now well known: the increase in abandonments of children and that of pre-marital conceptions began in the seventeenth century, and were probably largely due to the Christianization of the rural areas; the rise in the rate of illegitimacy, on the other hand, does not become evident in the rural areas until fairly late in the second half of the eighteenth century, and can probably be explained by the increased difficulties in getting married caused by the boom in population and the rise in prices; these would also explain the second wave of abandonments. Finally, one cannot fail to observe that illegitimacy and birth control developed in different social sectors: the workers, who had a particularly high rate of illegitimacy, were to remain fertile throughout the nineteenth century, and infant mortality, in this sector, was also to remain high; on the other hand, in the sectors where fertility had been most affected – the bourgeoisie and the peasant proprietors – people seem to have had (whether they procreated them or not) far fewer illegitimate children.

It is doubtful whether one can seriously admit the concept of 'demographic revolution' in connection with birth control, and yet deny this 'revolution' all ideological or, to put it more precisely, moral support. Either one sees contraception as selfish behaviour, opposed to family morality and the interests of society, in which case one considers that it is the act of 'immoral' and 'anti-social' individuals, incapable of founding a new order of society; or one acknowledges that it is characteristic of the customs of a given society, our own, in which, nevertheless, altruism, humanitarianism, patriotism and family feeling are no less honoured or less practised than in the society of former times – quite the contrary –

215

in which case it is supported by the morality of that society. The Christian moralists and the short-sighted demographers of the eighteenth century might adopt the former interpretation, at a time when contraception was still the practice of only a minority of Frenchmen. Two centuries later, however, knowing that it has become generalized in all western societies without the latter lapsing into decadence and that it is, therefore, socially viable, we can no longer do so. Nowadays it is absurd to explain the beginnings of what turned out to be a demographic revolution in terms of a 'deterioration of morals', in the same manner as those who, in the eighteenth century and afterwards, so patently deceived themselves as to the underlying nature and the consequences of what was going on before their eyes. On the contrary, one should try to explain it in terms of the construction of a new family morality.

It does, indeed, seem clear that between the sixteenth century and the end of the eighteenth century, the family changed in character and a new morality of family relations was adumbrated. We have maintained, in the first two chapters of this book, that ties of solidarity based on neighbourhood became progressively obliterated and were replaced by ties of family solidarity; that the sense of *lignage* and the 'spirit of the house' were severely damaged by the legislation of the Revolution and probably earlier, before 1789, by the rise of new values which explain that legislation; that the father–mother–children group gradually detached itself from the other kinsfolk and the domestic servants, who had always been included in the 'families' of former times, in the well-to-do sectors; and that it has acquired greater solidarity because putting babies out to nurse and the expulsion of the adolescents no longer happen in the families of today, whereas they were customary in past times. In Chapter 3, we showed how domestic morality had become more sentimental at the end of the eighteenth century than it had been at the end of the sixteenth; that it increasingly demanded of the husband a less brutal and more courteous attitude towards his wife, and that this courtesy constituted in the eyes of the bourgeois, at the beginning of the nineteenth century, a basic test of the degree of civilization of customs; that this morality increasingly insisted on the duties of parents towards their children, which may have developed in the parents both the sense of the responsibilities that they were assuming in procreating children, and the desire to avoid them by not procreating children. Finally, in the present chapter, we have demonstrated that the demographic system of past times, based on uncontrolled fertility, was murderous to the children, in a 'full country' such as France – despite the corrective, which was certainly important, provided by late marriage; that infant mortality decreased at the same times as the rates of fertility; that the system was aggravated by the practice of putting babies

216

out to nurse; that Enlightened opinion was conscious of its detrimental effects; and that these effects were aggravated in proportion as the towns grew in size. It is in terms of these transformations of society and of morality that one must try to explain the transition to the demographic system of the present day.

The refusal of conjugal duty by the wife

Birth control was first of all of benefit to the wives. One can argue about the physiological and psychological need of wives to be mothers. It is, however, indisputable that perpetual pregnancies are fatiguing: 'Always going to bed, always pregnant, always giving birth', sighed the pious and fertile Marie Leczinska. Confinements were always distressing and, if Montaigne was right to say that they were all the more so because they were held to be so,[68] we may assume that they were more painful than today. Above all, they often resulted in death. Let us quote as one example among many others the five wives of Guillaume Versoris: of the first, nothing is known; the second, Jeanne Houdon, gave birth to a child on 9 April 1523, and died a month later, on 10 May; the third, Loise Barjelonne, married on 13 July 1523, gave birth on 8 June 1524, and died on the 17th; the fourth, Ysabeau Gallope, married on 17 June 1526, died ten months later, on 21 March 1527, probably in the course of a confinement. When the diary comes to an end, in 1530, Guillaume had been married to his fifth wife for three years, and she was still living, but she had not had a child.

The few demographers who have tried to evaluate this risk suggest that 10 per cent of mothers died as a consequence of childbirth: slightly fewer among the peasantry, slightly more among the bourgeoisie. Be that as it may, all women dreaded the experience. To reassure them, there was a large number of magic stones, there were special pilgrimages, blessed girdles, invocations to the Virgin and Saint Anne, prayers to recite on the occasion of childbirth, which were as numerous in Protestant regions as in Catholic ones. However, neither 'superstitions' nor the most pure faith put an end to the anguish. In the enlightened and mystical home of the Josselins, each birth took place in an atmosphere of panic, in spite of the assistance of neighbours and kinsfolk, who were close observers of this almost public incident in domestic life.[69]

Furthermore, the 'conjugal due', which in principle was as much a matter of coercion for the husband as for the wife, was in fact much more so for the latter, who feared the consequences of coition. Probably reflecting the grievances of their women penitents, some confessors pointed out to husbands their selfishness and their lack of love, when they demanded their rights from a wife who had particular reasons for fearing pregnancy and childbirth. One cannot 'in good conscience render this due, when that...would greatly prejudice health, or life might depend on it', wrote Pierre Milhard in 1611. He referred thus to 'women who cannot bear children without a probable danger to their life' or to those who

> in their pregnancy suffer extreme pains and ailments, more than is usual with pregnant women. To this God has never intended to obligate women, with such prejudice to their health or probable risk to their life; for that would truly be an oppression, and the most severe and intolerable obedience and law ever to be seen among Christians; it would not be the law of love, and consistent with the nature of such a marital society, but most assuredly a tyrannical and utterly inhuman law, an obedience – I say – which would entail a greater obligation than that of children towards their Fathers; of Religious towards their Superiors; it would even surpass the obedience that all Christians owe to the Church; to which obedience God has never compelled anyone, when it has been a question of danger to life, or considerable damage to health, and even God Himself has not obliged people to obey in such cases as this, in any of his purely positive laws...This is, therefore, far removed from the fantasy or frenzy of those sensual men who desire that without exception or demur their wives should be obliged to acquiesce in and submit to their passions. No, this is an error, an act of impiety and a tyrannical abuse, that destroys such a society and sacrament of love or reciprocal charity: such love should not be founded on the flesh and its concupiscence, but should be a holy love, which considers the good of the soul and of the body. This opinion is not mine, but that of the Apostle, when he says 'You husbands, love your wives' – and how, or in what manner? – 'As Christ has loved His Church', replies the Apostle. This, then, is the rule and standard of marital love: it commands and teaches one never to expose the life of one's partner to death or to serious damage to health; a thing to which neither divine nor human laws oblige one, whatever temptations or frailties may be encountered.[70]

It may well have been on account of these observations, which were rare at the beginning of the seventeenth century, that the work was condemned by the Sorbonne. Anyway, they show us the contrast between the points of view of the man and the woman with regard to the conjugal due, and the moral problems that this provoked.

Although one does not know, directly, the complaints of wives to their husbands, one knows the warnings uttered by a loving and anxious mother, Madame de Sévigné. To her daughter, who had just given birth, she advised sexual abstinence. Thus, she wrote on 23 December 1671: 'I beg of you, my dear, do not rely on having two beds; it lends itself to temptation: have somebody sleep in your bedroom. Seriously, have pity on yourself, on your health and mine.' And, on 8 January 1672:

> I want to warn you of one thing that I will maintain, between your husband and you. It is that if, after being purged [that is, purified after childbirth], you have the mere thought – it is little enough – of sleeping with M. de Grignan, count on becoming pregnant; and if any of your midwives says the contrary, then she has been corrupted by your husband.

It is clear that Mme de Grignan – who no longer wanted to become pregnant – was hoping to take advantage of the period of sterility which always follows childbirth, even when the mother does not nurse the baby, while her mother put her trust only in continence. Furthermore, she did not hesitate, in her letter of 23 December, to upbraid her son-in-law directly, urging him to leave his wife in peace. One would have to be profoundly ignorant of the nature of the risks of childbirth in past times and of the anguish that they provoked among the women of the day to explain away this intervention on the part of a mother by jealousy that she may have felt for her son-in-law, however excessive, in the opinion of her confessor, may have been her love for her daughter.

Should one conclude from this that it was the wives who, without consulting their husbands, practised contraception? Fromageau, for example, quoted the case of Céline who, 'after paying the conjugal due, expels all or part of the male seed'. Sanchez had already referred, at the beginning of the seventeenth century, to 'the woman who, immediately after coition, urinates, stands up straight or does some other thing whereby she expels the seed'.[71] He himself, however, seems not to have believed in the efficacy of these measures, 'for it is very rare for the seed to run out. . .on account of the fact that, once the seed has been received, the aperture of the womb closes in such a manner that it does not leave room for even the point of a needle to pass'. There remained the solution of preventing it from reaching the womb by means of a vaginal tampon. This was probably the method used by prostitutes. The licensed prostitutes – for example, those in the brothels in the fifteenth century – must have known a method of avoiding pregnancy without requiring the active assistance of their clients. There was, in fact, frequent reference to such tampons in the heyday of prostitution, for example in one of Chaucer's tales. However, the confessors of the seventeenth and eighteenth centuries did not refer to them at all when they questioned married women.

If it was the women themselves who limited their fertility, it was more

219

probably by refusing to fulfil their conjugal duty, as Madame de Sévigné advised her daughter. In addition, between the sixteenth and the eighteenth centuries, the theologians increased the number of occasions whereby a wife could avoid the embraces of her husband. Sanchez enumerated thirty of them. Here are some of them, drawn from Fromageau's *Dictionnaire des cas de conscience*. We have already noted that of Jeanne, who was nursing her child: 'If, on account of her poverty, she cannot have it fed by another woman, she may absolutely refuse her husband the conjugal due.' There was also Louise, 'who had recently given birth', of whom her husband Gervais 'insistently demands his conjugal rights': 'It is an obvious fact that Louise, being in this condition, is not obliged in conscience to grant her husband what he demands of her, however much he may insist.' Eléonor, 'having been in quite evident danger of death in her previous confinements, and the Physicians and Surgeons having told her that she can no longer have children without dying. . .is not obliged to fulfil her conjugal duty to her husband when there is such great danger'. Junia is, perhaps, the most interesting case. She 'has a husband who is by nature very lustful and who sometimes wants to oblige her to render to him his conjugal rights, even though she is extremely ill'; Fromageau considered that 'in this case, Junia is not obliged by justice or by charity to render the due to her husband; the interests of her health having priority over the reasons that her husband may have for demanding it'. This was, perhaps, the reason for the epidemic of migraine which, for several centuries, afflicted married women. Finally, one may quote the case of Basin, who 'has the habit of demanding his rights of Louise his wife when he is drunk'; 'if Basin is so drunk that he has lost the use of reason, Louise is not obliged to render him the conjugal due'.[72]

Fromageau did not invent these cases of refusal of the conjugal due: they had all been cited already by Sanchez. In the Middle Ages, however, and as late as the sixteenth century, most of them were the subject of controversy, and many of them were given solutions at variance with those proposed in the eighteenth century. Moreover, most of the moralists did not exercise their ingenuity to find cases in which the conjugal due could be refused; on the contrary, they increased those in which, however paradoxical it may seem to us, the due was to be paid. As late as 1590, for example, Pierre Alagona wrote: 'The fury or the madness of him who demands the due does not excuse the woman from rendering it, if without danger of serious damage to the person of whom it is demanded it may be paid.'[73] Likewise, the woman should accept the embraces of a leprous husband.

The advent of birth control and its significance

At the same time as the moral possibilities of refusal were increasing in number, the woman was becoming, to a much greater extent than before, mistress of her own behaviour, since the husband had lost the right to beat her to compel her to fulfil her duty. Especially among the nobility and the bourgeoisie – the sectors to which about three-quarters of the women who petitioned the officiality of Cambrai for divorce on the grounds of ill-treatment belonged – the refusal to render the conjugal due may have been a quite common method of birth control. In addition, this transformation of the relationships of forces within the household was equally favourable to the spread of coitus interruptus.

Coitus interruptus and the transformation of conjugal relationships

This method of contraception, which historians and demographers generally regard as the principal agent of the 'Malthusian revolution' in France, is always represented as being the act of the man. This was not only because it depends on the man to practise it or not, but because the theologians have often represented the libertinous man as imposing on his pious wife this 'unnatural practice'. This interpretation does not date from the nineteenth century: for example, at the ecclesiastical conference held at Bricquebec in 1706,

> it was asked whether a woman sinned when she refused her husband, who demanded to exercise his conjugal rights in a manner indecent and against the natural order, knowing well, through having experienced it many times, that he would pollute himself as a result. The husband behaving in this manner only so as not to be overburdened with children, of whom he already had more than enough...One supposed this same husband to be so violent and angry that the wife was virtually certain that she would be seriously ill-treated if she did not obey, having already experienced this many times.[74]

Since this question of complicity in the 'unnatural act' had to be raised, one could clearly envisage only the complicity of the woman in the crime of the man, in view of the technique employed. At the beginning of the twentieth century, when industry had put on the market vaginal diaphragms and other female contraceptives, the theologians began to consider the contrary situation.[75] However, is this sufficient evidence to warrant the belief that in practising coitus interruptus the man was imposing his will on the woman?

These ecclesiastical problematics referred, most probably, not so much to the reality observable in the eighteenth century as to a millenarian tradition. In the Book of Genesis, Onan had refused to have children by his sister-in-law Sarah, who desired them to such an extent that she had them by her father-in-law Judah.[76] Therefore, Onan alone bore the responsibility for his act, and it was he whom God punished. This would have sufficed to lay the foundations of the ecclesiastical interpretation of the responsibilities involved in coitus interruptus. Furthermore, confessors referred to it, from the early Middle Ages onwards, at the same time and in the same terms as those other 'unnatural acts' which are not only infertile but are supposed to give gratification to the man alone. The discussion regarding the complicity of the woman had gone on continuously since antiquity in connection with sodomy or oral relations, and it was in the light of what the early theologians had said of these practices that one judged, in the seventeenth and eighteenth centuries, the question of the complicity of the woman in coitus interruptus. Should one command her to make the same categorical refusal, even when she was threatened with death? Some writers, such as Thomas Sanchez, pointed out that the case was different in that, up to the moment of withdrawal, the act of coition was 'conjugal', and therefore the wife should not and could not elude it. However, should she foresee that it would be, finally, 'unnatural' when her husband made a habit of this practice? These traditional problematics distracted the attention of the theologians from the real psychological conditions involved in the practice of coitus interruptus. Moreover, even when the debate took place at an ecclesiastical conference, among experienced practitioners of confession, it was couched in the terms of the hypotheses of the Scholastics. This continued until the declarations of Mgr Bouvier, in 1842, which envisaged the problem in entirely different terms.[77]

The husband, it is true, might have reasons for limiting the numbers of the offspring, and we will return to this subject. It is, however, difficult to understand why his wife would not have approved of this measure, especially in an age in which differences of religious opinion between men and women were less customary than in the nineteenth century. Moreover, it was the women and not the men whom the demographer Moheau and many other lay observers of the eighteenth century reproached: 'Rich women, for whom pleasure is the greatest objective and the sole preoccupation, are not the only ones who regard the propagation of the species as a trickery of past times.'

His observation also suggests that, before becoming widespread in ordinary households, contraception was practised only by rich women avid for gratification. Moreover, earlier he had specified that, normally, contraception took place only in extra-marital relations, because then the woman could not conceive without forfeiting her honour.

It is not to be thought that irregular unions may benefit the State: they are never productive, as are those unions approved by the law and of which the fruits may appear without dishonouring their author. We have observed that in France births, in relation to marriages, are in a proportion of over four to one. . .But which of the licentious girls and widows gives the same profit to the State? Women who have abandoned themselves to prostitution do not have children – they avoid them as being an obstacle to their trade; seduced girls or widows, who have renounced chastity, have not always renounced shame: they fear fertility as a proof of their dishonour, and out of two thousand girls or widows who consent to have carnal relations, there is not one who bears two children.[78]

One must, therefore, explain this paradox: both within marriage and outside it, it was the women who wanted to limit their fertility, and, apart from the haunts of prostitution, it seems that there was only one effective method of contraception, coitus interruptus, which can be practised only by the man. There is only one solution to this apparent paradox: coitus interruptus was practised when women were in a position to persuade men to practise it. They appear to have succeeded in doing so in the context of illicit relations at an earlier date than in that of marriage.

In the sixteenth century, according to Brantôme, it was the great ladies who had recourse to it, not in marriage – except for some scandalous cases – but in adultery. With their lovers, they did not deny themselves 'putting it in and frolicking until they are surfeited, but so that they do not receive any of their seed'. And he emphasizes that 'they *do not wish to permit* anything to be left inside them',[79] which means quite clearly that they had enough authority over their lovers to impose on them this measure of self-control and this curtailment of their gratification.

Now this situation had prevailed for a long time among the devotees of courtly love. One may judge of this, for example, by the Twelfth Precept of Love of André Le Chapelain (late twelfth or early thirteenth century): 'When giving yourself up to the pleasures of love, do not surpass the desire of your mistress.' When he had given proof of his perfect submission and of his ability to master his elemental impulses, the knight could obtain from his lady carnal favours – this seems indubitable – but moderate and infertile ones. Coitus interruptus was, most probably, one of the practices characteristic of the courtly relationship, in which the woman was the 'mistress', free to grant or to withhold her favours, and the man the 'servitor'.

Within marriage, the relationship between the man and the woman was entirely different, as is well attested by the pronouncement of the Countess of Champagne, reported by André Le Chapelain.

We state and affirm by these presents that love cannot extend its

rights between spouses. Lovers, indeed, grant each other everything mutually and gratuitously, without being forced to do so by
any obligation. Spouses, on the other hand, are obliged by duty to
submit their wills reciprocally and never to refuse anything to each
other. Furthermore, if spouses give each other caresses in the
manner of lovers, neither of the two shall draw further advantage
from it, and they appear to possess nothing more than that which
they possessed by right previously.[80]

Traditionally, the woman owed to her husband the service of her body,
and could not, apart from in exceptional cases, which were much less
numerous in the Middle Ages than in the seventeenth and eighteenth
centuries, either refuse his embraces or oblige him to render them infertile,
even when she was afraid of dying as a result. Besides, the canon
Si conditiones, based not on old, but on recently formulated precepts,
less than a century after the appearance of courtly love in the west, had
set the matter to rights properly: 'If conditions are stipulated which run
counter to the essence of marriage – for example, if one party says to the
other "I contract with thee if thou avoidest children. . ." – then the matrimonial contract is void. . .' Girls were, in principle, free not to marry, and
the most 'wise' among them voluntarily chose celibacy to escape from the
constraints of marriage. But once married, the woman should accept the
constraints and the risks inherent in her status as a wife: the conjugal due
and death in childbirth.

In law, there was no change in this situation until the twentieth century.
Nevertheless, the decrease in the means of coercion at the disposal of the
husband, and the increase in the number of cases in which morality
acknowledged the right of the woman to refuse the 'due', have perceptibly
altered the relationship between the partners. Above all, it appears that
the courtly relationship was introduced into marriage from the seventeenth century onwards. When, in the first half of the century, the
Précieuses tried to force husbands to behave like lovers, they appeared
ridiculous to the majority of the bourgeoisie and the nobility. Nevertheless, at the moment when Molière took them to task, they had already had
considerable influence on both the customs and the language of polite
society. As for the refinement of manners and speech, there is a gulf
between the 'century of Louis XIV' and the Rabelaisian humour of the
age of Louis XIII. It was, perhaps, the same in the sphere of marital
relationships: M. de Grignan still had too many children by his wife, but
his mother-in-law openly expressed her indignation about it, and the dukes
and peers, from the beginning of the eighteenth century onwards, began
to have many fewer children than in the past. One might, quite evidently,
suppose that their infertility was due above all to the fact that after a few

years of marriage they neglected their wives in favour of their mistresses. However, they had had mistresses in the reign of Henri IV, to the same or a greater extent than at the end of the reign of Louis XIV. Furthermore, the demographic study which has been devoted to them does not tell us whether those who led an exemplary married life were more fertile than the others. Saint-Simon, for example, who cherished his wife until her death, appears to have had only one daughter and two sons, in an age when in that sector of society the average number was 2.79 children per couple. There is a strong presumption, therefore, that contraception was practised from the beginning of the eighteenth century. However, as the dukes and peers were in a position to provide their younger sons with exalted appointments in the Church and the Army, and as it was in their interest to have large families in order to ensure their political power, they would have voluntarily limited their fertility only out of consideration for their wives.

In 1782, Father Féline, a confessor in Lower Normandy, analysing in his *Catéchisme des gens mariés* the motives of those of his penitents who committed the 'sin of Onan', wrote:

> The first is due to the excessive obligingness of husbands towards their wives. They become too sensitive to the complaints that the wives make about all that it has cost them to bring children into the world. [The husbands] deal gently with their excessive delicacy, they consent to spare them this trouble, without, however, renouncing the right that they believe they possess.[81]

In the eighteenth century, a gallant man no longer demanded the 'conjugal due' of his wife: he made love to her when she consented, and in as restrained a manner as she demanded. As early as the beginning of the century, Antoine Blanchard, even though he still referred to the 'conjugal due', did so only briefly and no longer insisted, as had Benedicti, that the 'body of the wife belongs to the husband'. He was concerned, on the other hand, about her 'arrogance', her 'lack of obligingness' and her 'indifference', which might give her husband 'occasion to transfer his affection elsewhere'.

Finally, at the beginning of the nineteenth century, the bourgeois had apparently been converted to *précieux* customs: their chaste language and the respect that they professed for the 'weaker sex' are evidence of this. This probably has some connection with the decline in their fertility in most regions of France.

Saving the children

Birth control by means of coitus interruptus became possible only as a result of a transformation of the conjugal relationship into a courtly relationship. However, the women's fear of pregnancy and childbirth was not the only reason that impelled husbands to adopt this practice.

Though very often lucid, Moheau appears, in this matter, to be blinded by his prejudices: his entire dissertation plagiarizes the arguments of a long series of Christian orators. Like them he classes coitus interruptus, an ascetic practice, as a hedonistic perversion on a par with other 'unnatural acts'. Like Lactantius, who described as 'parricides' those who squandered their semen, he compared non-procreation to an act of murder. This influence of the Christian tradition can be noted even in his style: thus, when he writes 'if these licentious customs, if these homicidal tastes', this, with its rhetorical balancing of terms and association of ideas, echoes the celebrated formula of Saint Augustine, *haec libidinosa crudelitas vel libido crudelis.*[82] In common with these orators and moralists, it was as a polemicist rather than as an analyst that Moheau approached this question.

However, he pressed this Christian tradition into the service of an end alien to Christianity, 'populationism'. In fact, in common with such men as Colbert, and all the French demographers of past times, he was arguing from the point of view of the State. Having a large number of children is never in the interest of individuals. Let us observe, on the other hand, the frequency with which he refers to the interests of the State: 'without morality there can be no properly constituted *Empire*'; the man who is moral is 'necessary to ensure the population of a *State*'; 'illicit unions' cannot 'benefit the *State*'; 'each married woman gives the *State* more than four individuals. . .which of the loose-living girls or widows gives the same profit to the *State*?' Contraception is 'fatal to the *State*', and it was with the 'good of the *State*' that the demographers who studied the subject were concerned. As for mothers who put their children out to nurse, 'they are failing in their *duties as citizens*'. On the other hand, he does not once mention God or specifically Christian virtues.

Moheau used in argument only one part of the Christian tradition – the most superficial one. There was another, centuries-old part, which preached continence even to married couples, when they had sufficient offspring: 'Even young people', exclaimed Saint Ambrose, 'when the fear of God calms and moderates their hearts, often renounce the activities of their youth as soon as they have children.'[83]

One finds a revival of the latter tradition in the writings of Malthus. To this Protestant, continence is not a good in itself, it is not meritorious in absolute terms, but it is imperative when the good of one's neighbour depends upon it. Now, it is criminal to procreate children without having the means of feeding and bringing them up properly; and it is an abominable and sacrilegious sophistry to make God responsible for the inexorable consequences of our incontinence.

> To the Christian I would say that the Scriptures most clearly and precisely point it out to us as our duty, to restrain our passions within the bounds of reason; and it is a palpable disobedience of this law to indulge our desire in such a manner as reason tells us will unavoidably end in misery. The Christian cannot consider the difficulty of moral restraint as any argument against its being his duty; since, in almost every page of the sacred writings, man is described as encompassed on all sides by temptations which it is extremely difficult to resist; and though no duties are enjoined which do not contribute to his happiness on earth as well as in a future state, yet an undeviating obedience is never represented as an easy task.[84]

There is nothing more alien to English Protestantism than the unconcern and fatalism which we believe we have discerned in the writings of the French Catholics. Moreover, since they did not associate continence with the exercise of the pastoral ministry, the Protestants were not tempted, as were the Catholic moralists, to render insoluble the dilemmas involved in the conjugal state, the better to extol the convenience of the ecclesiastical state or to demonstrate its social necessity.

For example, in one of Gerson's dialogues on celibacy, Wisdom says to Nature: 'Your Aristotle, when establishing the principles of politics, has observed that the multitude of children should be limited...; it must be understood that certain men, dedicated to higher things, are not destined to procreate children.' This dangerously controversial sophistry, character-istic of early and medieval Christianity, continues to explain the contra-dictions (sometimes, even, the sort of irresponsibility) which we have observed in post-Tridentine morality, which was, nevertheless, much more favourable to the family.

The reader may judge this by examining a sermon of La Tour on the feasibility of continence.

> Young people, excited by the fire of passion or irked by the yoke of dependence, you wait impatiently, like the Prodigal Son, for the moment when, as masters of your property and of yourselves, you will exercise over another the authority that you dread when applied to yourselves. Alas! that vain shadow of liberty that seduces you will serve only to enslave you more on account of the duties which it imposes on you. Duped by some idle tendernesses

that prevail in all ages to alleviate the burden of obligation, you will have all the more grounds for complaint. You congratulate yourself on being reborn in the fruit of your loins. This consolation will cost you dear: the most severe pains will bring [children] into the world, the difficulties and expense of their education will disturb your repose, and perhaps vicious behaviour will render them unworthy of you; sickness and death will carry them off; you will have a surfeit of them: *saturati sunt filiis* (Psalm XVI, 14).[85]

In the face of this line of argument, and this interpretation of marriage, one imagines his listeners setting out in quest of a means of plucking the rose without being pricked by it. Moreover, it is just possible that this contributed to the infertility that developed in France from the mid eighteenth century onwards, whereas in the Protestant countries married couples seem to have limited their fertility in circumstances unfavourable to the survival of children, and to have become fertile again in favourable circumstances. This hypothesis has been advanced recently on the basis of the decline in fertility in Colyton and Geneva in the seventeenth century.[86]

Fundamentally, however, French 'Malthusianism', like that which developed a century later in the other countries of western Europe, probably had as its purpose the good of the children. Sébastien Mercier, among many others, testified to this in the eighteenth century: 'There are others who would like to limit their fertility. Making a false calculation of the favours of Providence, which they distrust, they dare to fear to bring into the world a being which, according to them, will not find room enough on the earth, nor this earth abundant enough to feed them.'[87] There had been apprehensive parents as early as the sixteenth century – it was for their benefit that Benedicti had re-echoed the words of David – and even as early as the beginning of the fourteenth century, before the Black Death, according to Pierre de la Palud.[88] The principal difference, in the eighteenth century, was that their anxiety was no longer purely personal, but had become a philosophical theory, a heresy.

Rather than dwelling on the analyses of its adversaries, let us finally hear the observations of one of the rare *philosophes* who was bold enough to justify birth control – Condorcet.

Among all the species of animals that we have been able to observe, the voluntary act which serves to perpetuate the species is accompanied by gratification. This general natural law not only ensures the preservation of the species, but even leads to an increase in the number of individuals, which ends only as a result of the inability to subsist, and for some species the destruction to which they are exposed, either on the part of other species, or because of the inclemency of the climate. There is only established. . .a more or less regular equilibrium, encompassing the full extent of each of them, as a result of these two opposing forces, of which one produces too great an increase and the other compensates for the excess by a premature destruction. It is, therefore, the *sufferings* that accompany this destruction that counterbalance the effects of a superfluous abundance, of which the attraction of *pleasure* has been the cause.

In this introduction, Condorcet clearly breaks with the Stoic and Christian tradition which, when speaking of animals, ignored both the pleasure which they sought in the act of procreation and their sufferings in death, and consequently never emphasized the cruelty of the regulatory mechanisms of nature. In this respect, he anticipated Malthus's *Essay*. However, it was not continence and prolonged celibacy that he proposed as a solution.

Does this law of nature apply to man? He alone, among all the animals, has found a way to separate, in the act which should perpetuate the species, the gratification inherent in that act and the procreation which, in other species, is the involuntary cause of it. Not only do the motives of a more permanent and more long-lasting interest give him *the strength to resist this attraction*; but he may yield to it, and foresee the consequences of it. Thus, his will can, *without it even implying great sacrifices for him*, establish in a more pleasant manner for his species that equilibrium which can continue to exist in the others only as a result of violent upheavals and cruel destructions.[89]

The reason for which 'Malthusian' couples reproached the laws of nature was not that the latter restricted their pleasure, as Moheau and the Christian moralists maintained, but that they established demographic equilibrium by the death of redundant children. It was the refusal to acquiesce to infant mortality that gave them the 'strength to resist' the sexual impulse. Because he understood their fundamental motivation, Condorcet was not reduced to denying that birth control demanded a certain degree of asceticism, a reduction of gratification, whether it were effected by means of continence ('to resist that attraction'), coitus interruptus or any other contraceptive method. Although he emphasized that it did not necessarily imply 'great sacrifices', this was to encourage married couples to limit their fertility, and because, unlike Malthus, he acknowledged the legitimacy of contraception.

He was probably referring to coitus interruptus when he wrote:

Habit generally renders the success of this method almost certain for individuals with a sound constitution; it renders almost unnoticeable the sacrifice that it demands, and to make it more assured one might add certain new expedients, less generally known; the diminution of pleasure which may result from it is not enough to counterbalance important or long-term interests.

These 'new expedients, less generally known' were, apparently, male condoms, to which he later devotes a lengthy dissertation.

Now there exists a method of preserving oneself from at the same time a malady that destroys the human race and from involuntary fertility. Everyone knows that this malady shortens one's life, corrupts one's old age, destroys the talents and the vigour of those whom it does not kill, extends its influence from one generation to another, and above all is injurious to procreation; and great care has been taken to prevent this method from becoming more widespread, and thus becoming a practice more effectual, more easy and less expensive. A physicist who would compose a treatise on the nature of the materials that should be employed, the physical and chemical properties that they should [possess], the precautions that need to be taken in manufacture, with regard to both strength and all the other specifications that must be followed, such a physicist would be expelled from our academies. . .Similarly, this method has been until now absolutely useless to the human species because it remains little known, so that very few men can afford to make use of it, because the price, increased as a result of prejudice, and the difficulties of manufacture because of the unskilful workers who consented to undertake this work, have even led to the use of materials which make it much less safe, and, owing to the fatality that attaches itself to everything shrouded in a veil of mystery, this little invention which would have been of such great utility has been abandoned to quackery. How, then, has one been able to make into an object of shame something that has no other purpose than to preserve men and to prevent the birth of individuals doomed to that misfortune which almost infallibly awaits him whose birth is feared?

Asking himself since what era humanity had discovered the means of separating pleasure from procreation, Condorcet formulated a reply on the basis of what he knew of contraception in pre-industrial society.

The accounts of travellers do not tell us in what epoch of civilization this method became generally known. It appears that it must have been very close to that in which the fertility of girls became a cause of disgrace to them, and the birth of a child without a recognized father a misfortune for a family. The author of this dishonour, of this misfortune, though already punished by the reproaches and the sufferings of her whom he loved, found himself exposed to vengeance.

On this point, therefore, he shares the interpretation of Moheau, and confirms the analysis which we have carried out above regarding the earliest diffusion of coitus interruptus. First threatened in his very existence because he threatened the honour of his mother, it was the illegitimate child who was the first to be prevented from being born.

Saving the foster-children

Condorcet went on to imagine a second reason for recourse to contraception, which might explain the second stage of its diffusion, that is, its introduction into conjugal relations.

> Since in the human species, even at the lowest degree of civilization at which it has been observed, there are not for either of the two sexes exclusive periods, either for desire or for the possibility of satisfying it, it has also been necessary to seek and find the means of not being deprived of the woman during the nursing stage, without a new pregnancy injuring the first child.

Because they did not accept either contraception or marital infidelity, the Catholic theologians had found in the practice of putting the baby out to nurse the solution to the incompatibility of the functions of nurse and of wife. Enlightened opinion in the eighteenth century, because it did not accept either infidelity or putting out to nurse, saw as the only solution – before the advances in the artificial feeding of babies – contraception.

The fiercest adversaries of contraception confirm this analysis: Father Féline, for example, counted among the motives that impelled his penitents to commit the 'sin of Onan', 'the fear which the women have of finding themselves pregnant again too soon after their confinements', not wishing 'to injure the children whom they are nursing'. And he stated that 'it is this situation in which a great number find themselves'.[90]

Rejecting this interpretation of the origins of contraception, the demographers have not troubled to confirm testimonies of this nature. Nevertheless, these clarify a number of existing demographic data. Was it not to precautions of this nature that the couples of the south-west owed their low fertility? A recent study[91] has concluded that they probably did not practise contraception, because, between 1720 and 1819, one does not find among them the tendency – characteristic of present-day 'Malthusianism' – to group together all the births at the beginning of married life. But it is quite possible that in past times contraception was practised for reasons different from those of today. In an age when it was not known how to feed babies 'artificially', it was during the nursing stage that it was imperative to avoid conception. The women of the south-west, instead of having *average* intervals of two years between births, like those of northern France, had intervals of from two-and-a-half to three years. Was this merely because they had more often nursed their babies themselves or for longer periods? But we have observed that, in northern France, the physiological sterility of the nurse did not last as long as the period of nursing, and it would be astonishing if the women of the south-west were physiologically different. If they hardly ever became pregnant during the nursing stage, and if their nurselings, in consequence, hardly ever died (Figure 10 above), this was because they took more care not to conceive than did the mothers of the Paris Basin.

It might be thought that the cohabitation of the young married couples with their parents had some influence on this difference in behaviour. For example, perhaps the husband – even though his authority was in principle greater in southern France – was subjected to the combined pressure of his mother and his wife, and this persuaded him to make the necessary sacrifices. Moreover, there is no proof that it was by the practice of coitus interruptus that the married couples of the south-west avoided conception during the nursing period. It might just as probably have been by a refusal of coitus, attenuated by reciprocal caresses, as during the period of betrothal.[92] In fact, since coitus interruptus did not demand 'great sacrifices', and was effective once one had become accustomed to it, couples who had practised it during the nursing period probably would have recourse to it at other times as well, to solve other problems; and consequently their fertility would have been much lower.

Nevertheless, in the south-west, as in most other regions of France – and at an even more constant rate than elsewhere – the number of children per *complete family* slowly but surely declined in the course of the eighteenth century. This decline, which became accelerated in the nineteenth century, when it assumed the characteristics of present-day Malthusianism, can probably be attributed to the practice of coitus interruptus by an increasing number of couples. In short, if one considers coitus interruptus as one of the sacrifices which married couples could impose on themselves for the good of their children – the least demanding of those sacrifices, once one had become accustomed to it – it appears that the practice of more or less strict sexual abstinence during the nursing stage prepared the married couples of the south-west systematically to impose on themselves this small sacrifice, when the Revolutionary laws requiring partition of the inheritance among the children made necessary a draconian limitation of one's offspring in order to preserve the unity of the patrimony. It was, indeed, only after the Revolution that the couples of the south-west ceased to have children beyond a certain number or a certain length of conjugal life, and they adopted this behaviour more systematically than did couples in other regions of France. On this point, too, Le Play's analysis appears to be justified, as far as these couples are concerned.

What happened, however, in northern France, where contraceptive practices became widespread in domestic life from the mid eighteenth century onwards? In the Paris Basin, in particular, where mercenary wet-nursing was extremely common, can it be supposed that the desire to preserve the lives of the nurselings was the prime cause of this propagation?

In interpreting the decline in fertility in this region, one is hampered by the insufficiency of statistical data on mercenary wet-nursing. It is generally acknowledged that it expanded continuously throughout the course of the century, notwithstanding the 'Rousseauist' campaign in favour of maternal nursing. However, did it expand to a greater or a lesser extent than can be accounted for by the growth of the towns and the increase in the abandonment of children? It seems probable that, despite the possible overall expansion, the practice diminished in the social sectors in which there had been recourse to it most habitually, that is to say, the urban élites. Detailed testimonies have, in fact, been collected about the expansion of maternal nursing at the end of the eighteenth century.[93] In Nemours, for example, from 1785 onwards, 'the well-to-do women nurse their children there', whereas 'those of the people put them out to nurse, so as to be able to work unhindered'. In the towns of the department of the Meurthe, an observer in 1805 wrote that 'it is as rare to see a mother not nursing her child, as it was twenty years ago to find one who took this trouble: the censuses held at the end of Year IV confirm that 59/60 of babies at the breast were nursed by their mothers.' And this observer, who was certainly biased, added: 'It is a patent fact that this submission to the will of nature is one of the causes of the perceptible decline in the proportions of mortality.' One could cite analogous testimonies about Paris in 1786, Saint-Malo in 1790, and the department of Mont-Blanc in 1807.

The young mothers converted to the practice of maternal nursing were generally warned against its drawbacks by a circle of relations and in-laws who were traditionally hostile to this practice. They were warned of the excessive fatigue that would afflict them, of the ridicule to which they might expose themselves by coddling the baby, and of the risks which a premature conception might entail for the lives of their children. They could overcome these arguments and this opposition only with the support of their husbands. For this reason, the transformation of the conjugal relationship into a courtly one and the pressure of Enlightened opinion were needed.

It appears that the decline in fertility took place somewhat earlier in the towns than in the rural areas (see Table 17 and Figure 11, above), and also occurred earlier among the social élites than among the people (see Table 23 above). This is in accordance with what one might suppose regarding the spread of 'Rousseauist' ideas from the upper to the lower strata of society. However, it is still not known whether, within those social élites, the women who adopted the practice of maternal nursing began earlier than others to limit their fertility, nor by what means they did so. Future demographic studies will perhaps reveal that it was, on the contrary, among the couples that continued to put their children out to nurse that contraception first became widespread.[94] We shall examine this possibility later.

The decline in fertility in the rural areas of the Paris Basin, attested from 1760 onwards (Figure 11 above) could perhaps be explained simply by the increase in the practice of putting babies out to nurse, which, by a purely natural mechanism, would have prolonged the sterile period of the nurses. However, one must bear in mind that the sterility of the nurse does not last as long as the period of nursing, and that examples of the death of a nurseling when the nurse was pregnant were numerous in this region. Furthermore, despite the spread of mercenary wet-nursing, which should have provoked an increase in infant mortality, the rates of infant mortality declined perceptibly in the second half of the eighteenth century, except among the foundlings. It is, therefore, reasonable to suppose that the mercenary nurses living with their husbands in the country increasingly took precautions to avoid pregnancy. In the sixteenth century, mothers in the towns who were concerned about the survival of their children brought the nurse to live in their house, when they could afford this, and thus prevented them from having sexual relations.[95] In the eighteenth century, when these mothers knew how to avoid pregnancy without depriving their husbands of all sexual satisfactions, they would probably have passed on this information to the nurses who then stayed in the country. Above all, they would probably have exerted on the couple responsible for the nursing financial and even judicial pressure,[96] which would have compelled them to modify their conjugal behaviour.

It has not been demonstrated – because there has been no attempt to acquire data on this subject – that the nurses who lost least children had longer intervals between confinements than the others. There are already available, however, both for the towns and the rural areas, demographic data which suggest that contraception became established in conjugal relations in order to preserve the lives of the nurselings. In Meulan and the surrounding rural areas, it was not until after the Revolution that control of fertility became conspicuous by the grouping of births at the beginning of conjugal life, as is customary nowadays. Between 1740 and

1789 it is seen only in the larger number of families with long and very long intervals between births (see Table 23 and Figure 11, above),[97] as if the intention were, not so much to prevent the dependent children from increasing beyond a certain number – which varied from one family to another – as to space out the births. This can only be explained as deriving from a concern to avoid a premature conception injuring the life of the baby being nursed. It seems unlikely that it is because of a still inadequate mastery of the technique of coitus interruptus. It would then be necessary to suppose that this technique is so difficult to use that after several years of practice, and even when age had diminished the force of sexual impulses, couples still did not succeed in mastering it. One would have to suppose that their apprenticeship lasted for half a century in the Paris Basin and for over a century in the south-west of France. Such suppositions, at the present stage of research on the subject, are certainly not the most reasonable ones. On the contrary, everything leads one to believe that, for a period which varied in length according to the region, married couples had had recourse to contraception above all to preserve the life of the nurselings. It was not until after the Revolution that it seems to have been widely used for other purposes.

Contraception as a consequence of the Catholic reforms in France

It is, however, probable that those parents who continued to put their children out to nurse also took measures to limit their fertility, precisely on account of that practice, which was so habitual in their environment: before 1789, contraception was too evidently occurring in the Paris Basin, and mercenary wet-nursing remained too systematic there, for it to have been otherwise.[98]

It seems unlikely that recourse to contraceptive measures was taken because the excessive fertility physiologically entailed by the practice of putting out to nurse rendered intolerable the number of dependent children. There are several difficulties with this explanation. Firstly, it was the richest and not the poorest who were the first to become 'Malthusians'. This necessarily implies that economic constraints were not the only cause: the important factor is the mental attitude with which these were perceived. Furthermore, one would need to explain why this burden should have become intolerable from 1740 onwards – when circumstances were becoming particularly favourable to the rich – and why it had not been intolerable previously. Was it because the costs of education increased? However, with this hypothesis one is leaving the sphere of economics and entering that of the history of education. Except for the very poorest families – which seem to have been the last to be affected by the decline in fertility – it is impossible to explain these changes in conjugal behaviour in terms of purely economic motives. It is necessary to look for the explanation in terms of a transformation of mental attitudes.

We have emphasized that in almost all northern France, the great decline in fertility had been preceded by a rise, of more or less short duration, which cannot be explained simply by improved registration of births. This rise was probably caused partly by an improvement in the standard of living and a fall in morbidity, but it may also have been caused by a stricter enforcement of the traditional system, under the influence of the Catholic reforms. Might there not be a dialectical relationship between this rise and the decline that followed it? Might the rejection of the traditional system not have resulted from a stricter enforcement, which would have exacerbated the contradictions inherent in it? And might this not have happened first in the sectors in which these contradictions might have been most strongly resented, that is, among the élites? It was their members who, on the one hand, systematically put their children out to nurse and, on the other, had more rapidly been made sensitive, by the Christian moralists and the *philosophes*, to their responsibilities with regard to infant mortality.

Traditionally, the death of children at an early age had been attributed to the mysterious will of God, as had been their birth. Furthermore, the practice of putting out to nurse meant that the parents did not become too emotionally disturbed, because separation from the moment of birth prevented maternal and paternal love from crystallizing, and because the father and mother were not present at the death-agony of the child, and did not themselves struggle to save its life.

However, the parents who put their children out to nurse – especially the mothers – were the first to be held responsible for their death or their illness. As early as the sixteenth century, physicians had recommended maternal nursing, and they found in ancient literature extremely harsh comments on mothers who did not nurse their children.[99] As for Christian moralists, one may refer the reader to Benedicti. It is true that they did not actually forbid the practice of putting out to nurse, and even recommended it as a solution for the incompatibility of the nursing and the conjugal functions, but they made mothers who had recourse to it feel guilty. To realize that one is responsible for the life or death of one's child by the good or bad choice one has made of its nurse is a first step, and probably a fundamental one, towards a more general realization of parental responsibilities. It may be assumed that, between the late sixteenth and the mid eighteenth century, the increasing ascendancy of the clergy over the minds of the faithful involved, for the mothers, a growing tendency to feel guilty about this practice.

Moreover, the teaching of the moralists underwent a perceptible trans-formation: they increasingly tended to emphasize the sacredness of the child's life. When a mother was too poor to put her child out to nurse, the medieval theologians considered that she was nonetheless obliged to render the conjugal due, even if she had positive reasons for fearing that her child would die as a result. Pierre de Ledesma, at the end of the sixteenth century, seems to have differed from this opinion. However, his view was too novel to gain acceptance. Thomas Sanchez declined to commit himself: he certainly considered 'that she is dispensed from the obligation of rendering the due, the mother. . .who knows from experience that her breasts dry up when she conceives or that her milk becomes very injurious to the child'; but this was only out of condescension to the sufferings of a loving mother, and not because he regarded the life of the child as sacred: 'The mother', he wrote, 'is not obliged to expose herself to such suffering, nor to suffer such injury.'[100] Moreover, we have observed that, in fact, he was as generous towards the father, authorizing him to demand the conjugal due even when this imperilled the life of the child. In the eighteenth century, on the other hand, a conformist writer such as Fromageau considered that the wife could refuse to render the due to her husband, 'because he does not have the right to demand it in this case, at the expense of his child's life'.

At the same time, Enlightened opinion unambiguously condemned the practice of putting babies out to nurse: 'To surrender a child to a strange woman is a cruel and unnatural act, which, if it were an isolated occur-rence, would be regarded as an atrocity', wrote Moheau, for example. Many mothers among the élites were influenced by this propaganda in favour of maternal nursing. Not all of them, however, found in their immediate circle or in their husbands the support needed to translate these intentions into acts. One can divine, in many households at that time, a crisis in connection with the nursing of the children. Might not the refusal to conceive have been, on the part of a certain number of women, a reaction to this lack of understanding on the part of their husbands and their kinsfolk? Coitus interruptus might have been a means of alleviating the conflicts, a means more convenient for everybody than maternal nursing and sexual abstinence.

In more general terms, one might assume that many couples limited their fertility because the moralists of the Catholic reformation had made them realize the great extent of their duties towards their children – in terms of their moral, intellectual and professional education – without having given them sufficient reasons for accepting this servitude. The con-tinual tirades about the selfishness of the unmarried and of Malthusian couples are not necessarily without foundation: in an age and in the social sectors in which there was a consciousness of these duties, it was, perhaps, the most selfish and the most avid for pleasure who had least children. However, the transformation of mental attitudes which explains the appearance in history of 'Malthusian' practices consisted not of a growth of hedonism, but of a realization of the duties involved in procreation. All the evidence indicates that in the eighteenth century there was a greater realization than in the sixteenth century; pity for children was felt more systematically; their innocence was held to be sacred, and thus one was all the less inclined to tolerate the injustice of their death. The simple joys of family life became fashionable among the social élites. If hedonism was at that time a motive for sterility, the reason was that fatherhood, which previously had been above all a source of power, had increasingly become revealed as a source of servitude. And who had been the cause of this development, if not the moralists of the Catholic reformation?

Why France?

Birth control became widespread in France a century earlier than in England and the other countries – both Catholic and Protestant – of western Europe. This has long been considered to have been an effect of the Revolution, with its dechristianizing and egalitarian tendencies. The Revolution probably did accelerate the process, by liberating a part of the population of France from the prohibition that the Church had hurled against contraception, and because the Revolutionary laws regarding succession, by upsetting the system of reproduction in southern France, obliged couples to limit their offspring in a draconian manner. This explanation, however, does not apply at all to northern France.

More recently, an attempt has been made to find an explanation in terms of Jansenism, that other eminently French phenomenon.[101] But in what way could Jansenism have prepared the way for Malthusianism? Did it do so as a school of sexual asceticism, developing among the faithful a hatred of the works of the flesh and, as a result, inspiring conjugal continence? In this case, it would have to be proved that this condemnation of the works of the flesh was characteristic of Jansenist preaching, and one could then acknowledge that the decline in fertility in France – at least in the early stages – can be attributed to the growth of conjugal continence rather than to the sin of Onan. At present, one is far from being able to prove this. Can one say, instead, that Jansenist asceticism taught the faithful to control their bodies, thus making them capable of practising coitus interruptus? This idea, though interesting, is not supported at present by any evidence, and probably no evidence will ever be forthcoming. As for the suggestion that coitus interruptus may have been practised to attenuate the sin of the flesh that one imagined that one was committing in legitimate marriage, this is to make a totally unjustifiable amalgam between Jansenism and twelfth-century Catharism.

Jansenism might, however, have influenced developments in another way, by instilling into the faithful the habit of following the promptings of their conscience as against the directions of priests suspected of moral laxism – in this case, those who encouraged married couples to procreate without worrying about the possibility of feeding and educating their children, or the risks that a new pregnancy entailed for the baby being nursed by the wife. This explanation would be compatible with and support the theses maintained in this book. It must, however, be clearly stated that such a degree of moral independence could just as easily be a symptom of the irreligion provoked in France by two centuries of struggle between Catholics and Protestants and then between Molinists and Jansenists. France was, to a greater extent than other European countries, the scene of these conflicts, and today it is increasingly clear that the incredulity and the hatred of fanaticism which characterize the thought of 'enlightened' Frenchmen are the results of this experience. Unfortunately for this theory, this moral independence on the part of married couples also existed in England, both as a consequence of the violent religious conflicts of the sixteenth and seventeenth centuries and because the Protestant clergy intervened much less than the Catholic father-confessors in the sexual life of married couples.

We may turn this argument the other way round: it is not impossible that it was acts of indiscreet interference, particularly those of the more rigorous confessors, who were suspected on these grounds of Jansenism, which had driven married couples away from the confessional and made them more radically independent of Christian morality than Protestant couples in England. Clerics such as Mgr Bouvier vividly described this danger in the nineteenth century, and there is abundant evidence of its existence from the eighteenth century onwards: the orders to exercise discretion imparted to confessors, the development of the theory of good faith, or even the condemnation of works recommending the systematic investigation of the sin of Onan, such as that of Father Féline. Being allowed more freedom, Protestant couples were able to limit their fertility in hard times and to remove the restraints during periods of economic expansion, whereas the Catholics, principally in the areas where the Jansenists held sway, may have entirely abandoned the 'trickeries of past times'. Finally, if it is possible to establish a correlation between the presence of a Jansenist clergy and the spread of 'Malthusian' practices, this may be explained in different and even contradictory ways, and does not enlighten us very greatly as to the reasons for the emergence of 'Malthusianism' in France from the eighteenth century onwards.

Furthermore, the abandonment of Christian morality did not necessarily imply recourse to the act of Onan. As Condorcet observes, 'only rarely have the Philosophers bestowed a confident look on those objects placed between repugnance and ridicule, in which case it has been necessary to avoid at the same time hypocrisy and scandal'. And he is astonished at this: 'Why...would the Philosophers, who have defied the league of tyrants and priests, be afraid of that of the practical jokers and the moral hypocrites? Would their courage be brought to an end by the fear of ridicule and the anathemas of a false delicacy or an artificial austerity?'[102] It is quite probable. It was easier for them to denounce the celibacy of the clergy in the name of 'populationism' – the Protestants, Colbert, Louis XIV and many others having preceded them in this line of argument – than to oppose the Church on the point at which its morality came closest to the naturalism of their own.

Nevertheless, which of these *philosophes* were fathers of a large family? Most of them, in one way or another, sinned daily 'against nature'. It can be assumed that the 'Enlightened' people of the second half of the eighteenth century, freed from the prohibitions of the Church, behaved in their private lives like the *philosophes*, even if, like them, they affected in public to be 'populationists' and obedient to the laws of nature. The genius of Condorcet, in this sphere as in others, consisted in evolving a theory on the basis of their practice.

Finally, one may reckon the process of dechristianization to be one of the factors that explain the spread of contraception in France a century earlier than in other countries. However, from the eighteenth to the twentieth centuries birth control by married couples has been practised among Christians as well as among unbelievers. Besides, those who consider the rate of illegitimacy of births to be an indication of the rejection of Christian morality should observe that it was, in the eighteenth century, higher in England than in France. France is, perhaps, the country in which moral liberty was most harshly repressed in the seventeenth and the first half of the eighteenth century: the Mediterranean countries were traditionally more uncompromising as regards the virginity of marriageable girls; the other European countries seem to have been more tolerant of pre-marital intimacy. There are very few villages in France where the rates of illegitimacy, in the first half of the eighteenth century, approach the English rates (Figure 4 above). This harsher repression was a factor favouring the development of contraceptive practices in extra-marital relations.

We have maintained that birth control within marriage is essentially explained as a result of a change in the conjugal relationship and by an increased sense of responsibility towards the children. Should one, therefore, assume that these changes took place in England and the other countries of Europe later than in France? The question cannot be evaded; but one cannot, unfortunately, provide a serious answer, in the absence of truly comparative studies of family attitudes in France and England. Let us try, despite this, to reason on the basis of the little we do know.

The evolution of conjugal relationships is, quite clearly, not peculiar to France. In some respects, it may even have been more marked and chronologically earlier in England: the improvement in the legal status of women between the fifteenth and the nineteenth centuries may have been less ambiguous there.[103] Moreover, from the sixteenth century onwards, the Puritan moralists justified, to a certain extent, the marriage of love. Numerous travellers of the seventeenth and eighteenth centuries extolled the freedom of choice enjoyed by English girls and the familiarity existing between husband and wife in England. However, did these trusting relationships imply that the women were able, to the same degree as in France, to impose their will on their husbands in the marriage-bed? It was owing to gallantry that the situation of the French wife became transformed, and such relationships of gallantry imply a kind of distance, a sort of battle between the sexes, which was not, perhaps, part of the English tradition. 'I would find it more to my taste to have an English wife', wrote François de La Rochefoucauld, after observing that in England 'the woman...has an air of obligingness which has always pleased me'. Moreover, he concluded that in that country 'the union of husbands and wives has...a political advantage': 'Families are much larger in England than in France, nearly all the fathers and mothers have eight, ten or twelve children.'

In the domain of the relations between parents and children, the progress of the English is much more debatable. It is true that the Puritan or Anglican moralists informed parents as to their duties,[104] but we do not know whether they insisted on them as much as the Catholics did. This remains to be shown by a systematically comparative study. In any case, it seems that the Protestant commentators on the Fourth Commandment – like the Catholic ones before the Council of Trent – did not refer to these duties at all. All foreign travellers, from the sixteenth to the eighteenth century, were impressed by the brutality of the English towards adolescents. Aristocratic education, until the twentieth century, was influenced by the Spartan model to a much greater extent than in the other countries of Europe. The children of the people were driven out of the paternal home at the very beginning of their adolescence, and condemned to forced labour in the house of another person. The apprenticeship law of 1563 made this system general and this servitude obligatory both in the country and the towns. This expulsion of the adolescents

certainly solved some problems which the French peasants of the nineteenth century solved by contraception.

Being less conscious of their duties as parents, and more accustomed
than the French to losing their children at the beginning of adolescence,
the English of the eighteenth and nineteenth centuries must have had
fewer scruples about procreating children whom they could not support
with the ancestral patrimony. Besides, many other people in English
society at that time acted in the same way. The principle of the right of
primogeniture accustomed parents of all social classes to seeing their
younger sons living by their labour alone. The wage-earners were
numerically predominant in England from the eighteenth century onwards, whereas in France, even in the nineteenth century, small peasant
proprietors formed the majority of the population. The wage-earner – or
at all events the worker – seems to have been 'Malthusian' less often than
the small proprietor. This is attested, in nineteenth-century France, by
the high rates of fertility in the industrialized departments: Nord, Pas-de-
Calais, Seine-Inférieure, Moselle, Haut-Rhin, Bas-Rhin, Loire, Bouches-
du-Rhône, etc.; and, above all, by the rise in the national rates of
reproduction and infant mortality under the Second Empire, a period of
intensive industrialization. However paradoxical it may appear at first
sight, the earlier proletarianization of English society and the earlier
industrialization delayed for two centuries the 'Malthusian revolution',
just as they appear to have also hindered the growth of universal literacy.

Finally, there is the following paradox: in so far as it was a response to
the refusal to accept the deaths of new-born children, contraception first
became widespread in France because, as a result of the practice of
mercenary wet-nursing, infant mortality was probably greater there than
in any other country in Europe. It was the increasingly murderous nature
of this practice that aroused both in parents and in nurses a consciousness
of their responsibility for the deaths of the children, and impelled them to
refuse that death by refusing the gift of life. If, in the other countries of
Europe, parents only later realized their responsibilities, the reason was
that their culpability was less great or less perceptible, and at all events
less easy to denounce.

Notes

INTRODUCTION

1. *The Diary of Samuel Pepys*, ed. Henry B. Wheatley (8 vols., London, 1924), January 1659–60, vol. I, pp. 1–2.

CHAPTER 1. THE TIES OF KINSHIP

1. Michel de Montaigne, *Essais* (Paris, 1950), bk. I, ch XLVII, p. 313.
2. *Ibid.*, p. 314.
3. Pierre de Bourdeille, Abbé and Seigneur de Brantôme, 'Nombre et rolle de mes nepveux, petitz-nepveux, ou arrière-petitz-nepveux à la mode de Bretagne, que moy Brantôme je puis avoir, et que j'ay faict aujourd'hui 5 novembre M.DC.II', in *Oeuvres*, ed. Ludovic Lalanne (11 vols., Paris, 1864–82), vol. X, pp. 88–106, 91–2.
4. *Ibid.* p. 90.
5. Pierre de Lancre, *Tableau de l'inconstance des mauvais anges* (1612), quoted in Jean-François Soulet, *La Vie quotidienne dans les Pyrénées, sous l'ancien régime du XVIe au XVIIIe siècle* (Paris, 1974), p. 221.
6. Soulet, p. 221.
7. Claude Liberman, 'Démographie d'une paroisse basque sous l'Ancien Régime: Urrugne', unpublished M.A. thesis, University of Paris 8-Vincennes, 1976, pp. 10–12.
8. Brantôme, pp. 94–5.
9. Mgr Abelly, *La Vie du vénérable serviteur de Dieu Vincent de Paul* (Paris, 1664), bk. II, ch. I, sect. V ('Des missions faites en l'Isle de Corse'), pp. 73–4.
10. Louis Faletti, *Le Retrait lignager en droit coutumier français* (Paris, 1923), *passim*.
11. *Ibid.* pp. 153 and 162–3.
12. *Ibid.* pp. 178–9.
13. *Ibid.* pp. 176–7.
14. *Ibid.* ch. III, pp. 252ff.
15. Rétif de la Bretonne, *La Vie de mon père*, ed. G. Rouger (Paris, 1970), p. 27.
16. *Encyclopédie ou dictionnaire raisonné des sciences, des arts et métiers*, vol. XI (1765), p. 937, col. 1.
17. See, for example, Orest Ranum, *Les Créatures de Richelieu* (Paris, 1966), *passim*.
18. Duc de Saint-Simon, *Mémoires* (7 vols., Paris, 1947–61), vol. I, ch. VIII (1964), pp. 114ff.
19. *Ibid.*
20. Faletti, pp. 253–5.
21. *Encyclopédie*, vol. XI, p. 937, col. 2.

22. The wills utilized in this study have been published in C. Aboucaya, *Les testaments lyonnais de la fin du XVe siècle au milieu du XVIIIe* (Paris, 1961), pp. 182–216.

23. Faletti, p. 253.

24. Charles Lalore, *Ancienne discipline du diocèse du Troyes* (4 vols., Troyes, 1882–3), vol. II, pp. 72–4.

25. 'Deux bourgeois de Vitré; Journal inédit; 1490–1583', published by Emile Clouard, *Revue de Bretagne*, vol. LI (1914), pp. 70–91, 133–42, 197–237.

26. Nicolas Versoris, *Journal d'un bourgeois de Paris sous François I*, text selected and edited by Philippe Joutard (Paris, 1963), collection 10/18, no. 69.

27. Alan Macfarlane, *The Family Life of Ralph Josselin, a Seventeenth-Century Clergyman: An Essay in Historical Anthropology* (Cambridge, 1970), pp. 105ff.

28. A. L. Rowse, *Simon Forman, Sex and Society in Shakespeare's Age* (London, 1971), *passim*.

29. *The Diary of Samuel Pepys*, ed. Henry B. Wheatley (8 vols., London, 1924), introduction (vol. I) and index (vol. VIII).

30. G. Arbellot, *Cinq paroisses du Vallage, XVIIe–XVIIIe siècles*, AUDIR Microfiche no. 73.944.1.

31. For example, Claude Karnoouh, 'L'Étranger ou le faux inconnu', *Ethnologie Française*, vol. II, nos 1–2, pp. 107–22.

32. Maurice Garden, *Lyon et les Lyonnais au XVIIIe siècle* (Paris, 1970), pp. 405–8.

33. Soulet, p. 244.

34. *Ibid.* p. 240.

35. Rétif de la Bretonne, *Monsieur Nicolas* (14 vols., Paris, 1883), vol. II, pp. 417–18, quoted by G. Rouger with reference to *La Vie de mon père*, pp. 193–4.

36. De la Bretonne, *Monsieur Nicolas*, vol. I, p. 108.

37. *Ibid.* vol. I, p. 122.

38. *Ibid.* vol. I, pp. 93–4.

39. De la Bretonne, *La Vie de mon père*, p. 117.

40. De la Bretonne, *Monsieur Nicolas*, vol. I, p. 194.

41. *Ibid.* vol. I, pp. 198ff.

42. *Ibid.* vol. I, pp. 195–6.

43. *Ibid.* vol. I, p. 197.

44. *Ibid.* vol. I, pp. 20–1.

45. Saint-Simon, *Mémoires*, vol. I, pp. 228–30.

46. De la Bretonne, *La Vie de mon père*, pp. 110–11.

47. *Archives départementales de l'Aube*, Inventory series G, vol. III, p. 4.

48. David Houard, *Dictionnaire...de la coutume de Normandie* (4 vols., Rouen, 1780–3), vol. III, pp. 235–40, quoted in J.-M. Gouesse, *Documents de l'histoire de la Normandie* (Toulouse, 1972), p. 311.

49. *Archives départementales de l'Aube*, Inventory series G, vol. III, p. 3.

50. De la Bretonne, *Monsieur Nicolas*, vol. I, pp. 117–19, quoted by G. Rouger in *La Vie de mon père*, pp. 218–20.

51. *Les Cahiers du capitaine Coignet* (Paris, 1968), pp. 3–10.

52. De la Bretonne, *La Vie de mon père*, p. 108.

53. *Ibid.* p. 117.

54. *Ibid.* p. 116.

55. *Ibid.* p. 118.

56. *Archives départementales de Seine-et-Marne*, 22.G.41, enquiry of 9 May 1738.

57. *Ibid.* 22.G.40, dispensation dated 13 January 1737.

58. *Ibid.* series B, Bailiwick of Provins, declaration of pregnancy, 27 January 1748.

59. De la Bretonne, *La Vie de mon père*, p. 28.
60. This incident has been examined more fully in J.-L. Flandrin, *Les Amours paysannes* (Paris, 1975), pp. 71–2.
61. De la Bretonne, *La Vie de mon père*, p. 70.
62. 'He who has only daughters for sons-in-law will be at all times in a great wrangle': A.-J.-V. Le Roux de Lincy, *Le Livre des proverbes français*, 2nd edn (2 vols., Paris, 1859), vol. I, p. 234; 'An angered son is better than a calm son-in-law': Marie Mauron, *Dictons d'Oc et Proverbes de Provence* (Forcalquier, 1965), p. 92; 'Keep your son-in-law far away and your dunghill close by': F. Allemand, 'Proverbes Alpins spécialement recueillis dans le Champsaur et le Gapençais', *Bulletin de la société d'Etudes des Hautes Alpes*, vol. III (1884), pp. 369–80, no. 277.
63. *Les Cahiers du capitaine Coignet*, pp. 6–8, 14.
64. De la Bretonne, *La Vie de mon père*, pp. 26–7.
65. *Archives départementales de Seine-et-Marne*, 22.G.43, dispensation dated 4 February 1751.
66. Flandrin, *Les Amours paysannes*, pp. 141–6.

CHAPTER 2. THE HOUSEHOLD: SIZE, STRUCTURE AND MATERIAL LIFE

1. Frédéric Le Play, *La Réforme sociale* (Paris, 1864).
2. Pierre Bourdieu, 'Célibat et condition sociale', *Etudes rurales* (April–September 1962), and 'Les Stratégies matrimoniales dans le système de reproduction', *Annales E.S.C.* (July–October 1972).
3. Peter Laslett, *Household and Family in Past Time* (Cambridge, 1972), p. 623.
4. Pierre Goubert, *Beauvais et le Beauvaisis* (Paris, 1960), pp. 30–45, 61–2; Michel Fleury and Louis Henry, *Nouveau manuel de dépouillement et d'exploitation de l'état civil ancien* (Paris, 1965).
5. For example, R. Noël, 'La Population de la paroisse de Laguiole d'après un recensement de 1961', *Annales de démographie historique* (1967), pp. 197–223; and P. Lions and M. Lachiver, 'Dénombrement de la population de Brueil-en-Vexin en 1625', *Annales de démographie historique* (1967), pp. 521–37.
6. Laslett, *Household and Family in Past Time*, pp. 130–1, 133, 138.
7. Peter Laslett, *The World We Have Lost*, 2nd edn (London, 1971), pp. 66–71.
8. Louis Merle, *La Métairie et l'évolution agraire de la Gâtine poitevine, de la fin du Moyen Age à la Revolution* (Paris, 1958), p. 252.
9. Gerard Bouchard, *Le Village immobile, Sennely-en-Sologne au XVIIIe siècle* (Paris, 1972).
10. See, for example, Lawrence Stone, *The Crisis of Aristocracy* (Oxford, 1965), p. 569; and Elizabeth Bourcier, 'La Famille anglaise dans la première moitié du XVIIe siècle à travers les journaux privés du temps', *RANAM (Recherches Anglaises et Américaines)*, no. VIII (1975), p. 39.
11. Laslett, *The World We Have Lost*, p. 94.
12. *Ibid.* p. 95.
13. *Ibid.* p. 181; see also Stone and Bourcier.
14. Laslett, *The World We Have Lost*, pp. 98–9.
15. Jacques Dupâquier and Louis Jadin, 'Structure of household and family in Corsica, 1769–1717', in Laslett, *Household and Family in Past Times*, ch. 11.
16. This refers to the unpublished studies submitted in the Ecole des Hautes Etudes en Sciences Sociales to the seminar organized by J. Dupaquier and J.-P. Bardet, on 25 November 1974, by Jean-Claude Peyronnet and Mme Nicole Lemaitre on

Limousin, by Mlle Antoinette Chamoux on the Pyrenean Baronies, and by Alain Collomp on Haute-Provence.

17. J.-C. Peyronnet, 'Famille élargie ou famille nucléaire? En Limousin au début du XIXe siècle', *Revue d'histoire moderne et contemporaine* (October–December 1975), pp. 568–82.

18. Interdisciplinary study in ethnohistory by the Centre de Recherches Historiques, relating to the Baronies of the Hautes-Pyrénées (forthcoming 1979).

19. Alain Collomp, 'Alliance et filiation en haute Provence au XVIIIe siècle', *Annales E.S.C.* (May–June 1977), p. 445.

20. Jean Yver, *Egalité entre héritiers et exclusion des enfants dotés* (Paris, 1966). See also Emmanuel Le Roy Ladurie, 'Structures familiales et coutumes d'héritage', *Annales E.S.C.* (July–October 1972), pp. 825–46, which covers the essential elements in the work of Yver.

21. Article 1 of the compilation of customary laws of Bareges, quoted in Jean-François Soulet, *La Vie quotidienne dans les Pyrénées sous l'ancien régime du XVIe au XVIIIe siècle* (Paris, 1974), pp. 222–3.

22. Bourdieu, 'Célibat et condition sociale' and 'Les Stratégies matrimoniales'.

23. Evidence published in Abel Hugo, *La France pittoresque* (3 vols., Paris, 1835), vol. I, p. 266.

24. Document published by Jean-Noël Biraben in *Annales de démographie historique* (1970), pp. 441–62; and, in a more sophisticated form, in Laslett, *Household and Family in Past Time*, ch. 8.

25. Yver, pp. 158–9.

26. *Ibid.* p. 159.

27. There are, however, some statistical data relating to the villages of Escoutoux and Messeix, in Abel Poitrineau, *La Vie rurale dans la Basse-Auvergne au XVIIIe siècle* (2 vols., Paris, 1965), vol. I, pp. 595–9, and in Guy Thuillier, *Aspects de l'économie nivernaise au XIXe siècle* (Paris, 1966), pp. 33ff. See also Michel Morineau, 'Le peuplement de la généralité de Moulins', *Annales de démographie historique* (1973), pp. 475ff.

28. Yver, pp. 211–21 (for Valenciennes) and 203–10 (for Longuenesse).

29. A. Collomp, 'Famille nucléaire et famille élargie en Provence au XVIIIe siècle', *Annales E.S.C.* (July–October 1972), p. 971.

30. Yver, pp. 108–9 and 297–8 (on imposition from above), and pp. 279–89 (on Scandinavian law).

31. Quoted in Yver, p. 41, n. 65c.

32. Pierre de Saint-Jacob, *Les Paysans de la Bourgogne du Nord au dernier siècle de l'Ancien Régime* (Paris, 1960), pp. 38–9.

33. *Ibid.* p. 423.

34. G. Chevrier, 'L'Originalité du droit franc-comtois', *Tijdschrift voor Rechtsgeschiedenis*, no. XXVII (1959); and Simone Galliot, *Le Régime matrimonial en droit franc-comtois de 1459 à la Revolution*, unpublished law thesis (Paris, 1953), particularly pp. 32–5, from which source all the following examples have been drawn.

35. Chevrier, pp. 183–4; and Jean Gaudemet, *Les Communautés familiales* (Paris, 1963), p. 122, n. 108.

36. Emmanuel Le Roy Ladurie, *Les Paysans de Languedoc* (2 vols., Paris, 1966), vol. I, pp. 162–5; and, for more detailed information, Jean Hilaire, *Le Régime des biens entre époux dans la région de Montpellier* (Paris, 1957), *passim*.

37. Yves Castan, *Honnêteté et relations sociales en Languedoc, 1715–1780* (Paris, 1974), pp. 229–35.

38. Le Roy Ladurie, *Les Paysans de Languedoc* pp. 165–8; Hilaire; R. Aubenas, 'Le Contrat d'affrairamentum dans le droit provençal du Moyen Age', *Revue d'histoire du droit* (1933); Ch. de Ribbe, *La Société provençale à la fin du Moyen Age* (Paris, 1898); A. Dumas, *La Condition des gens dans la famille périgourdine, XVe–XVIe siècles* (Paris, 1908); M. Juillard, 'La Vie populaire à la fin du Moyen Age en Auvergne, XVe siècle', *Auvergne*, no. 28 (1951), p. 61.

39. Gaudemet, pp. 117–18.

40. *Ibid.* pp. 89, 97.

41. Guy Coquille, *Coutume du Nivernais* (1864), pp. 304–14.

42. Le Roy Ladurie, *Les Paysans de Languedoc*, p. 167.

43. There has been much discussion concerning the historical importance of this phenomenon. Be that as it may, its existence is unquestionable: it was denounced as early as the beginning of the sixteenth century by Thomas More (see *The Complete Works of St. Thomas More* (New Haven and London, 1963), vol. IV, *Utopia*, pp. 65, 67).

44. Poitrineau.

45. *Cahier de Vouzon*, published in C. Bloch, *Cahiers de doléances du bailliage d'Orléans* (2 vols., Orleans, 1906), vol. I, p. 441; quoted by Bouchard, pp. 230–1, no. 51.

46. Le Roy Ladurie, *Les Paysans de Languedoc*, p. 167.

47. Poitrineau.

48. Gaudemet, pp. 97–100.

49. Collomp, 'Famille nucléaire', p. 972.

50. Research carried out by Jean-Pierre Bardet, on Rouen; research by the Laboratory of Historical Demography of the Ecole des Hautes Etudes en Sciences Sociales, on Valenciennes and the neighbouring villages; results submitted by J.-P. Bardet to the seminar held on 3 February 1975.

51. Philippe Ariès, *L'Enfant et la vie familiale sous l'Ancien Régime* (Paris, 1973), pp. 441–61, and, for the iconography of family life, pp. 377–407.

52. *Les Caquets de l'accouchée* (Paris, 1890); see, for example, pp. 14–15.

53. S. G. Longchamp and Wagnière, *Mémoires sur Voltaire* (2 vols., Paris, 1826), vol. II, pp. 119ff., quoted in Franklin, *La Vie privée d'autrefois*, abridged edn (Paris, 1973), p. 234.

54. Norbert Elias, *La Société de cour* (Paris, 1974), p. 25, n. 1.

55. Françoise Janin, 'Crimes et délits sexuels dans l'ancien droit francais, XVIe–XVIIIe siècles', unpublished M.A. thesis (University of Paris I, 1973), e.g. pp. 53–7.

56. Mme de Campan, *Mémoires* (3 vols., Paris, 1822), vol. I, ch. IV, p. 104, quoted in Franklin, p. 234.

57. This idea has already been put forward by Ariès, pp. 443, 457–8, and by Bouchard, p. 236.

58. Maurice Garden, *Lyon et les Lyonnais au XVIIIe siècle* (Paris, 1970), pp. 405–22, particularly p. 408.

59. Richard Lick, 'Les Intérieurs domestiques dans la seconde moitié du XVIIIe siècle, d'après les inventaires après décès de Coutances', *Annales de Normandie*, 20th yr, no. 4 (December 1970), pp. 291–316.

60. J. Carrière, 'La Population d'Aix-en-Provence à le fin du XVIIe siècle', *Annales de la Faculté des Lettres d'Aix-en-Provence* (1958).

61. Félix Tavernier, *La Vie quotidienne à Marseille, de Louis XIV à Louis-Philippe* (Paris, 1973), pp. 109–11.

62. Noël du Fail, *Les Baliverneries d'Eutrapel* (1894), pp. 45–8; quoted by J.-L. Flandrin in *Nouvelle histoire de France* (36 vols., Paris, 1965–8), vol. XI, pp. 1298–9.

63. Richard Carew, *Survey of Cornwall* (1602), p. 66; Robert Reyce, *Suffolk in the XVI century: the Breviary of Suffolk* (1618), ed. Lord Francis Henry (1902), p. 51; quoted in Joan Thirsk (ed.), *The Agrarian History of England and Wales*, vol. IV (Cambridge, 1967), pp. 443–6.

64. Thirsk, vol. IV; pp. 442–54, written by Alan Everitt, are devoted to the domestic life of the 'farm labourers'.

65. According to Suzanne Tardieu, *La Vie domestique dans le Mâconnais rural pré-industriel* (Paris, 1964), pp. 47–55.

66. Hugo, vol. I, p. 154.

67. *Ibid.* vol. II, p. 154.

68. *Archives départementales de l'Aube*, Inventory series G, vol. II, pp. 438–9.

69. *Ibid.* p. 387.

70. *Ibid.* pp. 385–6.

71. Noël du Fail, *Les propos rustiques de Noël du Fail* (1547), ed. Arthur de La Borderie (Paris, 1878), end of ch. V and beginning of ch. VI.

72. 'Coarse linen, the clothing of many peasants, does not protect them adequately. . . but for some years. . .a much larger number of peasants have been wearing woollen clothes.' Fernand Braudel, *Capitalism and Material Life, 1400–1800* (London, 1973), p. 230. Specimens of this coarse linen clothing can be seen in the Musée des Arts et Traditions Populaires. In this connection, see also Robert Mandrou, *Introduction à la France moderne* (Paris, 1960), pp. 35–43, particularly p. 42.

73. Bouchard, p. 94.

74. *Ibid.* p. 98.

75. Ariès, p. 445.

76. The peasants of Gascony, 'seated round the fire, are accustomed to eat without a table and to drink out of the same goblet', wrote a sixteenth-century observer, quoted in Braudel, p. 212.

77. Charles Kunstler, *La Vie quotidienne sous Louis XV* (Paris, 1953), pp. 337–8.

78. Ariès, pp. 401–4.

79. Rétif de la Bretonne, *La Vie de mon père*, ed. G. Rouger (Paris, 1970), p. 131.

80. *Ibid.* pp. 191–2.

81. *Ibid.* p. 191.

82. *Ibid.* p. 191.

83. 'The women eat once the men have been served', wrote Gaetan Bernouville in the twentieth century, in *Le Pays des Basques* (Paris, 1930). Moreover, one finds in the eighteenth century similar evidence regarding other Pyrenean regions, for example the notebook of the mountaineer and geographer Ramond.

84. De la Bretonne, *La Vie de mon père*, p. 130.

85. *Ibid.*

86. *Ibid.* pp. 130–1.

87. *Ibid.* pp. 131–3.

88. Noël du Fail, *Les Contes et discours d'Eutrapel* (Rennes, 1603), ff. 52v–53v; quoted in J.-L. Flandrin, *Les Amours paysannes* (Paris, 1975), pp. 121–2.

89. 'Journal du sire de Gouberville (1553–1564)', *Mémoire Soc. Antiq. Normandie*, vol. XXXI (Caen, 1892).

90. Flandrin, *Les Amours paysannes*, pp. 119–22.

91. Hugo, vol. I, pp. 237–8.

92. Etienne Tabourot, *Les Escraignes dijonnaises* (Paris, 1614), prologue; quoted in Flandrin, *Les Amours paysannes*, pp. 120–1.
93. Grosley, 'Dissertation sur les écreignes lue dans l'Academie de Troyes le 15 novembre 1743', *Mémoires de l'Académie de Troyes* (1743).
94. Charles Lalore, *Ancienne discipline du diocèse de Troyes* (4 vols., Troyes, 1882–3), vol. III, pp. 257–8.
95. Castan, *Honnêteté et relations sociales*, pp. 174, 236–7.
96. Soulet, pp. 281–2.
97. Yves Castan, 'Pères et fils en Languedoc à l'époque classique', *XVIIe Siècle*, no. 102–103, pp. 31–43, especially pp. 40–1.
98. Elias, ch. I.

CHAPTER 3. DOMESTIC MORALITY

1. Abel Hugo, *La France pittoresque* (3 vols., Paris, 1835), vol. I, p. 202.
2. *Ibid.* vol. II, p. 154.
3. *Ibid.* vol. I.
4. Quoted in J.-M. Gouesse, *Documents de l'Histoire de la Normandie* (Paris, 1972), p. 313.
5. Hugo, vol. I, p. 266.
6. *Ibid.* vol. II, p. 203.
7. *Ibid.* vol. I.
8. *Ibid.* vol. I, pp. 237–8.
9. *Ibid.* vol. II, p. 234.
10. *Ibid.* vol. I, p. 299.
11. *Ibid.* vol. I, p. 291.
12. *Ibid.* vol. I, p. 202.
13. *Ibid.* vol. I, p. 234.
14. Sebastien Locatelli, *Voyage en France, 1664–1665*, ed. A. Vautier (Paris, 1905).
15. Census results published, with observations, by P. Lions and M. Lachiver, 'Denombrement de la population de Brueil-en-Vexin en 1625', *Annales de démographie historique* (1967), pp. 521–37.
16. A. Brette, *Recueil des documents relatifs à la convocation des Etats Généraux de 1789*, vol. I (Paris, 1894), pp. 75, 76–7, arts. 20 and 25.
17. Jean-François Soulet, *La Vie quotidienne dans les Pyrénées sous l'ancien régime du XVIe au XVIIIe siècle* (Paris, 1974), pp. 226–7.
18. Jean Benedicti, *La Somme des Péchez* (see note 31 below), bk. II, ch. IV, no. 47, p. 110.
19. In general, the Protestants acknowledged the need for social hierarchies only on the grounds of the corruption of man by Original Sin. In contrast to this Protestant outlook, Benedicti is here expressing that of the Catholic theologians.
20. Jean Gerson, *Instruction pour les curés* (1602), ch. 8.
21. Quoted in Jean-Claude Dhotel, *Les Origines du catéchisme moderne* (Paris, 1967), p. 423.
22. All the proverbs existing before the nineteenth century which are referred to here can be found in the collection published by Le Roux de Lincy, *Le Livre des proverbes français*, 2nd edn (Paris, 1859), vol. I, pp. 219–32 (157 proverbs relating to women).
23. M. Quitard, *Proverbes sur les femmes, l'amitié, l'amour et le mariage* (Paris, 1861).

24. The short legal dossier which follows has been compiled by Pierre Cuzacq and published in *La Naissance, le mariage et le décès...dans le Sud-Ouest de la France* (Paris, 1902), pp. 114–17.

25. *Ibid.* pp. 117–19.

26. Jean Gaufreteau, *Chronique bordelaise* (2 vols., 1876–8), vol. I, p. 58.

27. Roger Vaultier, *Le Folklore pendant la guerre de Cent Ans d'après les Lettres de Rémission du Tresor des Chartes* (Paris, 1965).

28. Henri Lalou, 'Des charivaris et leur répressions dan le Midi de la France', *Revue des Pyrénées*, vol. XVI (1904), pp. 498–9.

29. For example, Roland Mousnier, *Les Institutions de la France sous la monarchie absolue*, vol. I (Paris, 1974), pp. 74–5.

30. Pierre Petot and Andre Vandenbossche, 'Le Statut de la femme dans les pays coutumiers français du XIIIe au XVIIIe siècle', *Recueil de la Société Jean Bodin*, vol. XII (1962), pp. 243–54.

31. Jean Benedicti, a preacher in Lyons, was also a professor of theology and Father Provincial of the Province of Touraine Pictavienne of the Order of Friars Minor (Observants). His *Somme des péchez*, which was first published in Lyons in 1584, appeared in numerous expanded, expurgated or abridged editions. References in this book are to the full Paris edition of 1601, of which there is a copy in the Bibliothèque Nationale, classmark D.6502. Bk. II, chs. I to IV.

32. The Spanish cardinal Francisco Toledo, who died in 1596, bequeathed to posterity a voluminous work of moral theology first published in 1599 in Lyons and entitled *De instructione sacerdotum*. In the course of the seventeenth century there were about a hundred complete or abridged editions, in Latin and various vernacular languages. References to him here under the name of Tolet will be to the full French translation entitled *L'Instruction des Prêtres, composée en latin par François Tolet, et mise en français par M. A. Goffard*, published in Lyons in 1628, of which there is a copy in the Bibliothèque Nationale, classmark D.10281. Bk V, chs. I and II.

33. *L'Examen de théologie morale*, by the Portuguese Antonio Fernandes de Moure, appeared, from 1616 and perhaps earlier, in numerous editions in Latin and the vernacular languages. The Rouen edition of 1638, to which reference is made here, was probably not the earliest French one, because the translator of Tolet wrote in 1628, in his preface, that 'the *Somme* of Benedicti and the work of moral theology of Fernandes de Moure...already circulate in France, translated into the vulgar tongue'.

34. Antoine Blanchard, Prior of Saint-Mars-les-Vendôme, *Essay d'exhortation pour les états différents des malades...On y a joint un examen général sur tous les commandements et sur les péchés de plusieurs estats...*(2 vols., Paris, 1713). All references will be to the Paris edition of 1736, of which there is a copy in the Bibliothèque Nationale, classmark D.26150.

35. *Instruction du chrestien, par Mgr l'éminentissime cardinal duc de Richelieu, revue, corrigée, augmentée et remise en meilleur ordre par S[on] E[minence], XXVe édition, du commandement de Mgr l'Evesque de Meaux, pour servir aux Curez de son diocèse* (Paris, 1640), p. 199.

36. Alain Lottin, 'Vie et mort du couple; difficultés conjugales et divorces dans le Nord de la France aux XVIIe et XVIIIe siècles', *XVIIe siècle*, no. 102–3 (1974), pp. 68–71.

37. Quoted in Mousnier, pp. 76–7.

38. *Encyclopédie ou dictionnaire raisonné des sciences, des arts et métiers*, article entitled 'Puissance paternelle', vol. XIII (1765), pp. 560–3.

39. Council of Trent, Session XXIV, *De reformatione matrimonii*, ch. I, decree *Tametsi.*
40. J.-L. Flandrin, *Les Amours paysannes* (Paris, 1975), pp. 36–75.
41. Quoted in Gouesse, pp. 310–11.
42. Flandrin, *Les Amours paysannes*, pp. 46–7.
43. *Ibid.* p. 40.
44. Fernandes de Moure, p. 665.
45. Quoted, with comments, in Flandrin, *Les Amours paysannes*, pp. 25–7.
46. *De reformatione matrimonii*, ch. IX.
47. Benedicti, bk. I, ch. I, no. 3.
48. Lucien Carrive, 'La Vision de la famille chez les moralistes puritains', *RANAM*, no. VIII (1975), p. 65.
49. Tolet, p. 541, no. 12.
50. Fernandes de Moure, pp. 708–9, no. 5.
51. Council of Trent, Session XXV, *De regularibus et monialibus*, ch. 17 and 18.
52. Pierre-Joseph Dorléans, 'Instruction chrétienne aux personnes engagées dans le mariage sur l'éducation de leurs enfants', in J.-P. Migne, *Collection intégrale des orateurs sacrés du premier ordre*, vol. XIII (Paris, 1845), cols. 967–79.
53. *Ibid.* col. 977–8.
54. Richelieu, p. 196.
55. Blanchard, p. 200, no. 16.
56. J.-L. Flandrin, 'L'attitude à l'égard du petit enfant et les conduites sexuelles dans la civilisation occidentale', *Annales de démographie historique* (1973), pp. 143–205.
57. Migne, vol. XXXII, col. 1322.
58. Fernandes de Moure, p. 20, no. 2.
59. Migne, vol. XII, col. 842.
60. *Instruction du Chrestien*, pp. 189–90.
61. Carrive, pp. 62–3.
62. Migne, vol. XIII, col. 978.
63. *Ibid.*
64. Migne, vol. XXXII, col. 1319–20.
65. *Ibid.* vol. XXXII, col. 1315.
66. Benedicti, bk. II, ch. II, no. 41.
67. *De reformatione matrimonii*, ch. IX.
68. Migne, vol. XXXII, cols. 1324–6 and 1328.
69. Yves Castan, *Honnêteté et relations sociales en Languedoc, 1715–1780* (Paris, 1974), pp. 211, 223.
70. See two recent studies relating to orders under the king's private seal: François-Xavier Emmanuelli, 'Ordre du Roi et lettres de cachet en Provence à la fin de l'Ancien Régime', *Revue historique* (October–December 1974), pp. 357–92; and Jean-Claude Perrot, *Caen au XVIIIe siècle* (Paris, 1975), vol. II, pp. 836–8.
71. The catechisms which will be referred to were studied in the University of Vincennes in the spring of 1973, in collaboration with Jackie Ducatez, Suzanne Morin-Rozenfeld and Irène Musial-Optolowicz. All the texts quoted are from the chapter of each catechism devoted to the Fourth Commandment.
72. Luis López, *Instructorium conscientiae* (Salamanca, 1585), pt. I, col. 385.
73. Saint Jerome (v. 331–420), *Adv. Iovinianum*, I. 49.
74. Benedicti, bk. II, ch. IX, no. 59.

75. J.-L. Flandrin, 'Contraception, marriage and sexual relations in the Christian West', in R. Forster and O. Ranum, *Biology of Man in History, Selections from the Annales E.S.C.* (Baltimore, 1975), pp. 37–41.

76. John T. Noonan, *Contraception: A History of its Treatment by the Catholic Theologians and Canonists* (Cambridge, Mass., 1966), pp. 494–504, especially p. 501.

77. Michel de Montaigne, *Essais* (Paris, 1950), bk. I, ch. XXX, pp. 235–6.

78. *Ibid.* p. 235.

79. Luc Thoré, 'Langage et sexualité', in *Sexualité humaine* (Paris, 1970), pp. 65–96.

80. Pierre de Bourdeille, Abbé and Seigneur de Brantôme, *Les Dames galantes,* first treatise, ed. Maurice Rat (Paris, 1955), pp. 25–6.

81. Hugo, vol. II, p. 82.

82. Henrie Smith, *A Preparative to Marriage* (London, 1591), f. E2v (p. 56).

83. William Whately, *A Bride-Bush; or a direction for married persons...*(London, 1619).

84. Robert Pricke, *The Doctrine of Superioritie and of subjection contained in the fift Commandement* (London, 1609), f. 15v; and Robert Bolton, *Small Generall Directions for a Confortable Walking with God,* 5th edn (London, 1638), pp. 237, 239.

85. Thomas Gataker, *A good Wife Gods Gift,* sermon (London, 1623), p. 11; and *A Mariage Praier, or Succint Meditations,* sermon (London, 1624), pp. 7–8. See also Daniel Rogers, *Matrimonial Honour: or the mutuall Crowne and comfort of godly, loyall, and chaste Marriage* (London, 1642), pp. 147–50.

86. Joseph Hall, *Resolutions and Decisions of Divers Practical Cases of Conscience,* 3rd edn (London, 1654), pp. 322–4.

87. Suzanne Halimi, 'Le Mariage en Angleterre au XVIIIe siècle', *RANAM,* no. VIII (1975), pp. 75–80.

88. François de la Rochefoucauld, *La Vie en Angleterre au XVIIIe siècle* (1784), ed. J. Marchand (Paris, 1945), pp. 79–80.

89. Comte P. de Vaudreuil, *Promenade de Bagnères-de-Luchon à Paris* (2 vols., Paris, 1820–1), vol. II, p. 41; and W. Blackstone, *Commentaire sur les lois anglaises,* translated from the 15th English edn (Paris, 1821–3), vol. V, p. 300n. (This note is by the French commentator E. Christian.)

90. Hugo, vol. I, p. 291.

91. Study of the vocabulary of the titles of works for which a licence or tacit permission was requested between 1723 and 1789, carried out at the Centre for Historical Research of the sixth section of the Ecole Pratique des Hautes Etudes, under the direction of François Furet.

92. *Archives départementales de l'Aube,* Inventory series G, vol. II, p. 406.

93. *Ibid.* vol. III, pp. 2–10.

CHAPTER 4. REPRODUCTION AND SEXUAL LIFE

1. John Dod, *A godlie forme of householde government...First gathered by R.C. [Robert Cleaver]* (London, 1612).

2. Saint Thomas Aquinas, *Commentary on Saint Paul,* quoted in John T. Noonan, *Contraception: A History of its Treatment by the Catholic Theologians and Canonists* (Cambridge, Mass., 1966), p. 280.

3. Burchard of Worms, *Decretum,* bk. XIX, art. 174, in *Patrologie Latine,* ed. J.-P. Migne, vol. 140 (Paris, 1853).

4. Jean Benedicti, *Somme des péchez* (Paris, 1601), bk. II, ch. II, no. 20.

5. *Ibid.* bk. II, ch. I, no. 3.
6. Pierre-Joseph Dorléans, 'Instruction chrétienne aux personnes engagées dans le mariage sur l'éducation de leurs enfants', in J.-P. Migne, *Collection intégrale des orateurs sacrés du premier ordre,* vol. XIII (Paris, 1845), cols. 967–9.
7. *Ibid.* col. 970.
8. *Ibid.* col. 968.
9. Claude Joly, 'Sur les devoirs des chefs de famille', in Migne, *Orateurs sacrés,* vol. XXXII, cols. 1516–17.
10. Benedicti, bk. II, ch. IX, no. 63.
11. Guillaume Bouchet, *Les Sérées* (1873), vol. III, ch. 22, p. 290 and vol. IV, ch. 23, p. 10.
12. *Archives départementales de l'Aube,* Inventory series G, vol. II, pp. 413–14.
13. Flandrin, *Les Amours paysannes,* pp. 207, 210–15.
14. Alain Croix, *Nantes et le pays nantais au XVIe siècle, étude démographique* (Paris, 1974), p. 96.
15. Jacques Depauw, 'Illicit sexual activity and society in eighteenth century Nantes', in R. Forster and O. Ranum, *Family and Society, Selections from the Annales E.S.C.* (Baltimore, 1976), p. 181.
16. C. Pouyez, *Une communauté d'Artois, Isbergues, 1598–1826,* AUDIR Microfiche no. 73.944.37.
17. G. Arbellot, *Cinq paroisses du Vallage,* AUDIR Microfiche no. 73.944.1.
18. J.-L. Flandrin, *Les Amours paysannes* (Paris, 1975), pp. 223–9.
19. Jacques Rossiaud, 'Prostitution, jeunesse et société dans les villes du Sud-Est au XVe siècle', *Annales E.S.C.* (March–April 1976), pp. 289–325, especially pp. 294–6. An English version of this article is to be published in a third *Selections from the Annales* by R. Forster and O. Ranum.
20. Fernand Braudel and Ernest Labrousse, *Histoire économique et sociale de la France* (Paris, 1970), vol. 2, pp. 487–97.
21. For a recent restatement, see Claude Delasselle, 'Les Enfants abandonnés à Paris au XVIIIe siècle', *Annales E.S.C.* (January–February 1975).
22. Rossiaud.
23. *Archives départementales de l'Aube,* Inventory series G, vol. II, *passim.*
24. *Instructions pour les confesseurs du diocèse de Chalon-sur-Saône* (Lyons, 1682), p. 10.
25. Letter from Lancelot to M. de Sacy, quoted in G. Snyders, *La Pédagogie en France aux XVIIe et XVIIIe siècles* (Paris, 1965), p. 45.
26. Françoise Tolet, *L'Instruction des Prêtres, composée en latin par François Tolet, et mise en français par M. A. Goffard* (Lyons, 1628), bk. V, ch. XIII, no. 11.
27. According to a report by Dominique Julia, in *Annales de démographie historique* (1973), p. 299.
28. Benedicti, bk. II, ch. VIII.
29. F. W. H. Wasserschleben, *Die Irische Kanonensammlungen* (Leipzig, 1885), bk. LXVI, ch. XVI, p. 239.
30. Marcel Lachiver, 'Fécondité légitime et contraception dans la région parisienne', in *Hommage à Marcel Reinhard* (Paris, 1973), pp. 383–401.
31. Edward Shorter has drawn attention to this phenomenon and proposed the first of these hypotheses in his 'Female emancipation, birth control and fertility in European history', *American Historical Review* (June 1973), pp. 605–40. I have suggested the second hypothesis in *Les Amours paysannes,* pp. 149 and 243–4.
32. E. A. Wrigley, 'Family limitation in pre-industrial England', *Economic History Review,* no. 1 (1966), pp. 82–109.

33. These seem to have occurred at a rate of about 237 per thousand conceptions, and to have become particularly frequent from the age of thirty to thirty-five onwards; cf. Henri Leridon, *Aspects biométriques de la fécondité humaine*, INED, Travaux et Documents, no. 65 (Paris, 1973), pp. 47–80.

34. See, in particular, L. Henry, *Anciennes familles genevoises*, INED, Travaux et Documents, no. 26 (Paris, 1956); and *La Population de Crulai, paroisse normande*, INED, Travaux et Documents, no. 35 (Paris, 1958).

35. Jacques Dupaquier and Marcel Lachiver, 'Les débuts de la contraception en France ou les deux malthusianismes', *Annales E.S.C.* (November–December 1969), pp. 1391–1406.

36. See, for example, Philippe Ariès, 'Attitudes devant la vie et devant la mort du XVIIe au XIXe siècles', *Population* (July–September 1949), pp. 463–70, and 'Sur les origines de la contraception en France', *Population* (July–September 1953), pp. 465–72.

37. This is, in short, the argument maintained by Ariès in 1935, in reply to an article by Michel Riquet, S.J.

38. Cf. Noonan, especially pp. 257–95; and J.-L. Flandrin, *L'Eglise et le contrôle des naissances* (Paris, 1970), especially pp. 53–5.

39. Pierre de Bourdeille, Abbé and Seigneur de Brantôme, *Les Dames galantes*, first treatise, ed. Maurice Rat (Paris, 1955), pp. 38–9; quoted, with comments, by J.-L. Flandrin, 'Contraception, marriage and sexual relations in the Christian West', in R. Forster and O. Ranum, *Biology of Man in History* (Baltimore, 1975), pp. 41–5.

40. Saint François de Sales, *Introduction to the Devout Life*, trans. John K. Ryan (New York, 1950), bk. III, ch. 39, p. 170.

41. Claude Lévy and Louis Henry, 'Ducs et pairs sous l'Ancien Régimes: caractéristiques démographiques d'une caste', *Population* (November–December 1960); and L. Henry, *Anciennes familles genevoises*.

42. Cf. M. Lachiver, in *Hommage à Marcel Reinhard*.

43. J. Potter, 'The growth of population in America, 1700–1860', in *Population in History* (London, 1965), pp. 631–88.

44. J. Henripin, *La Population canadienne au debut du XVIIIe siècle*, INED, Travaux et Documents, no. 22 (Paris, 1954).

45. Since I wrote this book (1975), studies on childbirth in the seventeenth and eighteenth centuries have multiplied. See in particular: Jacques Gelis, 'L'accouchement au XVIIIe siècle: Pratiques traditionnelles et contrôle médical', *Ethnologie Française*, vol. VI, no. 3–4 (1976), pp. 325–40; Jacques Gelis, 'La formation des accoucheurs et des sage-femmes au XVIIe et XVIIIe siècles: Evolution d'un matériel et d'une pédagogie', *Annales de démographie historique* (1977), pp. 153–80; Jacques Gelis, 'Sages-femmes et accoucheurs dans la France moderne', *Annales E.S.C.* (September–October 1977), pp. 927–57; Mireille Laget, 'La naissance aux siècles classiques: Pratique des accouchements et attitudes collectives en France aux XVIIe et XVIIIe siècles', *Annales E.S.C.* (September–October 1977), pp. 958–92; J. Gelis, M. Laget and M. F. Morel, *Entrer dans la vie: Naissances et enfances dans la France traditionnelle* (Paris, 1978).

46. Method devised by J. Bourgeois-Pichat. An exposition of it can be found in Roland Pressat, *L'Analyse démographique* (Paris, 1969), pp. 134–8.

47. See, for example, Maurice Garden, *Lyon et les Lyonnais au XVIIIe siècle* (Paris, 1970), pp. 95–107, or the abridged edition (Paris, 1975), pp. 46–54.

48. Garden, p 131.

49. E. Shorter has recently discovered precise evidence of this for the years 1837–1838; cf. *The Making of the Modern Family* (New York, 1975), pp. 185–8.
50. Garden, p. 128.
51. Jean-Pierre Bardet, 'Enfants abandonnés et enfants assistés à Rouen dans la seconde moitié du XVIIIe siècle', in *Hommage à Marcel Reinhard*, pp. 28–9.
52. Moheau, *Recherches et considérations sur la population de la France* (Paris, 1778), pt. 2, ch. VI, pp. 102–3.
53. Yves Castan, *Honnêteté et relations sociales en Languedoc, 1715–1780* (Paris, 1974), pp. 211–14.
54. For example, among the Jews in the first centuries of the Christian era, according to Noonan, pp. 69–70.
55. G. Fromageau, *Dictionnaire des cas de conscience* (Paris, 1733), col. 1198.
56. Benedicti, bk. II, ch. II, no. 20.
57. Thomas Sanchez, *Disputationum de sancto matrimonii sacramento* (3 vols., Antwerp, 1607), vol. III, *De debito conjugali*, bk. IX, dist. XXII, no. 15.
58. *Ibid.* no. 14.
59. J.-L. Flandrin, 'L'Attitude à l'égard du petit enfant et les conduites sexuelles dans la civilisation occidentale, structures anciennes et évolutions', *Annales de démographie historique* (1973), pp. 143–210, especially p. 179.
60. So far, research has dealt only with Meulan (from 1660 to 1764), Cuise-la-Motte (from 1670 to 1819) and Germont (from 1700 to 1819). My thanks are due to M. Lachiver and L. Henry, who kindly allowed me to consult their family record cards.
61. L. Henry, 'La Fécondité des mariages dans le quart Sud-Ouest de la France, de 1720 à 1819', *Annales E.S.C.* (July–October 1972), p. 987.
62. Flandrin, 'L'Attitude à l'égard du petit enfant', pp. 193–6.
63. Pierre Milhard, *Inventaire des cas de conscience* (Paris, 1611), ch. entitled 'Droit de mariage', no. 6.
64. Thomas Malthus, *An Essay on the Principle of Population*, Everyman's Library (2 vols., London, 1933), vol. II, pp. 4–5.
65. Moheau, pp. 101–2.
66. Lachiver, in *Hommage à Marcel Reinhard*, pp. 383–401.
67. Unpublished research by Marcel Lachiver, submitted to the seminar held under the chairmanship of Jacques Dupaquier on 17 February 1975.
68. Michel de Montaigne, *Essais* (Paris, 1950), bk. I, ch. XIV, pp. 79–80.
69. Alan Macfarlane, *The Family Life of Ralph Josselin, a Seventeenth-Century Clergyman: An Essay in Historical Anthropology* (Cambridge, 1970), pp. 84–5.
70. Milhard, on 'Droit de mariage', no. 8.
71. Fromageau, col. 1220; Sanchez, bk. IX, dist. XX, no. 3.
72. Fromageau, cols. 1197–9 and 1201.
73. *Abrégé du manuel du...Dr. Martin Azpilcueta Navarrois...*, translated from Latin into French by M. Robert Segard (Douai, 1601), ch. XVI, no. 27. This brief manual had first been published in Latin in Rome in 1590, and subsequently there were many other editions and translations.
74. Quoted in Jean-Marie Gouesse, 'Le Refus de l'enfant au tribunal de la pénitence', *Annales de démographie historique* (1973), p. 238.
75. Noonan, pp. 549–50.
76. Genesis 38.
77. Noonan, pp. 506–12; see also Hélène Bergues, *La Prévention des naissances dans la famille*, INED, Travaux et Documents, no. 35 (Paris, 1960), pp. 229–31.
78. Moheau, pp. 99–100.

79. Brantôme, *Les Dames galantes*, pp. 38–9.
80. Noonan, p. 230; Flandrin, *L'Eglise et le contrôle des naissances*, p. 116.
81. Bergues, p. 227.
82. Flandrin, *L'Eglise et le contrôle des naissances*, p. 115, canon *Aliquando*.
83. *Ibid.* pp. 3, 117; Noonan, pp. 108, 113.
84. Malthus, vol. II, p. 164.
85. Bertrand De La Tour, 'Discours sur la Foi et la pureté', in Migne, *Orateurs Sacrés*, vol. LX, col. 372.
86. Alfred Perrenoud, 'Malthusianisme et protestantisme...', *Annales E.S.C.* (July–August 1974), pp. 975–88.
87. Louis-Sébastien Mercier, *Mon bonnet de nuit* (Neuchâtel, 1784), pp. 142–3; quoted in Bergues, pp. 292–3.
88. Noonan, pp. 282–3, 381–2; and Flandrin, 'L'Attitude à l'égard du petit enfant', pp. 145–7.
89. L. Cohen, 'Condorcet inédit. Notes pour le tableau des progrès de l'esprit humain' in 'La Revolution Francaise', *Revue d'Histoire moderne et contemporaine*, vol. LXXV (1922), pp. 193–212.
90. Quoted in Bergues, p. 228.
91. L. Henry, 'La Fécondité des mariages dans le quart Sud-Ouest de la France', p. 1001.
92. Flandrin, *Les Amours paysannes*, pp. 191–200, 241–2.
93. This evidence has been collected and published by Edward Shorter in *The Making of the Modern Family*, pp. 182–4.
94. M. Lachiver, to whom I owe the idea developed in the following paragraph, is already convinced of this.
95. This is the opinion of, for example, the physician Laurent Joubert, quoted in *Annales de démographie historique* (1973), pp. 208–10.
96. There are many examples of legal proceedings against nurses who, after becoming pregnant, fed the baby bad milk or weaned it prematurely. See, for example, Garden, pp. 121, 123, no. 87.
97. Dupaquier and Lachiver, pp. 1391–1406. See also the graphs of fertility by age-groups presented by Lachiver in *Hommage à Marcel Reinhard*, p. 391; they become concave after 1789.
98. In the absence of precise data regarding mercenary wet-nursing, I have relied on the opinion of Marcel Lachiver, who is at present the scholar with the most detailed knowledge of this region.
99. See, for example, Laurent Joubert, *Première et Segonde parties des Erreurs populaires* (Paris, 1587), pt. I, bk. V, ch. I, pp. 176–90.
100. Sanchez, bk. IX, dist. XXII, no. 15.
101. This is the hypothesis maintained by Pierre Chaunu in several publications. See, for example, *La Civilisation de l'Europe des Lumières* (Paris, 1971), pp. 133–42; and 'Malthusianisme démographique et malthusianisme économique', *Annales E.S.C.* (January–February 1971), pp. 1–19, especially pp. 16–19.
102. Cahen, p. 200.
103. For example, F. Jouon des Longrais, 'Le Statut de la femme en Angleterre dans le droit commun médiéval', *Recueils de la Société Jean Bodin*, vol. XII, pp. 235–41.
104. Carrive, pp. 59–67

Index

abortion, as birth control, 1, 79, 193
abstinence, sexual, 193–4
  see also behaviour, sexual; celibacy
agriculture, and employment of labour,
  85–6
America, population trends in, 198
Anjou, family attitudes in, 113
Aquinas, Saint Thomas, 47
archaism, and household size, 60
architecture, domestic, 92ff
Aries, Philippe, 89, 92, 93, 95, 102, 103
Augustine, Saint, 47, 175
authority
  and duties of kin, 48
  exercise of, and *lignage*, 15–16
  husband's, 118–29
  nature of, 1, 118, 119; in household,
    116, 117; in Roman Law, 112
  paternal, 130ff; limitations on, 134–5;
    and marriage, 131–2, 134, 135
  principle of, 145
  over servants, 140ff; misuse of, 149
  women and, 149
authorities, public
  attitudes of, 116–17, 125, 189
  see also State
Auvergne, 78, 80, 86, 88, 89, 107–8, 113
Aveyron, 112

Bardet, Jean-Pierre, 90
Basque country, 117
Basse-Alpes, 112
Bassigny, 23
bastards, 180ff
  see also illegitimacy
Bearn, 75, 124
Beauvaisis, 123, 199
behaviour
  models of, 112ff; monarchical, 118ff
  moral, 1, 94, 118
  sexual, attitudes to, 161ff, 189, 211,
    211–12; and fertility, 232; and pro-
    creation, 179; repression of, 189
    211

social, changes in, 93ff
Benedicti, Jean, 16th cent. moralist and
  theologian
  on authority, 120, 134
  on breast-feeding, 207, 236
  on conjugal duty, 126, 225
  on domestic morality, 156ff
  on love, 159–60, 162
  on marriage, 126–7, 128, 129, 133, 190,
    194
  on masturbation, 190
  on parental responsibility, 160, 176, 178
  on servants, 141–3, 157
Bergerac, 123
Berri
  inheritance in, 77
  paternal authority in, 130
birth
  registration of, 197–8, 199
  rate of, 231–2; and social class, 58–9
birth control
  and attitudes to children, 153, 229,
    240–1
  attitude of Church to, 179
  attitude of demographers to, 213
  benefits of, 217
  and infant mortality, 200, 229
  and marriage, 240
  and Revolution, 238
  see also contraception
Blanchard, Antoine, 18th cent. moralist
  and monk
  on family relationships, 126, 141, 143,
    144–56
  on marriage, 127, 128, 129, 135, 190,
    225
  on parental responsibility, 138
  on servants, 141, 142
Bordeaux, status of women in, 124
Borromeo, Saint Charles, Bishop of Milan,
  121
Bouchet, Guillaume, 19th cent. writer,
  180
Bourbonnais, 23, 77, 80

257

Index

Bourdieu, Pierre, 52
bourgeoisie
  attitude of, to eating, 102; to peasant customs, 112; to women, 114–15, 123, 216, 224, 225
  and contraception, 213
  family structure, 92
  houses, 92
  household type, 60
  kinship system, 29–33
  land ownership by, 59, 86, 186
  maternal mortality, 217
Boyer, Abel, 17th cent. writer, 5, 19
Brantôme, Abbé de, 17th cent. writer, 11–12
  attitude of, to coitus interruptus, 194, 223; to marriage, 165
  genealogy of, 26–9
breast-feeding
  attitudes to, 205, 206, 236
  and conjugal duty, 220
  and contraception, 231, 234–5
  and fertility, 53, 58–9, 180, 201, 203, 206, 208, 231–2, 234
  and infant mortality, 153, 203, 208, 233
  see also wet-nursing
Brittany, 26, 114, 130, 169, 194, 199
Brueil-en-Vexin, census at (1625), 30, 70, 71, 117
Burgundy, 77, 80, 108

Cambridge group, 53, 54, 65, 174
  see also Laslett
Canada, population trends in, 198
Cantal, peasant behaviour in, 115
capital, and household size, 60
Caston, Yves, 109
Catechisme de Bruxelles (1785), 170, 172
celibacy, 52, 188
  as Malthusian ideal, 212
  and marriage, 189–90, 224, 227
  and population growth, 210
censuses, and family structure, 116–17
Cevennes, employment of labour in, 86
Champagne, social life in, 109
charity, 212
chastity
  and communal sleeping, 100
  and celibacy, 188
  evidence of, 189
childbirth
  and conjugal duty, 220, 224
  and mortality, infant, 200; maternal, 53, 217
children
  attitudes to, 153, 216, 226–7, 237, 241; and birth control, 228, 234, 238
  duty of, 134, 136–8, 148, 150, 159

and family, 3, 57ff, 140, 145, 152, 153, 154, 175, 177
  illegitimate, 182
  numbers of, 53, 56–8, 232; and over-crowding, 95–6, 98; and sexual behaviour, 210
  and parental authority, 130–1
  rights of, 84, 131, 133, 135, 136, 140, 172, 177
  and servants, 59, 143–5
  as servants, 87–8
  status of, 118, 130, 136, 137, 152, 175
  unwanted, 180, 186
  wet-nursing of, 203–4
  see also authority, parental; family relationships; foundlings; orphans; parents
Christianity
  and concept of parental duty, 175, 176
  and reproduction, 179–80
  see also Church; moralists; morality, Christian
Church
  Anglican, and marriage, 131, 167–8
  Catholic, attitude of, to celibacy, 188, 210; to children, 131, 137, 211; to communal sleeping, 98–9, 110; to concubinage, 182–4; to conjugal relations, 118–29; to family, 110, 121, 174, 211; to married love, 161–4, 166, 169ff, 211; to paternal authority, 133–4, 120–1, 131; to servants, 142; to sexual behaviour, 189–90; to social problems, 179; to traditional social activity, 110–11; to wet-nursing, 206
  in conflict with State, 131–2
  see also moralists, Catholic; morality
clergy
  and concubinage, 181, 182
  and marriage, 133
  social status of, 33
Code, Civil, 75, 118
cohabitation, parents and married children, 89ff
coitus interruptus, 194, 221, 225, 229, 232
  and breast-feeding, 206, 231, 235, 237
  and illegitimacy, 230–1
  and Jansenism, 238–9
  and marital relationship, 226
  in Middle Ages, 223
  moralists' attitude to, 194–5, 226, 239–40
  see also birth control; contraception
Colbert, 2, 20
communities, 84–5
  communautés taisibles, 78, 84–5, 86
  egalitarian, 84, 89, 116; *frérèche*, 83, 84, 86, 87, 88

Index

family
  basis of, 79
  changing character of, 216
  definition of, 4–9, 11
  function of, 174
  historical analysis of, 50ff
  and industrial society, 50, 69
  institution of, 1; Church's attitude to, 211
  life, 92–3, 95; and communal sleeping, 98, 101, 110; and fertility, 211; and food, 103; nature of, 94; and prayers, 105–6; and recreation, 106; ritual of, 110
  relationships, 112–13, 145ff, 216; and the Church, 118–22, 145ff; and Civil Code, 117–18; and customary law, 122–5, 153; hierarchical, 148–50; between husband and wife, 118–29, 150, 152, 155–6, 161ff, 168, 216, 223–4, 226, 233, 240; between parents and children, 130ff, 148, 150–1, 152–4, 155, 158–60, 167–8, 241; and Roman Law, 117
  size, 53, 54, 232
  spirit, bourgeois, 30; and laws of inheritance, 75–6; of nobility, 48
  structure of, 2; and censuses, 116–17; and customary behaviour, 209ff; and infant mortality, 202–3; and inheritance laws, 77–8; and 'rootedness', 91; and sharecropping, 87
  study of, 3–4
  type, complex, 89ff; conjugal, 66, 69–70, 71, 90, 174, 203, 216; extended, 66–8, 86, 90, 203, 210; multinuclear, 68, 86, 72–4, 203; 'stem, 50–2, 53, 74, 75, 79, 87, 210; 'unstable', 50
  see also household
families, individual, 2–3, 20
famine, and fertility, 197
father, as patriarch
  duties of, 119, 129, 131, 141
  powers of, 130, 133
  see also authority, paternal; parents
fatherhood, as duty, 238
  see also authority, paternal; father, parents
feelings, and family relationships, 145ff
Fernandes de Moure, Antonio, 17th cent. moral theologian, 126, 129, 133, 135, 137, 141
fertility
  and age of marriage, 58
  and breast-feeding, 58–9
  changes in, 191–8, 199–200, 213, 228, 233–4, 237

control of, 52, 193–4, 212, 213, 219, 223, 228, 234, 237
  and household structure, 54, 71–2
  importance of, 180
  and incidence of foundlings, 191
  and infant mortality, 59, 180, 199, 200, 211
  level of, and family life, 211, 216; and population trends, 198, 228; in urban areas, 242
  see also birth control; contraception; duty, conjugal
foundlings
  death rate among, 204, 212, 234
  increase in, 184, 191, 198, 213
  see also illegitimacy
France
  age of marriage in, 210
  birthrate in, 210, 232
  breast-feeding in, 209
  fertility in, 199, 210, 236
  household structure in, 72
  inheritance laws in, 74, 77
  neighbourhood sense, 35
Franche-Comté, 80, 81–3, 117
frérèche, see household, types
Fromageau, G. 18th cent. moralist, 206, 207, 219, 220, 237
funerals, 36–7, 39

games, children's, 41
Gascony, customary law in, 124
Gatine, land ownership in, 59, 60
Gaudemet, Jean, 89
de Gennes, Jehan, 15th–16th cent. merchant, journal of, 29, 34
gentry
  households of, 58, 61, 69
  social duty of, 61–2
  see also élites, social
Gerson, Jean, 15th cent. moralist, 120, 190
girls, freedom of, 168, 169
  see also women; wife
God, as patriarchal model, 119, 176
Goodnestone, Kent, population of, 56–8
Goubert, Pierre, 54
Gouberville, Sire de, 16th cent, diarist, 106
Grosley, 18th cent. writer, 109

Hall, Joseph, 17th cent. Bishop of Norwich, on marriage, 167–8
Haute-Provence, 89
holdings, size of, 59–60
  see also land, ownership of
Houard, 18th cent. jurist, 133, 173
'house', 6–7, 11, 79
  and duties of heir, 78

260